EYES OF THE MIRROR

ALSO BY MARGARET EMERSON

Breathing Underwater: The Inner Life of T'ai Chi Ch'uan
North Atlantic Books, Berkeley CA

A Potter's Notes on Tai Chi Chuan
Artichoke Press, Bayside CA

*Wu Style Long Form (*videotape)
Artichoke Press, Bayside CA

MARGARET EMERSON WEBSITE

www.MARGARETEMERSON.com

CONTACT THE AUTHOR BY E-MAIL

memerson@humboldt1.com

EYES OF THE MIRROR

Margaret Emerson

ARTICHOKE PRESS
BAYSIDE, CALIFORNIA

Eyes of the Mirror

Copyright © 2003 and 2005 by Margaret Emerson. All rights reserved. No portion of this book, except for brief review, may be reproduced in any form without written permission of the publisher.

Published by
Artichoke Press
P.O. Box 16
Bayside, California 95524

Cover finger painting and book design by Margaret Emerson
Printed in the United States of America

Library of Congress Cataloging-in-Publication Data

Emerson, Margaret Jane, 1948—

Eyes of the Mirror/Margaret Emerson

ISBN 978-0-9620690-3-1

1. Memoir   2. Personal Growth   3. Women's Studies   I. Title

Library of Congress Control Number 2005903307

CONTENTS

Preface vii

Entry	**Page**	
1	1	Portland, Fall 1998
2	6	Wonju, Fall 1996
3	15	Wonju, Fall 1996
4	23	Wonju, Fall 1996
5	27	Wonju, Fall 1996
6	34	Portland, Fall 1998
7	49	Portland, Fall 1998
8	50	Wonju, Fall 1996
9	57	Wonju, Fall 1996
10	66	Wonju, Fall 1996
11	70	Wonju, Fall 1996
12	76	Wonju, Fall 1996
13	86	Wonju, Winter 1996-1997
14	93	Wonju, Winter 1996-1997
15	96	Wonju, Winter 1996-1997
16	98	Portland, Winter 1998-1999
17	99	Wonju, Winter 1996-1997
18	104	Wonju, Winter 1996-1997
19	107	Wonju, Winter 1996-1997
20	112	Portland, Winter 1998-1999
21	118	Wonju, Winter 1996-1997
22	122	Wonju, Winter 1996-1997
23	135	Wonju, Winter 1996-1997
24	139	Wonju, Winter 1996-1997
25	143	Wonju, Winter 1996-1997
26	150	Portland, Spring 1999
27	157	Portland, Spring 1999
28	160	Portland, Spring 1999
29	164	Wonju, Spring 1997
30	175	Wonju, Spring 1997

Entry	Page	
31	186	Wonju, Spring 1997
32	199	Portland, Summer 1999
33	209	Wonju, Summer 1997
34	222	Portland, Summer 1999
35	230	Wonju, Fall 1997
36	233	Wonju, Fall 1997
37	243	Portland, Fall 1999
38	247	Portland, Fall 1999
39	254	Wonju, Winter 1997-1998
40	257	Wonju, Winter 1997-1998
41	261	Wonju, Winter 1997-1998
42	269	Portland, Winter 2000-2001
43	273	Portland, Winter 2000-2001
44	276	Wonju, Winter 1997-1998
45	277	Wonju, Winter 1997-1998
46	280	Wonju, Winter 1997-1998
47	281	Portland, Winter 2000-2001
48	283	Wonju, Spring 1998
49	285	Wonju, Spring 1998
50	291	Portland, Spring 2000
51	294	Portland, Spring 2000
52	297	Portland, Spring 2000
53	299	Wonju, Spring 1998
54	305	Wonju, Spring 1998
55	313	Portland, Summer 2000
56	318	Wonju, Summer 1998
57	327	Wonju, Summer 1998
58	331	Portland, Summer 2000
59	334	Portland, Summer 2000
60	337	Arcata, Spring 2001
Epilogue	340	Arcata, Summer 2005

PREFACE

Names have been changed; characters have been combined; events have been telescoped. But this narrative is as close as I can get to the truth about myself.

M.E.

Entry 1
Portland, Fall 1998

People say life is short. I think it's very long. They say you only go around once, but here I am starting again. The question is, do I want to?

You're supposed to be exuberant and daring (or else prudent and cautious) because your time on earth is brief. People have admonished me in both directions. What's the proper advice for a two-life person?

I look at it this way: I've lived my life. I went all out. Fifty years seems an adequate lifespan to me. It's time enough to do the important things if you start on them right away, as I did. I followed my passions. They provided a life and a living. I did my best. I could have done more and better, but I did okay. It was rich and full—plenty of exhilaration, frustration, contentment, unhappiness, joy, depression, and gratification. My body served me well. It was strong, generally healthy, and sensually responsive. I've done hard physical work and savored the sports I love. Now I'm spent.

However, it seems I am not finished. I imagine two hoops beside each other. I circumnavigated the hoop on the left. It forcibly ejected me, so I made a desperate grasp for the second hoop. I now feel like a trapeze artist whose ankles are still hooked around the first bar while her hands are clutching the second. The two bars are spreading apart. How far can she stretch before committing to the new swing or plummeting to her death?

Alternatively, I see it as a figure "8" on its side. I completed one half, then at the juncture of the two halves the tracks switched and now I find myself poised to begin the second half. This implies the desperation I feel may not be necessary. After all, having decided to live, and having completed one loop, presumably all I have to do is continue and the second loop will gracefully pull me on board. That's much easier, isn't it? One leads into the other inevitably. But if I stick with this metaphor it leads me back into the first loop, and on and on infinitely.

Enough is enough. Besides, life is more likely to let one sink than pull one on board. So much for the New Age.

Let's assume my life is over. Success has already happened, and failure has surely happened, and now a kind of death, too. So I'm over those things, right? As for loneliness, I have met it and it is I. My life now is as a ghost looking on. I get to observe, absorb, and expand. Sometimes I see myself hovering above the ropes that used to hold me down. They lie in limp curls on the ground, and look puny from up here. The gift of middle age: detachment.

The things that used to be important to me don't seem important now. My hormones have subsided; they don't drive me the way they used to. My life isn't about mating any more. Mother Nature has played out her trick—her first trick, anyway. Maybe this next life will be a theater for a different trick. Or maybe she's done with me and indifferent since I can no longer serve her. (I thwarted her, you know, during those fertile years— it wasn't easy.) So now at last I'm on my own. An adult without that implacable agenda. Free to set my own.

Which raises the question, what is my agenda now? What's important to me? What will be my source of joy? My antidepressant? Nature has set me free and I'm adrift.

I thought I wouldn't have a midlife crisis because I was already doing exactly what I wanted to do. I thought other people's lives came to a crisis in their forties because they had made bad choices early in life and couldn't sustain them—they had married foolishly or chosen work solely on the basis of money or status. Decades later their souls were starving, crying to be fed and cared for. Not very charitable of me. Maybe for all of us it's an *endlife* crisis—the natural death of one life and the potential for beginning a new one. Maybe our life phases are naturally self-limiting, the way a single cell in our bodies has a set life span.

Maybe also programmed within our DNA is our time of physical death. My father died in his early fifties. By his own hand, it's true, but our emotional capacities are part of our biology too. Are my cells expecting to die now? Am I preserving them past their natural time with all my natural remedies from the health food store? As a competitive swimmer I excelled as a sprinter—my talent did not lie in endurance. It occurs to me that I may not be a long-distance survivor.

There is a natural pattern for humans to live first a more physical, active, outwardly oriented life, and later to become more cerebral, introverted, contemplative. I guess both periods serve Mother Nature—the first for family raising and doing the hard physical labor, the second for contributing to a community in intangible ways—by doing its thinking and advising.

I was immersed in my body for such a long time. For almost thirty years I had my hands in clay and did the earthy, vigorous work of a potter. Simultaneously I was preoccupied with the imperative of finding a mate. Now I'm turning back to thought and words. (This is where I started, really, as a preadolescent girl scribbling in her diary and planning to be a writer.) The two forces advance and retreat within us—yin and yang, earth and sky.

It could all boil down to something very mundane—a period of work and then retirement. A person expends physical, mental, emotional, and sexual energy for some decades, then slows down and coasts. In a practical sense, this is predicated on making enough money during the active years to allow for withdrawing from the fray. I haven't done that. But even if I had, I would still have to be engaged, to have reasons for living.

I'm tired. It's my tiredness that brought me to the end of my first life. And maybe boredom too. Toward the end I strained against the millstone but it gradually slowed, grew heavier and heavier until at last it refused to move. I adjusted my stance, my position, and tried again and again. Still it didn't budge. It used to roll without so much effort. Finally I was forced to abandon it and look for another wheel—a much lighter one, and preferably headed downhill.

The effort of closing out one life and arranging for the beginning of another added to my exhaustion. The ensuing deprivations of two years in an alien country—where I went hoping to find rest, as well as new ideas, new influences, and some real money—further depleted me. It's a wonder there's anything left for this starting up again in Portland.

I look at my aging friends and see their eyes sinking, retreating into their faces. They peer out from a hiding place, looking less certain, more fearful. But mostly just tired. I can see why the gravestones have "Rest in Peace" on them. Life does kill you in the end.

Right here, right now I'm looking out the window at the brick wall of the neighboring apartment building. The view is redeemed by the age and varied patterns of the bricks as well as the sword ferns and holly bushes growing against the wall. I'm in a city again, but this time in my own country, and I have a lovely park just up the hill for practicing T'ai Chi in the mornings.

I have chosen a place in the park and fallen in love with it. T'ai Chi does this. It opens me up so that trees, bushes, and sky seem overwhelmingly, inexpressibly beautiful. I wonder that everyone else isn't drawn to stand there and stare. Every color, texture, and shape stirs me physically. The green color of the grass isn't just visual. It's a thrill that goes straight to my abdomen and sends a vibration radiating outward, like a finger plucking a guitar string. I open the T'ai Chi sequence facing a straight, tall fir tree that shows how simple it is to be lovely and graceful and strong.

Here in my apartment I've created a home that pleases me when I look at it. The office part of my living room is arranged conveniently. My files are in order. There's a feeling of space—I have very little extraneous stuff, and that's important to me. But I've learned not to leave things too stark.

I worry over the quantity, volume, and weight of what I own. Can I lift it by myself? How difficult is it to move? How long would it take? As I prepared to teach English in Korea, I bragged to my friends that all my worldly goods fit into a five-by-twelve-foot storage space that was only two-thirds full. I strive for lightness but it's hard to make a home without some weight. I tell myself—because I need to—that I can remain here in Portland for a while, maybe a long time. Long enough, I hope, to forget the strain of this last move.

I give myself permission to relax, but I don't always have that authority. Anxiety is an over-zealous sentinel that pounces every time my heart slows, prodding it to keep up its forced march. Still, slowly I make friends again with sleep, settling into my daily T'ai Chi practice, my running and swimming. At the "Y" I use the steam room, hot tub, and sauna to cleanse and warm. My muscles soften and stretch. I'm rusty at cooking, after allowing my repertoire to shrink to ramen and veggies, or cereal with soy milk while in Korea. But I'm getting back into the swing of it. The everyday activity, the smells, the delicious, healthy food are all a comfort to me.

Beside me are my journals from the last two years and some months. I feel raw from the time in Korea. I'm not sure I want to look through them. A friend gave the first journal to me just before I left my home in far northern California. I was about to go to school for one month in San Francisco to earn my certificate in teaching English as a second language. The journal is lovely, with an affectionate inscription. I have loved all my journals. I like to hold them in my hands. They contain me. Out of all the tangles and knots a pattern emerges, and I'm able to understand, forgive, and sometimes admire—both others and myself.

Entry 2
Wonju, Fall 1996

It's late September and I'm in Wonju, staying with a Korean family until school officials find me an apartment. I signed a contract with the South Korean government to teach English to middle school girls for one year, with the possibility of renewing for a second.

Wonju is in the middle of Kangwon-do, the northeasternmost province. I chose to be here, away from the really big, polluted cities and close to the mountains. The Koreans say the air and water are clean in this part of the country. Two hundred forty thousand people live in Wonju. It's a town of military bases—five in all. The one American base is visible from my school. This is a town undergoing rapid change. There are Italian clothing stores, expensive even by Western standards, within a block of traditional markets where elderly men and women (more often women) sit on the cold cement with their chestnuts, cabbage, squid, or shrimp. Cramped clothing stalls, some indoors and some out, stretch the length of several blocks.

My Korean host family is composed of Park Shi-eun, a fifteen-year-old student at my school, and her parents. No housing had been arranged for me when I arrived, so I stayed at the apartment of my "guide teacher" the first night. The next day he called around to the parents of some of his students to find a family willing to have me in their home for a couple weeks. It took several attempts to find the Parks. The lack of planning for my arrival was startling and a little humiliating. It was evident my guide teacher and his wife could not accommodate me along with their two preschool daughters in their cramped apartment. I was being unloaded on the Parks. However, they're kind, cheerful, and genuinely warm. My only objection at this point is that they watch too much TV. Anyway, with luck my stay here won't exceed the promised two weeks.

The Parks have a very compact three-bedroom apartment. It's a typical working class home on the ninth floor of a fifteen-story building. All around, in varying shades of gray, are other apartment buildings, businesses, and parking lots. There are no concessions to beauty here—inside or out. There are few decorations on the walls other than a calendar and a handful of long-dried flowers (a gift from a guest) hung upside down. The wavy, colorful wrapping paper and ribbon holding the bouquet together provide most of the visual interest, since the flowers are drained of color. There is a small, hard couch in the living room, and no chairs other than the bench in front of the piano Shi-eun plays. This is a culture of floor sitters.

I have been given Shi-eun's room and she has moved into her brother's, who is away serving his compulsory time in the army. There's a bed, a desk, and an armoire. The room is clean and the apartment seems fairly new. I understand how most things work here, but I'm puzzled by the single pair of plastic slippers on the threshold of the bathroom. Whose are they? Why do I never see more than one when there are three people in the family? And why is the bathroom floor almost always wet?

Mrs. Park and I rise at 5:15 to half walk, half jog on a trail that climbs a foothill behind the neighborhood. (I call her Mrs. Park to make this writing easier to follow, although Korean women don't use their husband's names.) The morning is cool, humid, and dark when we start out; it will be light when we start back. We follow a web of trails that I'm gradually getting to know. I have to remember to pick up my feet to avoid tripping over the tree roots that crisscross the path. The trail is one person wide. After twenty minutes we pass a small, flat area to the left. This is where the men who frequent the trail pause to do their calisthenics. We never stop here, but in the brief glimpses I get, I occasionally see some men practicing what look like Ch'i Kung exercises. Five minutes later we arrive at a larger clearing where hula hoops and jump ropes hang from tree branches. They seem to be public property because the women who gather here use them freely. Other activities include massaging backs against trees, or just sitting and talking. The time we spend in this space is not enough for me to complete my sequence of T'ai Chi, but I do as much as I can before Mrs. Park signals that we're starting back. I'm conscious, as usual, of being a closely observed curiosity.

People come and go continuously from this spot. These trails and clearings are well used. At any given time there are about eight of us here, all adults, mostly middle aged or older. It's rare to see a male-female couple on the trail. I'm beginning to learn that the sexes keep separate from each other in this country. There are more women than men on this hill, and maybe that's why the women have the choice spot.

One morning a man blocked our way on the trail up the hill. He took his time, acting oblivious to the presence of Mrs. Park, myself, and some other women bunching up behind him. He never stepped aside. We had to wait for a widening of the trail in order to pass. No one asked him to move over. Women, on the other hand, always stand aside to let people get by.

I think Mrs. Park is in her mid forties. She's a stocky, sturdy woman with abundant energy. Her face is ruddy and her movements are brusque. She carries her extra weight in front of her, in a round and solid stomach. Her legs and arms are very muscular. She likes to wear the velvet or satiny tops that are fashionable in Korea.

Mr. Park has a ruggedly handsome face. He's normal height by Korean standards; I consider him short. He, too, seems to be physically very vigorous and healthy. Of course, like almost all Korean men, he smokes. Mr. Park repairs appliances—videos, televisions, fans, and more. He works in his shop, which is a few minutes' walk from their apartment, seven days a week. His hours are 9 A.M. to 9 P.M. Mrs. Park gets there around 10:00 in the morning after doing chores at home. She comes and goes from the shop as her domestic duties allow. But mostly she's there at the business with her husband.

The shop is like a lot of small businesses in town. The front part (about twelve feet by twelve feet) has merchandise, and you can walk in there with your shoes on. The back part (extending an additional eight feet) is raised up one step and constitutes the "living room" for the proprietors. Shoes must come off for this space. The floor is heated; the ubiquitous TV is there, the food, pillows, calendar, and the miscellaneous detritus of living. The front of Mr. Park's shop is cluttered with appliances he's working on or trying to sell. It's purely functional space, and there's no attempt to pretty it up.

Shi-eun is about five feet, three inches; her frame is generously filled out. She has a sweet face framed with black hair cropped in the standard schoolgirl style. She smiles a lot and hides behind her bangs as much as she can. (Her complexion is acting up and she will have to endure much worse before it gets better.) Her hand is quick to cover her mouth when any kind of emotion threatens to escape. When we walk together she takes my arm. This is the way two females (and often two males) accompany each other. It's endearing and I try to conceal the fact that I don't know what to do with the arm she has linked onto. My guide, Mr. Young, is her English teacher and he tells me she's a "diligent" student. That's the English word most commonly used to compliment someone's schoolwork. I can see already that diligence is prized above everything else here. Shi-eun is not in any of my classes because she's a "third grader" (third grade of middle school, meaning ninth grade in American terms.) I teach only the first and second graders (seventh and eighth graders). English conversation is a luxury that third graders can't afford—they must use the year to prepare for their high school exams. The results will determine the course of their lives from that point on.

No one in the Park family speaks much English. Shi-eun does the best, but she's so shy that she often speaks too softly for me to hear her. Still, she serves as the interpreter and we manage to exchange most of the necessary information. Her father is eager to communicate with me, and enthusiastic about helping me learn the names of common household items. He's *too* zealous about this as far as I'm concerned. I know that my hearing him pronounce a word once while he's pointing to an object will not be enough for me to retain it. But he apparently thinks it should be. I struggle to write the words in the Korean alphabet (*Hangul*) on napkins, envelopes, any paper that's available. Later I copy them into a notebook. Sometimes my brain is just too tired to take in the information along with everything else it's having to process in this new environment. I try to conceal my exasperation.

Mr. Park drives Shi-eun and me to school in his van in the mornings. We take the bus home, a forty-minute ride across town. We arrive at an empty apartment at 6:30 in the evening. Dinner is a sometime thing for Shi-eun. And I'm glad to be left to my own devices, since eating Mrs. Park's traditional breakfasts is an awkward challenge. Dried, salty fish and seaweed soup are not what my stomach expects. I eat the white rice and she thoughtfully prepares a "salad" of grated cabbage with dollops of ketchup and mayonnaise. She shakes her head at me. So in the evening I'm happy to stop at the tiny, stuffed grocery store at the base of the apartment tower and pick up a few things that seem compatible with my Western tastes. At the apartment I boil ramen and throw in some vegetables or just resort to cereal. Shi-eun's not very interested in my attempts. Sounding like an American teenager, she says she's too fat, and is trying to lose weight.

....

After only one full week of school, this week was shortened by a major national holiday—*Chusok* or "Harvest Moon Festival." Comparable to our Thanksgiving, it's not much of a vacation for the women who spend it feverishly preparing the dozens of traditional foods. Koreans use this long weekend to return to their hometowns to honor parents, grandparents, and dead ancestors. It means a road trip from Seoul to Kangnung that would normally take four hours will take eight to twelve. Fortunately for my homestay family, Mr. Park's widowed mother lives only a block away.

We walked to her home in the morning for breakfast. The house is old and built of brick. It's roofed with the typical thick, green, humped ceramic tiles. Just the fact that she has a single-family house impressed me. As we entered her walkway and approached the small concrete yard, a ferocious snarling dog, flaccid tits flailing, bared her teeth and strained against a clattering chain to get at us. She seemed equally belligerent toward all of us; there was no softened treatment for relatives. In the background were five tiny, spherical, black puppies that were dusty and scruffy looking. They were none too friendly either.

In Korea I'm learning the meaning of the phrase "miserable cur." The dogs here are filthy, malnourished, runtish, cowed, and hostile. As much as I miss my two cats and long to cuddle an affectionate, furry animal, I recoil even from the few dogs that trot up to me hoping for food. They might be contagious. Now and then I see a well-groomed, relaxed, and happy-looking dog with its owner. Most are like Grandma's dog, although hers is unusually aggressive.

Grandma's house is packed full of miscellaneous goods. Of course there's the large TV and the usual household clutter—stuffed animals, calendars, artificial plants, things that look like plastic souvenirs. There are some big, heavy pieces of furniture including a cabinet with glass-paned doors. Behind the glass is a supply of Amway products. On that day a large table that sat low on the floor of the living room was laden with dishes holding mounds of rice cakes, vegetable pancakes, kimchi, fish, and mysterious roots and vegetables under a red sauce that by then I knew would be hot. There's a small kitchen and a bedroom that doubles as another living room. (This is common in Korea. The bedding is folded and stored in a closet during the day.) The bathroom is an outhouse in the yard. Grandma was very proud to show me the "storm bed" in her room. It's a slab of marble with heating coils underneath. This one is divided into two halves, each with its own controls.

Overall, the house struck my American eye as a poor and shabby place. On our way in we passed something I'm very curious about. Between the house and the road are two trampolines with a heavy black net forming a ceiling over them. One trampoline is rectangular, about ten or twelve feet by eight feet. The other one is round, about eight feet in diameter. All day long various neighborhood kids played on them. I tried to question Shi-eun about them, but she either didn't have the English, or didn't want to talk about it. Everyone ignored them. Is this another source of income—like the Amway products?

Grandma is spry and lively, a real extrovert, and was very welcoming toward me. Also there were Mr. Park's brother, his wife, and their two sons, aged twelve and twenty-six. Shi-eun's uncle was silent and did not participate in the conversation, at least not while I was there. Her aunt is attractive and vivacious, and gave me a great deal of friendly attention. The younger cousin is cute and good-natured, not at all subdued by the presence of a foreigner. The older cousin is a fashion model in Seoul, I'm told. Strikingly tall and handsome, he was dressed in the current clothes of a sophisticated Seoulite. He was polite but distant. I'm a woman, and women are mostly ignored by men here.

Over the course of the day, we ate breakfast, lunch, and dinner at Grandma's. All day long I was exhorted to eat. *"Mani tuseyo!"* I stuffed myself gamely but finally had to get adamant about refusing. Late in the day, Grandma asked if I wanted more *pindae-dok* (bean and vegetable pancake). I said, *"Ani,"* a shortened form of "no" that I've heard Shi-eun use with her friends. Shi-eun curtly corrected me: *"Aniyo,"* and I realized my informality was inappropriate toward an older person. I was surprised at Shi-eun's tone of voice, embarrassed by my mistake, and felt unfairly rebuked. I understand the concept of different levels of speech for different people, but do not always remember to apply it. Can I be expected to after only a few weeks in the country?

In the afternoon I went to an amusement park with Shi-eun, her parents, her younger cousin, and a female friend of the family who runs a beauty parlor next to Mr. Park's business. The park is called Dreamland and is located in a town about forty-five minutes away. There are carnival rides, loud music, and a pretty lake.

The only photographs I have of the Parks were taken there. The colors are bright and the air looks clear. We stand smiling, arms linked. I am flanked by Shi-eun and the hairdresser, or by Shi-eun's parents. I'm such a contrast with my white hair and fair skin. Even my clothes are lighter. At five feet four inches, I'm the tallest. The pictures remind me of how new I am to Korea, and how eager I am to please, to fit in, to not offend, to do my part to refute the stereotype of the Ugly American. In the background is the noise and confusion of the amusement park.

Shi-eun and I rode the Viking, an inexorable pendulum dressed up like a Nordic ship. My rear end lifted from the seat at the apex of each swing. I really felt I would fall out if I didn't grip the bar in front of me with all my strength. I marveled that others—plenty of them frail looking—weren't dropping to the ground. At the same time I was trying to smile at Shi-eun's parents on the hard black asphalt, to look animated and happy while hoping each climb upward would be the last. My facial muscles were tense, tired, and finally quivering under the strain. At last the ship returned to land in one piece. I was the one that was a wreck.

After this, I knew better than to try anything more thrilling than the merry-go-round. But that ride was almost as bad because I felt silly—a sitting duck to be watched while I had nothing to do but revolve slowly and try to keep my face from sliding into its normal passive mold.

Back at Grandma's, and in between feedings, the females gathered in the bed-living room. Grandma kept prodding me, cupping my breasts, pressing on my stomach, and telling me I'm too thin. She doesn't believe in doctors. She is a member of a cult centered around a Korean man who is no longer alive. A solid yellow circle (invoking the moon) is the group's symbol. She claims praying to him has cured her ailments, though her fingers are noticeably swollen and deformed by arthritis. She's sixty-nine.

Holding her palm about twelve inches away from me, she repeatedly ran it over my body from head to toe, as if to wash out impurities and disease. Her hand paused in front of my stomach and she asked if there was anything wrong in that place. I said no, and other than being uncomfortably full, was indeed feeling very well. Since then, I've deliberately reimagined this "no-touch" massage in order to experience the same soothing shivers I enjoyed under Grandma's hands. It's one of the few gentle experiences I've had in Korea.

Shi-eun's mother apparently had a problem with her calf muscles. She sat on the floor with the soles of her feet together, her knees bent and falling outward. Her sister-in-law pounded the exposed calves with her palms continuously and loudly. I wondered how Mrs. Park could withstand this beating, but she seemed to relish it. (The next day her legs were black and blue.) Then it was Grandma's turn. She lay on her side and opened the zipper of her skirt that was held closed with a safety pin. By pulling up her blouse, the smooth skin of her hip was bared. The aunt applied the same vigorous, noisy slapping to this client. Afterwards, the women insisted that Shi-eun and I take a nap on the storm bed. It's something I would not normally do during a visit. But eventually we both obeyed. For me it was a chance to slide through some of the hours unnoticed.

Being in such an extraordinary place, being expected to respond and participate at all times without a shared language was enervating. And all the proceedings in Grandma's house were accompanied by boisterous music and talking coming from the TV. There were nonstop programs relating to Chusok, and they were no less obtrusive than having American football blared at you all day. It was torture. In addition, burping, slurping, gasping, smacking, and snorting are all part of a working-class Korean meal. My sensibilities had been thoroughly assaulted by the end of the day. By 7 P.M., I was so relieved that we were leaving. When we got home I showered and retreated gratefully to my room to read, sleep, and luxuriate in privacy.

Mr. Young says the Parks are a good example of the common people in Korea. He seems to think my exposure to them constitutes a useful cultural experience. He's right, of course. They're good people. But he has mentioned this several times and I wonder if he doesn't feel a little guilty about placing me with this family. I'm satisfied with my situation, but only because I believe it will end soon.

Entry 3
Wonju, Fall 1996

I'm the first occupant of this apartment—it's one of two on the third floor of a new three-story building. The gates of my school are visible from the window. I'm sure my colleagues consider this place luxurious. I think it's pretty spiffy too. There are two bedrooms. The kitchen and living room are one space with a wide floor-to-ceiling window at one end. The floor is the usual linoleum with padding underneath. It's yellow. Like other Korean homes, this apartment is heated with coils that carry hot water under the floor. The bedrooms are small, and there are no closets. I'll have to get an armoire. The bathroom reminds me of the one in the dorm at the University of Copenhagen—a memory going back twenty-six years. Walls and floor are solid tile. There is no separate shower stall, just a hose running up to the showerhead mounted on the wall. A toilet, a sink, and at the far end, my clothes washer. Everything can get wet, and does. Of course there was the joke in Denmark about being able to sit on the toilet and take a shower at the same time. I've acquired my own pair of plastic slippers to wear in the bathroom, and guests slide into them as they cross the threshold.

The "key money" (a lump sum paid in lieu of rent) demanded by the owner was too high for the government's budget. But my guide teacher, Mr. Young, managed to talk him down. He's quite proud of that. This place is far superior to the dingy high-rise apartment he and I looked at with officials from the school's financial affairs office. That one was a long bus ride away from work. And there was the other apartment in this neighborhood that smelled overwhelmingly of urine. No one else seemed to notice—not the present occupant, or Mr. Young, or the school official. I'm lucky to be here.

Fortunately my stay at the Parks' wasn't prolonged. They told Mr. Young they wanted me to remain with them for my entire stay in Korea. Perhaps my suspicions are unfair, but I wonder if they hoped for advantages Shi-eun might derive from her connection with an American. Everyone seems to want to go to the U.S. Shi-eun says she wants to go to school there. I told her I would help if I could when the time came. I was sincere, but unclear what form that help would take. I was afraid the word might be interpreted to mean money. Who knows what misconceptions they have about me—they very likely think I'm rich.

I'm full of unanswered questions about the Parks. I didn't understand Shi-eun's behavior at times. Toward the end of my stay she could be thoughtless and inconsiderate. One day I waited as usual for her to come to my desk in the teachers' room at 6:00 when she was done with her classes. I hung out for at least forty minutes before taking the bus by myself back to the apartment. It was raining, I had no umbrella, and no key to get in. I expected to find her there. When she wasn't, I walked to her father's shop in order to get a key. I was exasperated, exhausted from the whole day, and soaked. She showed up much later that evening, having gone for dinner downtown with her friends. She offered no apology or explanation. I was angry, but swallowed it. Other times she seemed irritated with me. Perhaps I was just interfering with her normal plans with friends. Yet there were times when I thought she regarded me as a fellow teenager. Did she think I was sixteen years old like her because I'm unmarried? Unmarried women here live like minors in America. They live with their parents and have curfews.

Did she and her parents perceive my moving into my own apartment as a rejection? How was I acting? I thought I was doing well at eating the food prepared for me. Did they think I was hard to please? Was I too private and reclusive for them? I had the impression Shi-eun thought I should have been able to speak Korean with her almost immediately.

It's true I chafed while living with them. I would have had many of the same problems living with a similar family in my own country. And maybe the same trouble I have living with anyone. When it comes down to it, I don't like people very much.

However, I do appreciate Mr. Young. He looks after me, and he's responsible for my getting this place. The mechanics of creating a home for me here make it necessary to talk often with him. His English is spotty, and his accent almost impenetrable at times. Although he is an English teacher, this is probably one of the few times in his life he has actually had to speak the language. Communicating with me is a real effort for him. My half of the conversation is equally strenuous. Sometimes I congratulate myself for learning his language so quickly. Then it occurs to me that all I'm doing is deciphering my own. It's a combination of listening as alertly as I can and guessing or intuiting his meaning.

In orientation there was some discussion about how important it is to Koreans not to lose face. I have taken that obligation on myself—to make their English look as good as possible by understanding them, and making my English as easy to comprehend as I possibly can. I try to keep the conversation from bogging down, and save them any embarrassment—especially if other people are around to witness the exchange. Koreans are very curious about each other's ability to converse in English with a native speaker. And many are loath to reveal their own level of proficiency in front of others. What I was told in the school for teaching English in San Francisco was true: Koreans are good at reading and writing, but their speaking and listening skills are poor.

As for this apartment, it's mostly empty except for my personal belongings—a suitcase full of clothes, my daypack, camera, and laptop computer. Over the weekend, I bought some small household items and a two-burner stove that is not yet hooked up to the propane tank outside my door. The "owner" (their English word for "landlord") provided me with a single-burner stove that operates on a canister. The furniture that is supposed to be provided by the government will, I hope, be bought and delivered this week. I'm sleeping on a quilted, not-very-thick mat that I double over to make a softer bed. Each night I cover myself with flowers in the form of a bright pink, green, and blue comforter that I bought. The sheets were brought from home, because I was warned Koreans don't use them.

Every delay, every snag makes me feel anxious, impatient, and distrustful. By now it's clear all the arrangements for my presence here are being handled on a minute-to-minute basis with no previous planning—both with regard to my housing and my teaching. Other Western teachers working for private schools here have so many horror stories about how they've been treated by school authorities—they're overworked, cheated out of their money, and miserably housed. I keep waiting for the other shoe to drop. Day by day, as each task *must* be handled, things are getting ironed out. To be honest, no shoes have dropped yet, or at least no boots.

Welcome home to a room of my own.

....

Having a five-day workweek is novel and welcome. I always spent six days a week in my ceramics studio, in addition to teaching T'ai Chi two or three evenings. As I adjust to this new job, I'm gradually expending less energy. I sleep well. I ran and did T'ai Chi in the schoolyard at 5:30 this morning. I'll do the same tomorrow.

One of the English teachers, Mr. Lee, took me downtown yesterday so I could buy the transformer that makes using my computer possible. I enjoyed being with him, talking, and having lunch. His English is tortured, but the best I have encountered so far. He seemed nervous and a little excited. I'm sure I don't appreciate what a strange experience it is for a Korean man to have lunch in a public restaurant with a Western woman. Mr. Lee is thirty-two and single. Mr. Young made a point of telling me early on that he will marry in January. I wonder what these people think of this way-past-marrying-age single American woman.

I teach in a girls' middle school with fifteen hundred students. They wear red plaid skirts, white blouses or sweaters, and a blue blazer. There are close to fifty in a class, and I see almost one thousand different girls once a week. I'm supposed to be "team teaching" –sharing the class time, even developing lessons with a Korean English teacher. But we never discuss the content of a lesson other than their telling me what part of the chapter they want me to handle. (I teach the dialogues, speaking practice, and sounds.) During class, I generally do all the teaching while my colleague sits in the back of the room. Some of them pay strict attention and are there to lend a hand with a translation when necessary. Others daydream, and at times seem satisfied to see me flounder, as if it confirms their opinion of me as a teacher, or as an American, or as a native speaking teacher who is not fluent in Korean.

The work is exhausting. I prepare very carefully because the girls understand so little English. I have to choose my words, sticking to vocabulary and sentence structure they're familiar with. As often as possible I use photos, actual objects, and miming to get the point across or elicit a word or sentence from them. I'm learning to keep my mouth shut and talk selectively and sparingly. Every word I utter goes through a mental screening process either before or during class. The Korean teachers are concerned with keeping a class quiet and subdued during the forty-five minutes. I, on the other hand, am always trying to rev them up, get them talking and participating in exercises that are physically active. Then I have to deal with fifty rambunctious students.

The girls are in school for a minimum of nine hours a day (8:00 to 5:00) and a half day on Saturday. Most attend academies after school until 9 or 10:00 at night. They're sleepy and dull at times, but considering what their daily schedules are like, they're amazingly energetic and good humored.

I work from eight to five and am protecting my Saturdays from any requests to teach private conversation lessons. My contract states I'm not allowed to take a second job, and I'm hiding behind this. The Koreans are quick to dismiss my excuse. But I really wouldn't feel comfortable violating the contract, and I have enough of teaching in five days. I *need* two days to recuperate and tend to other business.

At first the students seemed guileless. Now I'm not so sure. They're quick to parody and mimic me. They can be quite derisive—toward their peers and toward me. When I first arrived (I have only been teaching here a few weeks) they were all consistently shy and respectful. The newness of being addressed by a Westerner was almost too much for them—they clutched both hands of the friend sitting next to them, grinned breathlessly, and did their best to answer. I wish they would return to being that way. Many still are, and some are genuinely interested in learning from me.

Shyness is just another cover for someone's true personality—for someone's will. Everyone has a will. Even pretty, sweet-acting, petite, quiet little girls. And wills are for exerting. Yesterday a student executed an exaggerated, down-to-the-ground bow as I walked by. Today two girls passed me outside the school and one gave out a loud, scornful, obviously forced laugh as she went by. I thought it was meant for me.

William, a young American English teacher who works at an academy in town, tells me just the fact that I allow them—encourage them—to say hello or hi to me, to look me in the face and address me directly sets me apart (and some notches down) from other teachers on their hierarchical ladder. William has been here two and a half years, and speaks and understands some Korean. He says he overhears slighting comments toward Americans wherever he goes. Our soldiers have preceded us, and eighteen-year-old boys don't make the best ambassadors. Perhaps it's worse for men. William claims American men are automatically perceived as sex fiends.

What do these girls think of me? What do their parents think and say about me, or foreigners in general, or Americans in particular? Do they resent the American? For being associated (synonymous) with power? For being rich? For rescuing them? For being necessary to their safety? For requiring them to learn a complex and often totally illogical language? Their ambivalence toward me is obvious. They are eager to make contact with me and they derive status from it. They also resent me. I've adopted an assiduously self-deprecating and America-deprecating attitude that seems to have the intended effect—on some people, at least. I avoid making any criticism of Korea and am well prepared for the frequent question, "What do you like best about our country?"

"Koreans work very hard—they are diligent people."

"Koreans are very kind."

"Korea—especially Kangwon-do—is beautiful."

"I like to climb Ch'iak-san and Sorak-san." (These are local mountains, and the centerpieces of national parks.)

"The trees here are red and orange and yellow in the fall."

"Many people think some of the best ceramics in the world come from Korea."

The Korean government is spending a lot of money on me. (I'm certain every teacher and official at school knows *exactly* how much. Privacy in such matters does not exist.) They should be spending more on sending their own teachers to English-speaking countries for a year or two. That sounds like a better investment, and the teachers like to hear me say this. However, they will always need native speakers here.

....

I have two women friends, Bo-ra and Ae-ja. I met both of them on the street, although at different times. Bo-ra came up to me just as I was about to enter a bakery in downtown Wonju. She's a pleasant-looking, well-dressed woman in her early thirties. She introduced herself and asked if she could talk to me. I said yes without any reservations. We sat in the bakery and ate croissants that weren't bad at all. She told me her story in between asking questions about me, and remarking repeatedly on how young I look for my age, and how beautiful I am. (This is a common approach for Koreans—telling Westerners how beautiful they are.) She's a single woman, an "old miss" (a woman past the usual marrying age of twenty-six), and a student at a religious college in Seoul. She has her bachelor's degree already, and commutes to Seoul for graduate study in theology. She told me she wants to be my friend, help me in any way that she can, and practice English with me.

Ae-ja approached me on the sidewalk outside of my apartment. She lives in my neighborhood, and is an attractive housewife in her early thirties with three children. She also was full of compliments on how young I looked, how beautiful. She was very eager to help me cope with life in Wonju, and also wanted an opportunity to practice her English. I had no qualms about getting to know either of them. The white-haired, blue-eyed American gets lots of attention here. People are lining up on the street to be my friend.

Both of them have helped me get mundane things done and assisted in my first attempts to study and speak Korean. It must be frustrating for them to expend all the energy it takes to communicate with me. They were here for tea on Sunday, a welcome chance to entertain people in my new home. It turns out they went to the same high school, separated by only one year. Bo-ra and Ae-ja enjoyed talking with each other, and I was glad they had a chance to lapse into their own language after the slow, halting dictionary-rifling process of talking to me in English.

....

I'm not homesick for any of my friends or acquaintances yet, but I long for familiarity—for the comfort and relaxation that it can bring. My home is still barren. I'll have to wait until next week for my furnishings. The education office in Chunchon has not gotten around to sending the money. Yet I'm comfortable here—just glad to have my own place, and be able to write on my computer.

Entry 4
Wonju, Fall 1996

It's 7:30 on a Saturday evening. I just did T'ai Chi in a darkened playground, then walked once around the perimeter. I heard a cat's crying and tried to lure it with a high-pitched "kitty, kitty, kitty." I only caught a glimpse. Not only do these cats not speak English, they also don't respond to an affectionate tone of voice. I was missing my cats, Tigger and Piglet. For almost ten years they were my best buddies, and it was more difficult to leave them than it was to leave any people in my life. My primary concern as I prepared to go abroad was to find them a good home. My heart physically aches for them.

They came into my life as strays. Some friends and I were riding bikes on a rural road in Humboldt County, California. When we stopped at the top of a hill to rest, two tiny kittens pranced up to us, meowing importunately. They were both brown tabbies; the insides of their ears were lightly veiled with delicate hairs. One was round with a truncated corkscrew tail that formed a bushy plume. The other was long and thin with concentric stripes and a tail like a squirrel's. Everyone else already had cats, so one of my friends informed me these were mine. I was reluctant. I love cats, but am also allergic to them. I suggested taking just one. That embarrassingly stingy idea was immediately shot down. I put the round one—eventually to be named Piglet—into my bike bag. Someone else put the long one—Tigger—into hers.

When I got home, I discovered they were so small that I could hold them both in one hand and pet them with the other. They slept with me, kneading my scalp with their needle claws and sucking on my head. I threw them down to the end of the bed; they marched back. We did this over and over again until I gave up. I woke with a sore, wet head. For almost two months my eyes and palate itched and my nose ran—until I became immune to the allergic symptoms. The fact is I may have loved those cats more than I have ever loved anything. They delighted, amused, angered, and entertained me. They also reciprocated the attention and affection I lavished on them. At the end of every day, when I walked up the driveway to my apartment, I waved to Tigger who was perched on the windowsill looking out. One day she raised her paw—a little hesitatingly, as if she weren't quite sure want she was doing. She was waving back.

The night before we went on that bike trip, I dreamt that I had a baby, but the baby was a cat. She was wearing a flouncy yellow dress. As I lifted her joyfully in my arms I could feel her little spiral tail—Piglet's distinctive tail—in the palm of my left hand. Apparently I'm a cliché: the single woman with her cats. I cried as I finished another turn around the playground—the first time since well before leaving the U.S.

....

I felt wasted today, lethargic. Mostly I reread *Jane Eyre*. I gave myself the day off from some of the required activities I've wasted no time in setting up. Didn't feel like studying Korean— I'll put it off 'til tomorrow morning. I'm driving myself as I always have. I want to be a good teacher, learn the language, make myself look good, and not disappoint people. I try to remember that I want to take care of myself too, and that's why I'm here.

Last week I showed Mrs. Jong, one of the teachers, the photos I brought with me of family and friends. She said she thought I missed them. I tried to look wistful and said yes, but in truth they are scattered all over the U.S. and my contact with them was infrequent even when I lived there. I'm used to existing by myself, accompanied mostly by my work in clay and my T'ai Chi practice. Besides, I have only been gone six weeks and still feel like an escapee. I have written no letters yet.

I think the Koreans do wonder what I'm doing here alone. How many of us native English teachers are runaways? Couldn't find jobs, were frustrated with relationships, or just plain desperate? Korea isn't the most alluring place, and for all their national pride, they're aware of that. I'm here because they pay well and I knew of no better place to go. It gives me a way to make some money while I figure out how to begin my second life. All the other stuff I've been telling people here and at home—wanting to see the famous Korean ceramics; study brush painting and Tae Guk Kwan (the Korean word for T'ai Chi); visit the temples, parks, and historic sites—is rationalization after the fact, though nonetheless true.

....

This is a three-day weekend. Last week would have been my first full week of teaching, but Mr. Young and I took Friday afternoon to go shopping for my household goods. He drove us downtown to one of the many furniture stores. In about ten minutes I selected (from very few choices) a "sofa" that is really a big stuffed chair, a desk, office chair, coffee table, armoire, two dressers, mirror, hall tree, and single bed. My. Young was in what I have come to recognize as a typical Korean hurry. I didn't mind accommodating him by making snap choices.

I am learning that this is the way Koreans shop. They don't inspect the merchandise, mull it over, possibly even leave and come back. They walk in, point, and pay. Any other behavior by a customer just irritates a shop owner. Already I avoid entering a number of shops because of this. However, it didn't bother me to rush through the furniture-buying task. I don't take these purchases all that seriously—this is a temporary home and the furniture reverts back to the government when I leave. It's not my intention to re-create my American home here in Korea. The dresser drawers are painted alternately pastel pink and green. The armoire, coffee table, and sofa are all a matching green. None of my usual tasteful antiques—I want color.

We returned to the school office where I picked out appliances from a catalogue—TV, refrigerator, phone, washing machine, vacuum cleaner. All the afternoon's purchases were delivered later the same day. The school bestowed these purchases on two stores—chosen on what basis? I had nothing to do with it. I was just glad to get it done.

Instantly, almost two weeks after moving in, I have a home. The phone won't be hooked up until next week, and the hot water is frustratingly sparse, barely enough to eke out a shower. I've mentioned this to Mr. Young in the hopes that he will alert the owner. There is also a persistent sewer gas smell because the kitchen sink (unlike the bathroom sink) doesn't have a trap under it. I'm told this is common in Korean homes. I did my first load of laundry today. Fortunately Ae-ja stopped by around 5:00 and gave me a general working translation of the labels on the control knobs.

Entry 5
Wonju, Fall 1996

I've been ambushed. I'm forty-eight, but at times my libido is as wildly intense as it was in my twenties. Romantic, erotic fantasies keep me preoccupied and sleepless—I bloom like a rose during the day and hover above my bed at night. This is a crush as strong as any I've ever experienced. My heart's idle is set way too high. I churn out endless, urgent fantasies that I try to transfer to someone else—an old boyfriend from my distant past. This never works for long. As these things always are for me, it's pleasurable and painful at the same time. And distracting.

It has been years since I felt this way, and I didn't expect it—especially with such an unlikely object. I'm thirteen years older. He's an Asian male, married, with two little girls. The language barrier stunts our conversation. But, of course, none of these things are taken into consideration by whatever part of me it is that chooses the target and launches the campaign. My intellect is not consulted. Opposites, apparently, do attract. Is this the gene pool's attempt to avoid stagnation? Maybe it's my reproductive system's last hurrah. I'm on the cusp of menopause, and my never-say-die drive to procreate may be leaping at one final chance.

I have not yet described Mr. Young. He's a handsome man. He's slightly taller than I, with a solid build. He has a boyish face with even features, high cheekbones, and warm brown eyes. He often looks *too* young to me. His black hair is cut short so that it stands up like a velvety nap on the back of his neck. I like his voice, his smile, his mischievousness. He strikes me as entirely male.

From our first meeting, when he drove me to Wonju after I finished the orientation period in Chunchon, he seemed surprisingly Western in his thinking. I liked the fact that he had a critical, even cynical perspective on Korea. He told me not to think of Korea as a developed country, and that simple advice has helped me slough off many inconveniences and irritations. He is a true advocate, heading off problems before they get to me; he's a buffer between me and other teachers and officials who are less amenable to the presence of a foreigner in their school.

Mr. Young has been married seven years. Long enough to be well past the infatuation stage, and deep into the drudgery of raising small children. His domestic life has to be maintained while he's coping with an impossibly demanding five-and-a-half-day week that spills over into Saturday afternoon and Sunday. And the years stretch out in front of him just the same.

Korean lives generally follow a strict schedule: marriage by twenty-six for women, thirty for men. They immediately begin having children. They are part of a tightly woven extended family and divorce is very uncommon. If you know a person's age, you know whether they are married or not, and how many children they have. Their lives are preplanned for them, their marriages often arranged, and there's no room for spontaneity or divergence. Where is their outlet? No wonder Korea is full of "love motels" owing their existence to illicit meetings. People need some change, excitement, and joy in their lives.

I would like to know what Mr. Young's feelings are for me. I believe he's attracted, fascinated. Maybe because I'm exotic—a single American, blue eyes, white hair (my hair started turning silvery white when I was twenty-eight). American women are supposed to be easy. And we are: We have sex outside of marriage. As an American friend living in Singapore once said about this cultural feature, "Thank you sweet Jesus!" Maybe a Korean man thinks that means we're willing and eager to sleep with just about anyone.

I have always yearned to know people's unspoken thoughts and feelings about me. Although my intuition along these lines is persuasive, I'm reluctant to rely on it because I know how easily colored it is by fears or wishful thinking. (I also have a strong sense of direction. The problem is, it's usually wrong.) Not wishing to deceive myself, I have doubted, maybe frequently underestimated, my effect on other people. I marvel at the confidence with which some conduct themselves in personal relationships with me. They seem absolutely sure of all sorts of innermost information I have never uttered, and don't hesitate to use that information as leverage—sometimes benignly, sometimes not. They don't seem to lack any assurance in *their* ability to affect *me*; more often than not they overestimate it. I may be transparent, but I'm also strong.

....

  Two weeks after I arrived in Wonju, Mr. Young and I took a three-hour drive to the city of Tonghae on the coast so that I could register as an "alien." (I can tell it will be a long time before Korea replaces this word and the word "foreigner" with the more politically correct "international." Korea earned its title The Hermit Kingdom, and is ambivalent about giving it up.) In the days before we left, he told me more than once that he was looking forward to the trip because we would travel through the mountains and the trees are beautiful in the fall. When he was younger and single, he started his teaching career in that town. He has fond memories. I suspected some of his enthusiasm had to come from the one-day reprieve from school. It sounded like fun to me, too. Autumn is my favorite season, and I was enjoying the pleasant stimulation of a burgeoning attraction for my guide teacher.
  The day came and it was overcast and windy, a damper on our high expectations. We were both counting on sun. During the drive he played tapes of the kind of soft jazz I used to hear in the fifties and sixties. It struck me as quaint, a little old fashioned, and achingly romantic.
  We found the Alien Registration Office in Tonghae where I filled out the forms for my identity card. They told us it would be an hour or so before the card could be printed, so we drove to the harbor. Mr. Young pulled his car into a parking space and I reached for the door handle. He wasn't done parking yet, and placed his hand briefly on my thigh to stop me from opening the door. I was stunned. Everyone told me that Korean men and women don't touch each other. In an instant, feelings of being taking advantage of as a foreigner, and embarrassment at the response his touch evoked (that melting sensation) clashed with each other. I was angry, pleased, and confused all at once. Just as

quickly, I decided to pretend it was nothing. After all, I rationalized, I'm a Westerner—a Californian!—and where I come from, touching between friends who are opposite genders is commonplace, even required. Maybe he was counting on this. The incident rattled me.

    We walked to the dock from where we could see a long line of anchored squid boats with their strings of transparent light bulbs suspended high above their decks. They fish at night, and the squid are attracted to the lights. A new load had just come in, and the catch was darting around in waist-high, red plastic vats filled with water. They squirted us as they tried to propel themselves out of their prisons. Mr. Young chose fifteen to take back to his family and to friends at school. A woman immediately slit them open and gutted them. Then she chopped one into narrow strips and we squatted on the wet cement to eat it. The meat itself was bland, but we were provided with a container of spicy red sauce for dipping. Mr. Young ate a lot; I ate a little. Struggling to be a tolerant guest in this strange country, and shamelessly wanting the object of my crush to like me, I concentrated on holding my nausea at bay. Barely a minute ago this creature was thoroughly alive and in obvious distress.

    Since I had eaten so little, Mr. Young decided we needed to go to a restaurant so I could eat a real lunch. We found a dark and formal place—an imitation Western restaurant that was depressing to me. The food served in these places is a facsimile of middle-class American food from the fifties—the kind that our Korean War soldiers hungered for. As a mostly-vegetarian, I would have been much happier in a less pretentious Korean restaurant. But I think Mr. Young thought he was pleasing me, and he ordered the veal cutlet that I reluctantly chose. The waiter must have misunderstood, because he brought two meals. We accepted them and began eating. I felt uncomfortable and awkward throughout this lunch. I was in an oppressive restaurant eating food I didn't want to eat with a man I had difficulty talking to, and had feelings for that were inappropriate. What's more, I knew we were being scrutinized by the help. When we finally finished, I picked up the check because I knew the meal was expensive, and we were only there because of my inexplicable lack of enthusiasm for raw squid.

After taking care of the bill at the counter, I walked out through a narrow hallway where I encountered Mr. Young to my left. He was standing in a tiny room barely big enough to hold him, the door propped open by his back. (I'm not sure it *could* have closed with him in there.) He was facing away from me, and I could tell from the position of his arms that he was urinating. But my first shocked reaction was that he was exposing himself to me. After a fleeting double take, I grasped what was happening, and continued walking out of the restaurant. Still, I was jolted by the casualness, and, as usual, not sure what the intention was on the part of the Korean, if there were any intention at all. Most Americans like privacy when they use a bathroom, and expect others not to inflict the sight of their elimination processes on them. I composed myself.

I'm getting used to the fact that many restrooms in Korea are shared by men and women simultaneously. The women go into the stalls, and the men stand at the urinals. I was shaken the first time I was washing my hands at a sink and a man walked into the restroom and used the urinal.

We took a different route home, this one on narrow country roads instead of the highway. He said he wanted to show me some of old Korea. The traditional houses were small and low with thickly tiled, curved roofs. This was the picturesque rural Korea, sparsely populated and lushly green. The mountains reminded me of the eastern United States—old, rounded, soft, not too steep or rocky. They're hospitable.

Mr. Young asked me, as had almost every Korean I had met up to then, why wasn't I married. I had a prepared answer that saw a lot of use in Korea. I said I was very involved in my work as an artist, and, although I liked children, had never wanted any of my own. He didn't seem to hear that I had *chosen* not to marry. He expressed sympathy, and told me he hoped I would marry some day. He asked if I had had a boyfriend, and I selected one of my past lovers to tell him about, expressing in generalities the incompatibility that had caused us to split up.

Selecting and simplifying my history in order not to scandalize Koreans is something I do often here. It's a decision I made before I finished my first week of orientation. I knew from talking to a Korean-American friend that people here would have a hard time understanding my singleness. Partly on her advice, I decided not to add to that the fact that I was divorced—twice, by the age of twenty-eight. This proved to be a sound decision. Single women are viewed with a combination of pity and contempt. A divorced woman is a shameful thing.

My past, I resolved from the beginning, would be as private as I chose. This was a novel tack for someone who is only gradually (at this late date) learning not to feel obligated to answer with utter candor every question put to me by a friend or a stranger.

The road back to Wonju took us close to his wife's hometown. He told me how, as a child, she took the train to and from school every day. I asked how they met, and he told me they taught at the same school—he as an English language teacher, and she as a Korean language teacher. The fondness and respect with which he talked about his wife touched me. It made me trust him more, while it conflicted with other signals from him, as well as with signals I was giving myself.

....

I walked into school last Sunday around noon to use the phone since mine wasn't connected yet. Mr. Young happened to be there. He gave me a manila envelope full of mail that had been forwarded to me from the university where I had my first two weeks of orientation. Then he said, "Why don't you start a school?" meaning why don't I start my own English language academy. I told him I needed more teaching experience before I could consider something like that. He briefly disagreed with me, then got around to what he was really thinking about. He said he is considering starting an English language academy in his hometown in the southern part of the country. There is none there now. He looked me in the eye and pointedly said, "It is an opportunity for me." I sensed, as I sometimes do, that he had prepared and practiced this English sentence. He went on to say that he's not really a dedicated teacher. He's just putting in his time with an eye toward retiring as early as possible and starting a business in his hometown, which is smaller and cleaner than Wonju. It's where he wants to be. He asked if I would want to teach there. I reiterated my reservations about my lack of experience, and my inability to speak Korean. But as he talked about it, I gradually started thinking it could be fun to embark on an enterprise like that with him. As he described it, my work would include teaching and administration. I could recruit teachers from the U.S., perhaps through the school in San Francisco, and help make their experience as problem-free as possible. Mr. Young thinks there is some money to be made. I believe him; I think he's basically well-meaning and honest. It would definitely be more of an adventure than teaching here a second year, although at this point that doesn't sound bad. Could I stand working that closely with him for that long? It would take considerable restraint, if I continue to feel toward him the way I'm feeling now.

Entry 6
Portland, Fall 1998

    I lived the last two years before Korea in a state of bewilderment. In many ways I'd been successful—I had managed to make a living doing the things I most wanted to do. For twenty-four years I had been a full-time potter; for the last eight of those years I had taught T'ai Chi, another passion in my life; and I had realized my childhood aspiration of being a writer by producing two books. It had all happened so naturally—there were no hard choices or decisions. But one essential part of that success was missing: money.

    My crisis in faith engulfed me slowly over a period of at least two years. My work had been accepted by prestigious galleries, the kind that I thought signaled my arrival as an artist, and triggered the anticipation of modest financial security. That never panned out. The galleries took as much as sixty percent of the retail price, and I couldn't produce the work fast enough. I never wanted to develop a "line" that would lend itself to mass production and the hiring of help. Occasionally I hired someone to help with shipping. I knew I couldn't sustain the level of work required in my studio indefinitely. Clay is heavy and I was getting older. I was also getting bored. If something sold well, I had to keep doing the same sort of thing for too long. I spent less and less time experimenting.

    Part of my problem was that I was alone. I had no other source of energy—physical or emotional. Almost all the people I know who work full time as artists have a spouse or family lending some form of assistance, often monetary. Or they spent a long time teaching and accumulating assets and a reputation before they ventured into the chartless world of a full-time artist. Lovers came and went in my life and some contributed energy, others drained it. I never received money from lovers. In the midst of my poverty I actually was contributing to someone else's household over the two years that we dated. A woman friend of mine offered to buy an eighty-dollar plane ticket for me so I could visit her along with two other mutual friends. I accepted. I believe this is the only financial help I received after college other than the money I got from my mother's estate. That $35,000 helped me move from Illinois to California and afforded me the time to write my first book.

I had an IRA that had been growing on its own, with no help from me since I moved to California. I also had a savings account, but I had not added to it either since I moved. My decision to stop drawing on this source after living in Humboldt County for four and a half years constricted my life to a point of having to skimp on food. I remember the stinging distress caused by a friend's simple request to bring a salad to a potluck dinner. At that moment I wasn't able to buy the ingredients for a presentable contribution. A month later, a family of four stopped in at my house on their way through town on a summer trip, and if it hadn't been for a timely fifty-dollar check from a gallery, I would not have been able to feed them without dipping into my savings. When I attended a T'ai Chi workshop out of town, I stayed with friends. I told them I wanted to take them to dinner at one of our favorite vegetarian restaurants as a way of thanking them. During the course of the weekend I felt obligated to buy a video for fifteen dollars. This made me apprehensive about paying for gas on the way home. When a group of us went to dinner at the end of the weekend, I pretended to forget about my promise of hosting my friends as the check was being divided. The man quickly picked up his cue and paid for their meals. I felt miserable, small, powerless, and craven. Money had made me lie.

In the midst of my crisis, I was invited to attend a "career day" at a local high school. A painter whose work I admired and who had had good success marketing his work all over the country shared a table with me. We represented the arts as a career. It was a depressing day for several reasons. The high school was located in a working-class neighborhood, and the most popular tables were the ones where people were recruiting for the military, day care centers, and beauty salons. Those kids had no reason to be interested in art as a career—most of them were already poor and didn't aspire to more of the same for the rest of their lives. All the other options represented that day offered more security and more money. My friend and I had plenty of time to talk, which is how I discovered that he was wearily fending off the same worries that I was. How could I recommend art as a career? Even after more than twenty years of working six days a week, there was no letup. Anyone who has their own business has to be willing to work long hours for some years in order to get established. But eventually that hard work is expected to pay off—in the form of money or time or both.

Even though I have always known there is no place for art in academia, I reluctantly applied to grad schools for an MFA. At least that would give me the option of teaching, a possibility I had deliberately shunned when I started out as a potter decades before. It would have been easy for me to go on to graduate school then, probably in any school I would have chosen—given my degree from Ohio State, one of the top schools for ceramic arts in the country, and the recommendations of supportive teachers who carried some weight in the field. But I did not want teaching as "something to fall back on" as my mother so frequently warned. I wanted to be forced to make it as an artist. I had often listened to the best professors I had in college wishing they were full-time artists instead of earning their livings as teachers. My strategy worked, until I ran out of steam.

I applied to the four schools considered to have the best ceramics departments in the country. No sense in submitting myself to the arbitrariness and artificial pressure of school again if the degree I emerged with didn't have some clout. I visited a respected ceramic arts department—one I didn't apply to—and was shocked by the general chaos and clutter in the studios. There was a show of work by current MFA students in the gallery. Only one or two pieces looked mildly interesting to me; the centerpiece was a five-foot-high penis. The penises produced in the ceramics department at Ohio State didn't interest me back in 1970. How far behind me this sort of thing seemed now! I didn't want to try to fit into an adolescent atmosphere. However, I figured I could put up with almost anything for two years.

To my anguish and humiliation, I was not accepted. All sorts of conflicting feelings collided within me: my work was not appreciated—even my book about the parallels between art and

T'ai Chi (art and meditation) had not persuaded them to accept me. I was surprised and confused. I probably shouldn't have been. My work was my own—it was not current; it wasn't "in the pipeline." I have never looked outside myself to determine what sort of work I would do. And my work was too varied. This is something I've always considered one of my strong points, but in the art world, if someone doesn't stick with one idea and beat it to death over a period of years (maybe a lifetime), they're considered not serious.

This sounds like self-justification. The other possibility was that my work wasn't good enough.

It's my fault, though, isn't it? This sorry story. I should have done things differently—sold directly from my studio as I did in Illinois, or through art fairs instead of using galleries. The galleries were good for my ego. I wanted to show that my work was on a level with some of the best. And I was no longer involved directly in the tainted realm of sales. Instead of frittering my time writing and then setting up a new ceramics studio, I should have bought a house with that $35,000 as a down payment as soon as I arrived in California. But then I wouldn't have written that first book, or received those letters from readers in Scotland, Canada, South Africa, or the kind words from T'ai Chi practitioners in this country. Or maybe I would have found a way to write it. I wrote my second book while working six days a week in my studio which meant writing in the evenings when I wasn't teaching T'ai Chi, and on Sunday.

My T'ai Chi classes were popular and brought in an extra several thousand dollars a year. But the sparse population in that northern Californian county wouldn't support expanding the number of classes. My books—*A Potter's Notes on T'ai Chi Ch'uan* and *Breathing Underwater: The Inner Life of T'ai Chi Ch'uan* were selling well by small press standards, but the income I derived wasn't enough to make any significant difference in my living standard, or in the level of my security.

I was pissed at Joseph Campbell and the whole "follow your bliss" philosophy. I had followed my bliss, but my bliss lay outside the economy. If anyone at the time had accused me of being a New Age hippie expecting a just and benevolent universe to keep me afloat, I would have denied it. Yet I have to admit that in the back of my mind there was a whispering belief that if I worked hard enough and smart enough at the things that felt right to me—that fulfilled me—I would be rewarded. With material prosperity, among other benefits.

Joseph Campbell never set foot outside of academia in his whole adult life. He learned a lot of what he became famous (and rich) for from the young women at Sarah Lawrence. But if *they* had said the same things publicly, no one would have paid any attention. It had to come from a male academic. There was one hitch that Campbell failed to see—if your bliss is not embraced by the mainstream economy, devoting yourself to it can lead to exhaustion, poverty, and a sense of failure.

It was frightening watching my spirit shrink. I found myself growing angry and resentful toward people with money. (As an artist and a well-educated person, I have moved easily through most levels of society, so had constant contact with wealthy people.) I knew that even my friends with modest but comfortable incomes had no idea what I was experiencing. This was not something I discussed with people in detail.

Statistics say rich people live longer than poor people. I just heard on the radio that acquiring $100,000 produces as much happiness in a person's life as getting married.

One of the few things I enjoyed about Korea was the fact that I was actually making decent money, and not just while I was working. It was a new experience for me to feel that I was automatically and constantly generating money—on a weekend, over a holiday, while I was taking photos of the girls at Sports Day, during a class picnic, at night, even on days when I didn't teach well. The same amount of money came to me every two weeks. I was used to earning it pound by pound, from the finished products that had been squeezed through my hands several times and then finally chosen by people who were willing to pay for them. Piece by piece. No assurance that any money would come from it at all. It might get broken up at the end of the month or the year, and taken to the dump. I would pay to dispose of it. What a revelation to simply be under contract and *know* a certain amount of money would appear in my bank account.

On a long-distance phone call from America, a friend asked me about my new-flowing income, "What do you buy?" I told him I bought flowers for my table, meals out, winter clothes. And I didn't have to look at the price on every item I bought at the grocery store. Nothing extravagant. My material needs have always been small. But it was so refreshing not to have to think about every fraction of every dollar I spent—that's a wearing, stultifying life.

Before Korea, I was overworked, underpaid, and not saving any money—which meant I was losing ground. I decided I had to start "taking care of myself," I had to elevate money to the highest priority in my life. It's fear. The constant presence of fear.

These were my grumblings: I'm a smart, hardworking, responsible person. And that's more than I can say for lots of people who earn many times what I do. Certainly I can come up with a way to make a livable income that would allow me to do my ceramics, my writing, my T'ai Chi in my spare time and without the pressures of the marketplace.

Suddenly I found myself having to make decisions—something new. Until this point, my life had followed its own path, its only path. It wasn't a conventional one, and there was no leader to follow, but my life flowed by itself. Decisions were not made, they happened. Now, I told myself, I had to use my intellect. It was about time I used my head (instead of my gut) to make choices about how to make a living. This was difficult because there was no directional pull, no inner conviction, no confidence or joy behind any of the possible doors.

I closed out my studio (a huge effort when I was already depleted), moved my belongings into the storage unit and bolted for San Francisco where I could get certified for teaching English abroad. A few years away, I reasoned, could provide me with savings and time to figure out what I should be doing. I would also have acquired a marketable skill. Two years earlier, I would not have believed I'd be making such a move. When my friend who had been teaching English in Singapore talked about her experiences, I thought that was nice, but not for me. I was busy; I was engaged in my own work, excited about it. It wasn't long until the crisis in faith overtook me.

I'm a bitter woman. At first it was hard to admit it. I thought bitterness was taboo and represented the only real failure—you could suffer all sorts of setbacks and injustices, but each time you had to come back and persist. Letting life get to you, letting it alter you was the only thing to be ashamed of. Now I think bitterness is just another emotion, like anger or joy or sadness. The Chinese include it in the five tastes—salty, sour, sweet, pungent, and bitter. Westerners want to limit themselves to sweet and salty. At times bitterness is the only appropriate response. Especially for a woman over fifty and perhaps for anyone who's paying attention. In *Shirley,* Charlotte Bronte says bitterness is strength—it is a tonic.

When I returned from Korea, I considered resettling in Humboldt County, California, but was afraid of getting dragged back into the chronically depressed economy. I briefly scouted out Seattle, but its size scared me. I chose Portland because I have a sister and a brother here, and it seems a manageable city.

I'm a fifty-year-old woman living in a society listing dangerously toward the male side. My confidence is low. How will I make money? What shape will my life take? How do I go about shaping it?

....

Almost twenty years ago when I lived in Illinois, I remember writing this down: "This morning I woke up, stepped into myself, and I was a perfect fit." What a state of grace! I eventually outgrew that self, and had to shed that skin. After thirteen years, Illinois was no longer fertile ground for me. That's when I moved to northern California. I have not since achieved that Illinois state of comfort, and now I'm altogether skinless, casting about for a shell, a new home. Portland is a fecund place—I admire daily its greenness and moistness. Perhaps the nutrients are here for sprouting and nourishing a new life.

....

As I prepared to move to California from Illinois, I worried that I would not be able to fit my writing table into the U-Haul truck. I had gone so far as to contact the antique dealer who sold it to me to see if she wanted to buy it back, assuming it couldn't accompany me. It's an elegant and sturdy library table—solid walnut with walnut veneer. Its long, narrow shape is not ideal as a desk, but it was the home of my typewriter back in 1985, and the place where I sat to write.

I hired two men from a moving company to come to my home and pack the truck. This was a precaution intended to prevent my belongings from achieving a colloidal state by the end of the 2,400-mile trip. The night before the scheduled loading, I lay in a room empty of everything but the bed and window blinds and a few clothes hanging in the closet. I was in a quietly wakeful state with my eyes closed when I heard this sentence (from within or without my head?): "You will take your table with you."

It fit in easily, and I wrote both my books on that table—the first using the Smith Corona typewriter left over from college, the second using a word processor. *A Potter's Notes* was written at the window of my apartment overlooking Main Street in Ferndale, California—a Disney-like Victorian town, population 485. (I could tell you who was late for work, and who was returning to their own home after spending the night elsewhere.) *Breathing Underwater* was written at the window of a cottage in Bayside, a small town twenty-five miles north of Ferndale and adjacent to Arcata.

When I left for Korea, a friend took the table into her home. When I returned, it became an issue again—she and her husband were on vacation when I was planning to load a U-Haul for the trip to Portland. How would I get it there if I couldn't take it in the truck? The Honda Civic that I purchased within a week of my returning to the U.S. wasn't built for moving furniture. A delay in my schedule solved the problem.

Now the table holds my computer and printer and I sit here looking out a different window. I feel guilty that I have not maintained this table in the pristine condition in which I bought it. The veneer is bubbling in one place where the overflow water from a hanging plant dripped onto it. (One should not water plants and then leave home before determining whether this will happen.) There are cat scratches along the upper edges—not from my cats, but from an annoying, aggressive neighbor cat who lost no time in being destructive as soon as he gained entrance. We're friends, this table and I. Both of us have seen some hard wear, and are showing it.

....

    I bought this computer used. So far so good. It whirrs and buzzes unevenly and sometimes loudly—an unwelcome change from my silent laptop. It occurred to me that this is a poor substitute for the purring of my cats.

    They aren't with me. I did find a good home for them before I left for Korea. I told their new keepers that I would like to reclaim them when I resettled in the U.S. But I couldn't find (at least not quickly) an apartment in my price range that would allow cats. I was in a hurry to make a home for myself—I spent a total of two restless, sleep-deprived months with friends or family before I could move into this one. It's possible my cats have forgotten all about me, but I think of them daily, dream about them, and feel that I've deserted them. I tell them in my mind that I had no choice but to leave. I knew I would have to lose my studio soon because the property on which it was located was up for sale. Moving the studio and rebuilding a thirty-five-cubic-foot kiln would be time-consuming and expensive and would require more energy than I had. The landlord at my home whose suggestive and totally inappropriate remarks I had tolerated from the beginning of my six-year tenancy had finally threatened to shoot my cats for using his garden as a litter box. (Mostly it was other cats in his garden—I saw them in the morning as I did T'ai Chi. Unfortunately for me, mine preferred to come in from playing and hunting outside for the sole purpose of using their litter box.)

    My next move will be to a place where I can have cats. After about a year and a half, my friends gave Tigger away to an elderly woman who was looking for a companion. Tigger was not happy when they brought a new baby into the house. She spent whole days moping under their bed. Piglet is still with them. I hope I can at least retrieve her.

When I first returned from my travels, I considered what it would be like to build my life around my cats—choose my place to live and to some extent my lifestyle based on the necessity of living with them, resuming our relationship, and my responsibility for them. It seemed truly eccentric. Does one ascend or descend into eccentricity?

....

This buzzing computer. I intended to defray its cost by selling the laptop I used in Korea. I was never able to follow through on that intention. I've heard rumors that when you delete files—even from the recycling bin—they remain accessible somewhere in the far reaches of the computer's innards. And someone who understands computers much better than I do (which means most people) could retrieve those files. This made me feel squeamish. It would be like selling one of my journals. I rationalized that I should keep it as a backup, and for traveling. Although it's outdated in some respects, it has come in handy once so far.

I need to improve my computer skills. Most of the well-paying jobs anymore require them. I'm considering taking courses at the local community college. I've been using a popular CD that teaches the use of the keyboard. Until now it was always hunt and peck—albeit a pretty fast one. The CD will not let me exit the program; no matter what I do, I can't escape Mavis Beacon's classroom. No one has been able to help me with this problem. I just shut down Windows and hope for the best. Sometimes it works, and other times I have to go through some mystifying rigamarole when I turn on the computer again because it was "not properly shut down." The typing teacher's grammar and spelling are incorrect at times.

I paid a man to come to my apartment and help me set up the computer and give me some training in its use. He told me I must have a battery backup in order not to lose material. I went to the office supply store and priced them. The salesperson said computer aficionados like himself start with mere surge protectors and buy battery backups (at a minimum of ninety dollars) as they accumulate the money. How do I decide if I can afford it or not? He has a job; I don't. But I have considerable savings—including the $30,000 I saved in Korea—and no debts. I bought it. It was defective. I had to return it, buy another and set it up again. I also had to return my new keyboard—the keys were sticking and it was falling apart.

Every expert who has helped me with my computer has at one time or another said something like, "Gee, I wonder why it did that?" or "Hmm…that's really strange." Yet I have never sought to do anything on the computer other than the most basic procedures: set it up, add a printer, hook up to the Internet, use disks and CDs, and use it as a word processor.

I used the word processing program that was installed in my laptop when I bought it—Microsoft Works. Now I'm using Word. Why Microsoft failed to design the newer program so it could read the files of its predecessor is baffling. After much ado—failing to successfully download Microsoft's patch to correct this oversight and consulting many people in the field—a friend came up with a fairly simple way to deal with it.

Signing up for the Internet was another unwelcome adventure. I inevitably had questions, but was hard pressed to get in touch with an actual person who could answer them. The server representative had no idea how the billing worked, and was telling me I would be paying twice the actual cost. When I explained the arithmetic to him, he kept saying, "I'm no mathematician" when all he needed was common sense. I spend as little time as possible on the Internet. It's slow to offer up concrete information that I'm searching for and barrages me with unwanted data.

Personal computers are in a primitive stage. They're the undeveloped products of adolescent, relatively uneducated computer-centered people. They're supposed to be communication tools, but understanding them and communicating with them seems to be beyond even the experts.

Computers lack English language skills, not to mention common sense and logic. Yet people worship them. When something goes wrong, users assume they are at fault—not the computers or the shoddy programs. Some day computers will operate as easily and reliably as the telephone. It can't happen too soon.

Humans are becoming slaves, adjuncts to computers. They lead unhealthy, irradiated, sedentary lives as they peck away at the keyboard and stare into the flickering screen.

At least now my computer is running smoothly, I'm hooked up to the Internet, and my E-mail is restored to me.

Under the direction of a friend who has ten years' experience as a freelance copyeditor, I'm training myself to do copyediting and proofreading. I study forty pages a day of *The Chicago Manual of Style,* and have only a hundred pages left out of eight hundred. I'm up to thirty-five words per minute on the keyboard. Every Sunday I peruse the want-ads for likely jobs and have been working on various resumes aimed at various lines of work: writing, copyediting, teaching English as a second language, teaching ceramics. I think I'll be teaching T'ai Chi for a local community college beginning in the spring. And I'll start graduate courses in English at a nearby university in January. As a fifty-year-old single woman, I want the weight that a graduate degree can give me—almost any degree would do. It would have made a vast difference in my possibilities and compensation in Korea; it would mean I could teach T'ai Chi within the for-credit curriculum of a college or university instead of in their community education program; and it will look good on a copyediting resume.

Through all this preparing and planning, I'm writing about Korea. I'm in danger of falling in love with the writing—I need to be concentrating on making money.

....

Why do I want to write about Korea? When I tell people about my time there, I'm often embarrassed that I stayed so long. They look askance. I tell them I had a good T'ai Chi teacher, and I needed that time to learn the forms he was teaching me; I studied the language; I learned a lot about Korea and Asia. But I wonder too. Was it worth it?

I bartered my happiness for money there. I asked myself, "How important is my unhappiness? How much damage am I sustaining? Is it worth it?" Like a prisoner in an old movie, I crossed off the days until my contract ended. Why dredge up this misery?

Because I'm fascinated by the variety of human life and wish I could understand it. Because the experience provided some good stories. Because it seems necessary to try to make something meaningful, beautiful out of the muck and mire of day-to-day life: the lily that rises out of the mud.

I think about the dream I call The Spoon Dream. It came to me while I was still in the U.S. I was toiling in a vast field, digging my way through successive mounds of dirt with a shovel—I was clearing a path for myself. The mounds were long, narrow, and maybe waist high. They tapered down to the ground at either end, and were parallel to each other, dotting and effectively occupying the entire field. No matter what direction I chose, I had to dig through. While I shoveled, I was conscious that my tool was also a spoon, and the dirt I moved was my nourishment. I had a feeling of resignation, understanding that this hard experience was the fuel for my production, my creativity.

One day, many months after having that dream, I stood at a school window in Korea and looked out over the playground. There was my dream. Trucks had dumped hillocks of dirt that would be spread out to make a new surface. They were in the same formation and the same rich brown color of my dream. I had the same feeling of resignation, perhaps even more dogged, because it had not been a good day at school.

In *Shirley,* Charlotte Bronte says that unexpressed feelings exert their force against "the walls of their prison." Writing is one way of discharging my emotions, preventing them from accumulating, stagnating, and forming into hardened obstructions. The Taoists believe that ch'i, or internal energy, can be compared to electricity. A toaster works on the principle of restricting the flow of electricity; the result is a buildup of heat.

This works well with bagels in the morning, but not with the organs of the body. In autopsies, the Taoists say, diseased organs look as if they have been cooked—they are shriveled and hard. Ch'i is neither positive nor negative. It's just energy. If its movement is impeded, it can be very destructive.

Writing is like radio signals sent out into space in the hope of making contact with other like-minded beings. I've been the receiver of some of those messages through my reading. It may be something written hundreds of years ago by someone who shared one of my spiritual realizations—something I have not seen or heard any other reference to. Transcending time and space, we touch. My past transmissions have drawn life-sustaining responses.

There's so much bad stuff I swallowed and stored within me while in Korea. Somehow I will have to exorcise it—through dreams, T'ai Chi, tears, this writing. I question whether the experience nourished or poisoned me. When I first came home, I had unwelcome flashbacks of moments in Korea. Heavy, dreary feelings, verging on panic, flooded me. I'd rush to reassure myself that I was no longer there. A few times, waking up, I had to ascertain that I was in my bed in Portland, not in Korea. A suffocating feeling gave way to relief.

I'm fraught with anxiety and deeply, crushingly depressed at times. What's the point. The struggle is unremitting. My father, a physician, was very interested in the work of Hans Selye. Dad told me about one of Selye's experiments. He put some mice into a refrigerator with the temperature set at its usual cold temperature. He provided the mice with everything they needed to survive—food, water, air. The mice thrived, they were industrious, and their coats were sleek and shiny for about two weeks. At the end of that time, they were dead. Organisms can do well under stressful conditions for only so long. I talked to a friend from California on the phone last night. I told him I was sleeping better, feeling stronger. (Accent the positive.) He wanted to know why I hadn't been sleeping well. I told him about my aging face and body, the disadvantages of being an older woman in an ageist, sexist society. I told him that I had done what I passionately wanted to do in my first adulthood, and now wasn't sure what to do in my second. How much time do I have left? How much do I want?

These problems don't loom so big if you're having fun. "Are you having fun?" he asked. "No," I said.

Entry 7
Portland, Fall 1998

On my way to Washington Park this morning, I climbed a sidewalk littered with damp, matted leaves. The tree trunks on my left were thick and generations old. Their invisible snaking roots buckled the concrete beneath my feet. On either side of the street, the big, well-tended houses looked equally established as the trees. As I passed a lacy Japanese maple, my right arm lifted, my palm opened, and I brushed its leaves, drawing in the orange-gold-yellow-red-pink through the center of my hand. The Chinese call this point the *lao gong,* the opening that receives ch'i from the air. I reached the corner across from the wide cement stairs to the park. There I paused under the umbrella of another, taller maple. A soft shower of deep red-purple light fell onto my tingling head and shoulders, ran down my body. I have never before seen the colors I saw in those trees—never seen it reproduced in paint or dye.

    I continued up the stairs, past the skyward-pointing monument, and down the other side of the hill, leaving a slightly darker trail in the cool, wet grass. The green easily penetrated my shoes. I resumed my climb for another five or ten minutes until I reached the city's rose garden. At its edge is a clump of ginkgo trees. The ground around them was solid gold with their sheddings. The trees themselves emitted a bright yellow light, even on this sunless morning. I circled them, angling my body toward their glow, and breathed it in.

Entry 8
Wonju, Fall 1996

"Maple" and "ginkgo" were two of the first words I learned in Korean. Wonju is a forty-five minute bus ride from Chi-ak Mountain, one of the jewels of Korea. In the fall, these trees grace the slopes and pierce the heart with their colors.

Ae-ja and a friend of hers—a piano teacher—invited me to hike the mountain. We set out on an elegant Sunday in the prime of autumn. At the base of the mountain the parking lots were full and people swarmed around the vendors' stalls, buying hot corn on the cob, roasted chestnuts, buttered and salted potatoes, boiled fish sticks, and souvenirs. On a day like this people come from all over Korea, and there is a steady, sometimes bottlenecked parade to the top. I was reminded of ants that have found syrup on the shelf.

Clothes are important to Koreans—they are quick to judge people on their appearance, and they like to wear the appropriate outfit for every activity. In this case it's heavy, brightly patterned wool socks pulled up over their calves; serious hiking boots; Nordic sweaters; flak jackets loaded with pockets; and a jaunty, Tyrolean-looking cap or hat. But it's not unusual to also see young women dressed as if they're going shopping downtown: thin, tight-fitting clothes, high-heeled shoes, and full pancake makeup.

No one minded the crowds. Some came only to admire or pray at the beautiful, intricately painted Kuryongsa, ("Nine Dragon Temple") which is a ten-minute walk up a gentle slope. But the goal for most visitors is Pirobong, at four thousand feet the highest peak in this national park. It's a ritual climb and the jostling company of your fellow travelers is part of it. The overall mood that day was ebullient.

The trail is steep and sometimes pure rock. It would be impossible without climbing equipment if there were not occasional steel ladders, ropes, and chains installed to help people surmount the boulders. It took about three hours to get to the top, and it got colder as we ascended. Close to the summit the bare earth had a paper-thin, slippery coating of ice. The top of the mountain was packed with people admiring the full-circle view, taking pictures of each other, adding stones to the huge rock piles, and eating lunch. Little kids and elderly women were there. They all managed to make it to the top. Everyone was very free with their food; I shared some of my peanuts.

    I attracted almost constant attention on this trip. Children came as close as they dared and said, "Hello, how are you?" or "What's your name?" and then giggled and ran. Adults who wanted to demonstrate their English ability asked me where I was from, and sustained a conversation of a few sentences. As I was headed up the trail, a man who was on his way down handed me a pair of white cotton gloves. At first I demurred, but he pushed them toward me and I accepted. I was glad to have them—they kept my hands warm and helped me grip the slick metal railings beside the stairs. A little later a woman who was also descending handed me her walking stick. And when we paused to rest on the return trip some young men gave all three of us apples. I saw only two other Caucasians that day, and they were on the lower part of the trail. The Koreans were energized, proud of their mountain, and eager for me to appreciate it with them. As I crossed a rocky, utterly clear stream, a woman turned to me, stretched out her arms to include the entire surroundings, and said in Korean, "Doesn't it taste good?" I was too confused by this statement to answer, but nodded anyway. Later I learned she had really said, "Isn't it beautiful?" the words are the same except for one subtle vowel. I was sorry I hadn't more vigorously affirmed her. I brought home some of the luminous ginkgo leaves, but it's like carrying coals to Newcastle—the schoolyard is lined with ginkgos.

    Ae-ja and I made use of the long day to study English and Korean. As usual, she carried her dictionary—she is indeed diligent. I picked up new vocabulary and struggled to reproduce the correct sound for the word "sun." It's spelled *hae* in English, but the vowel is not a short *a* or a long *a*. It's somewhere in between, and I found it very elusive.

....

  The teaching is going as well as can be expected—some good classes and some bad. As things become more routine, they become easier. My teaching skills improve each week. The girls are mostly cute and endearing—a mixture of raucous and shy. I'm still touched by their bowing to me. The extra-curricular conversation classes are giving me some discipline problems, and I'll try to remedy that next week. The girls know I won't hit them like almost all their other teachers do. I have to devise some sort of punishment. Isolating the most talkative ones by making them stand in the back of the room is often enough. I can't imagine making them hold their arms straight up in the air while they stand—as the other teachers do.

  I was asked to take over two weekly conversation classes that Mrs. Ferguson, the wife of the commander at the nearby U.S. Army base, has been teaching. She didn't show up for her class Monday afternoon and gave neither warning nor excuse. The teachers who organize these lessons are thoroughly exasperated with her. Mr. Young said succinctly, "She breaks promises." One time she told me she had been given a schedule of her classes but had lost it. That was her excuse for missing a session. Another time she told me, "I forgot," as if that were an adequate reason for not appearing. Her behavior is an embarrassment; she's reinforcing their resentment of Americans.

  Donna Ferguson is tall, pretty, and very young—about twenty-five. One day she came into the teachers' room after a conversation class. She said her hands were very cold (the stoves have not yet been installed in the classrooms for the season). To emphasize her point, she reached out to place her palm on Mr. Young's face. He shrunk away, as if she had tried to strike him. All the other teachers standing around oohed. Did she know how intimately this gesture would be received by a Korean? Did she guess? Was she playing with this understanding while pretending ignorance? I'm sure occurrences like this are thrilling to Korean males. But they also breed resentment on the part of both males and females.

I agreed to take on her courses although my workload, at thirty-three teaching hours a week, is a strain already. They pay me extra for these classes, but that isn't an incentive. I make enough money. I'm doing it because I don't like to disappoint the teachers, and want to be as useful and effective as possible while I'm here. My ego enjoys a chance to "save" the situation.

....

It's Sunday again. My time to record some things in my journal and write to friends. Last night I got into bed at about nine o'clock and read a few pages of Wilkie Collins's *The Moonstone* before falling asleep. I awoke at eleven, read for two hours, then slept until five thirty. I guess I dozed until seven or seven thirty when I got up and fixed myself a bowl of corn flakes and soymilk with a banana. I crawled back into bed with my breakfast to finish the mystery and sleep a little more. I have always relished timeless Sunday mornings. There's nothing better than getting up when I wake up, eating what I want for breakfast, and going back to bed with the newspaper or a book—and sinking back into sleep again.

Reading is vital to me here. It helps me escape into a familiar world of flowing English where the vocabulary and sentence structure are unconstrained. It's a relief to enter into other people's lives and substitute their concerns for mine. Their dilemmas and irritations don't penetrate my skin as my own do. It's difficult to find books in English. I go to Kyobo bookstore in Seoul where they sell mostly classics. That's fine. I'll reread them and try out some of the warhorses I missed the first time around. I have never read Wilkie Collins before. His writing seems graceless to me, and the characters and story only superficially interesting. But he'll do.

Sleep is elusive for me in Korea just as it often was in my own country. A friend once told me that going to bed exhausted, sleeping for a couple hours, then lying awake for a good part of the night is a classic sign of depression. This is often my pattern now. It's true I've been struggling to function in a low-lying internal fog. It comes and goes, thins and thickens like fog.

....

Sports Day at school helped lift it. I took my camera which made me wildly popular with the students. At times they mobbed me, trying to get their grinning, posing faces into the frame. Other teachers came to my rescue, shooing them away. One of my best shots was of the *chuldarigi* (tug of war) contest with a military helicopter directly overhead. It struck me as an appropriate image for the two Koreas. I got some good photos of teachers too. Two days later when I showed my colleagues the prints they surprised me by keeping them. I'll have reprints made. The camera, I learned, is an effective tool for generating good will.

Toward the end of Sports Day I made a point of calling Mr. Young outside to take his picture. He acted pleased. As we left the teachers' room, the young female art teacher whose desk is beside his shot us a knowing, insinuating smile. This was one of the first and certainly the most pointed indication that teachers think something beyond a working relationship exists between Mr. Young and me. I resent her unspoken comment for many reasons. It seems disrespectful to both of us, and I feel it's an invasion of my privacy. Despite the fact that I have strong feelings toward him, I have exercised considerable restraint in not expressing those feelings in any way. And this barb came from someone I dislike, who has, from the first, impressed me as sly and mean-spirited.

This incident prompted the usual flood of questions without answers. My time in Korea is like a too-familiar dream, the sort in which I can't fully open my eyes, can't really see what's going on. Like the blind person trying to describe an elephant, I know only pieces, and I'm aware of the incompleteness of my understanding. Why did she smile that way? What does she think is happening between Mr. Young and me? Based on what? It was embarrassing. Am I so easily read? What has Mr. Young done or said to encourage these suspicions? I don't know this man well. For that matter, I don't know this culture well. I don't trust him not to start some self-serving rumors about himself and the American teacher. I don't trust him not to blame me or invent actions or words on my part that would make it seem that I am pursuing him. Or it could be pure, eager invention on the part of teachers looking for something to talk about. One of the English teachers recently assured me I'm a major source of conversation among the faculty. Maybe they're just paranoid about having a single American among them, assuming I'm bound to loose my sexually liberated self on some Korean man or other, and have no qualms about disrupting a marriage. Then again it may be my face. It's true I've been looking younger by the day. People notice these things.

By the time I left for Korea, I wanted to be dead—meaning beyond feeling. But I keep popping out of my grave with this silly, hopeful, expectant look on my face. It *does* spring eternal, damn it. I look shamelessly for signs from a caring universe: "This way to love." "This way to fulfillment." "This way to happiness."

Age is my advantage. I have fallen in love many times, weathered many intense crushes. I know this will pass. There is nothing for love to grow on: no compatibility, no shared perceptions or experiences, no opportunity. Just the object of my affection.

I respect passion. I've devoted my life to my passions—first clay, and then T'ai Chi. I believe in the life-bringing necessity of passion. I've drawn on love affairs, fantasies, and unfulfilled crushes most of my life for energy and optimism. It is a hard thing to deny this feeling, to not even tell him how I feel. I wrestle with it, I debate with myself. It has always seemed unhealthy, even dangerous, to smother or ignore such emotion. And such a waste.

I say I have fallen in love many times, but this gift has been absent from my life for several years. I've looked back and rued some of my relationships with men, thinking they were only draining and destructive. I've wished I'd waited longer, been more selective. The result of finally acting on that wish is that years have gone by without intimacy.

For many reasons I'd regret any relationship with Mr. Young. Most of all I care about his marriage—his wife and children. But even if all the obvious impediments were not there, if he were single, I would choose the same course. I don't want to be with a Korean man; American men are bad enough. I'd grow tired of him. Our unsynchronized likes and dislikes, our conflicting cultures would surface very soon. My attraction is an attempt at survival—a struggling psyche and body looking for sustenance.

Then there is the other part of me that bristles at the rigid confines of this Asian culture. It evokes a knee-jerk rebelliousness that makes me want to give these busybodies something to really talk about.

However, already the honeymoon is waning between my love and me. Something happened during the last week—our good will faltered, my feelings dampened. They had to; I'm wearing out. Recently he has been brusque at times. Once he made a point of telling me, "I always feel sorry for you." That angered me. "Don't be," I said. He seemed to be rationalizing the time he has spent helping me. Maybe he has taken some teasing from his friends or even questions from his wife. For now my fantasies have mostly evaporated. Even so there was a time a few days ago when I had a chance to look at his face and found myself exploring it with my eyes and was amazed at how pleasurable that was. Instinctively I wanted there to be some reciprocal feeling in him. I sensed its existence, but was unwilling to credit my intuition.

If nothing else, this experience lets me know I'm not dead yet. The idea of living the rest of my life without romance and without love from a man is painful. My accumulated resentment toward men, my cynicism about people and relationships hasn't inured me to this attraction. Life lives me in the end, more than I live it.

Entry 9
Wonju, Fall 1996

Living beside the school is a mixed blessing. I'm constantly scrutinized. If I come or go during school hours, I have to wade through a stream of curious students. Girls start arriving at 6:45 A.M. and the third graders don't go home until 9:00 in the evening during the week. They're around between 7:00 and 2:00 on Saturdays. The second floor of the building I live in is occupied by a "hogwon," or academy, where students study after school. Kids are often hanging out on the sidewalk beneath my windows socializing and waiting for their rides as late as 10:00 at night.

Some of my students have told me they want to come and see me in my apartment. Because I don't want to disappoint them, I have said they can come, while cringing at the idea of playing host to fifteen hundred girls over the course of my stay. I'm banking on only a few being brave enough to enter the foreigner's home. (It would be a first for virtually all of them.) So far I've had several visits of two or three at a time. I give them sodas or tea, fruit and peanuts as we sit on the magenta carpet of my living room with our dictionaries, communicating in occasional words of English or Korean. There are long pauses. We peel our oranges and try to think of something to say. They whisper to each other, rifle through their dictionaries, and then the one who gets nudged delivers the words—or even a full sentence—in English. I'm impressed and touched by their effort. They get up and crowd around the pages of Korean words and sentences I've taped to the wall. Each page has a heading: "Body Parts," "Greetings," "Shopping," and so on. I'm pleased when they make corrections because I like to enlist their help in my study. My only misgiving about this is that I know I'm acting out of character by exchanging roles with them. In such a rigidly hierarchical society, perhaps this is another way—like encouraging them to say hi to me—that could undermine respect. None of these visits is short, and they're a strain to get through. I soon learn that the girls will stay indefinitely if I don't tell them I have to go somewhere. Yet their presence is also soothing to me.

They want to see the entire apartment, and I don't mind showing it. But I have to keep an eye on them. They would open every drawer in the place if they could get away with it. The photograph of a man—a good friend whom I correspond with often—sits on my desk and naturally attracts attention. They want to know who he is; I can tell they're evaluating his appearance and dismayed by his receding hairline. Very few Korean men lose their hair, and balding is a source of tittering amusement to these girls.

Inevitably one of my visitors will ask to use the phone. Like the photograph, this is on the desk in my spare bedroom that serves as an office. Knowing how curious they are about my life, and how uninhibited about exploring my apartment, I try to remember to make sure the desk's top surface is clear and the drawers locked before anyone arrives. If I forget to do this, I have to make an excuse to go into that room while the student is on the phone so I can check to see that no personal letters are lying around. Many students wouldn't understand the content, but generally it's the brighter girls who come to visit, and their reading ability far exceeds their verbal.

One day I was home after school and very glad to be there by myself, shut off from my working life. I heard some excited, boisterous talking on the cement balcony outside the entrance to my apartment. The girls pounded on the door and shouted my name, "Emerson!" Although I knew they had probably seen me go in, I decided to pretend not to be there. The window beside the door was wide open so I had to duck behind a wall in my office in order not to be seen sitting at my desk. I waited a minute until it was quiet, then I peered around the corner to see if they had gone. Protruding into my apartment through the window was the entire head and torso of one of my brasher students. She had removed the screen and done everything but crawl in to look for me. (I wonder if she *would* have come in if I had not appeared.) I walked up to her and told her firmly in both Korean and English that I was busy and could not visit with them. I was outraged and amused at the same time. Sometimes I perceive Koreans as a liquid that would flow into any space left open, and I'm constantly building dams to restrict their encroachment on my life. It's these kinds of incidents that accumulate and constitute culture shock.

Not long ago I invited all sixty-five teachers to a house warming—just some refreshments after school—as a gesture of goodwill and because I knew they were curious to see my apartment. With Mr. Young's help I composed an invitation to post on the bulletin board in the teachers' room. A couple days before the event, Mr. Young informed me that the principal thought I would have to spend too much money if all the teachers came. Therefore he decreed that only members of the English department could go. Mr. Young was fuming. I was bemused and regarded it as a lesson in Korean culture. When I was in college we called this *in loco parentis*. But I was eighteen then.

Almost every day I'm asked what I eat for breakfast, lunch, and dinner, and what I do in the evenings. They assume that everyone's life is wide open to them, as if everyone is a part of their immediate family. They can't understand someone's living by herself. Why would I want to? Aren't I lonely? (The Korean words for "single" and "lonely" are some of the first I come to recognize because I hear them so often.) I tell them I'm lonely sometimes, but I keep busy.

I wonder if they understand the existence of an inner life. Fortunately I have one and I brought it with me to Korea. It's made of my reading, writing, daydreaming, running and T'ai Chi. The last is a wonderful traveling companion—it helps me stay centered and healthy. And it's an excuse to be outside, breathing in and appreciating the day, even if it's one most people would grumble about. My inner life used to include swimming and meditation, but I have not yet found a place to swim here, and after seventeen years of meditating daily, I rarely sit and tap into that still space inside me now that I'm in Korea. I probably need it more than ever, but I seem to be unwilling to let go, relax my guard. T'ai Chi, my moving meditation, my slow motion martial art, will have to serve.

This is a homogeneous culture that isn't used to differences. Americans are—diversity brings friction and problems, but we manage and are enriched by it. We're used to hearing accents coming from other Americans and from visitors and students. Often they're regarded as charming or alluring. Outside of Seoul, Koreans don't see many Westerners, and they definitely aren't used to hearing a foreigner speak their language. One of the reasons I have a hard time making myself understood here when I attempt to communicate in Korean is that initially they're convinced I'm speaking English. The dial just isn't set for deciphering their own language. They don't know what Korean sounds like with a foreign accent.

....

It's late November and I've been teaching more than two months. I was asked to write "my impressions of Korea" for the school year book. I thought I was keeping it short and simple, but as I reread it, I realize it's long and complex, and I probably gave them much more detail than they wanted. I feel sorry for the English teacher who had to translate it. I put as positive a face on everything as I could.

I began the essay by talking about the astonishing energy of the Korean people—the incredible work and study regimens they maintain. I said that I was struck by the communal élan of the audience at a huge outdoor music concert. (I appeared on national TV news that night. The cameras couldn't resist the one white-haired person.) Every kind of music was in the program—pop, traditional, and opera—and it was all received with equal joy by every age group and economic class. I was uplifted. In many ways, I said, Korea is one combined spirit and one enormous family. They even refer to a car as "our car," a husband as "our husband," and a wife as "our wife." I theorized that their cohesiveness was partly a product of their homogeneity and partly a result of their embattled history. They have always faced outside threats from Russia and Japan. I mentioned that my lifestyle—that of a single, childless woman—made me a curiosity here, whereas it's commonplace in the U.S. It was something I was frequently explaining and defending in Korea. Differences in customs and behavior startle me every day, I wrote, and I wondered how often I've unknowingly surprised or offended the people around me. I complimented the Korean diet as generally superior to America's, and said I liked their food. I congratulated the girls on their diligence and skill. I marveled at how accomplished they are as scholars, artists, musicians, and athletes. And, I added, the students become more and more dear to me every day. Finally I thanked the teachers and Mr. Young for their help and goodwill.

After the translation of this essay came out in the school's yearbook, several of my colleagues brought single women teachers to my desk, introduced them to me, and said, "Single not bad." Maybe they wanted to let me know they didn't think less of me for not being married. Maybe they wanted to show that Koreans could handle diversity. A bright third grader brought by an article written in English by a British woman in Korea. It was about the constant haranguing she got from Koreans on the subject of her singleness. She was tired of it too. My comments had evidently catalyzed a great deal of discussion within the school. The student with the article acted sympathetic and seemed to want to let me know that Koreans really do think "single not good."

....

I'm constantly weighing this culture—contrasting and comparing it with my own or with that of other countries I've visited. Several Americans have told me Korea is like the U.S. in the fifties. They mean it contemptuously: Korea is behind. (It's easy to become impatient with undeveloped countries. They're inconvenient and uncomfortable.) Most if not all the adults I know here were dirt poor when they were kids. They lived on farms and ate the few things they grew. They're delighted with the increase in their standard of living since then. They give their kids a better education, they have cars and TVs and plenty to eat. Not too many are restive yet. They don't have much personal freedom, but they believe they're sacrificing that for the preservation of their families and the progress of their country.

If Mr. Young wants to return to his hometown, he would almost assuredly have to quit teaching in the public schools. The government assigns teachers their schools based on where teachers are needed and how many "points" the teacher has earned. They can accumulate points by working in rural schools and performing other tasks beyond their usual teaching requirements. Acquiring points is a lifelong project. Mr. Young hasn't been teaching long enough to earn many points, and English teachers are needed in this province.

I hate this kind of control. The tightness (what I see as the smothering quality) of the family is also anathema to me. However, they have very ordered lives with a minimum of confusion because the choices are few. This will change with time. Once they get used to being relatively affluent, they will start demanding more personal freedom, at home and at work. Parents are losing control of their grown children as they scatter to take jobs in the cities. And families are becoming smaller. The teachers I work with commonly have seven or eight siblings, but they have only one or two children. What do human beings (Korean or American or any others) have that can take the place of the family? Consumerism? We'll have to do better than that.

What's the Korean impression of Americans? Mr. Lee recently told me a story. He went on a picnic with his fiancée, their female friend, and an American soldier who is engaged to their friend. Several young Korean men approached them, challenging the American to fight. They taunted him in Korean (which the soldier could not understand) saying, "Come on, Green Eyes, let's see who's tougher." To the great relief of Mr. Lee and his friends, the men eventually walked away without managing to provoke the fight they were looking for. Mr. Lee's assessment of this incident surprised me. He said he thought the Koreans were insecure and defensive, and that's why they acted in such a hostile way. I was glad to hear this from a Korean, because it agrees with my own interpretation of the behavior I've been experiencing.

Ae-ja and I were coming back from downtown on a bus. We were standing close to some third-grade students from my school. They were speaking in Korean, of course, but I could tell they were talking about me and laughing at my attempts to speak their language—mimicking my pronunciation. Creases appeared in Ae-ja's forehead and got deeper and deeper. Finally she turned to the girls and asked if they could speak English well. That quieted them. On the way out of the bus, I dropped some of my change to the floor and almost fell down the steps as I tried to retrieve the money and keep walking at the same time. I was tired, disoriented, and humiliated. The girls had had their effect. I felt bumbling, therefore I bumbled.

I was naïve when I first arrived in Korea. I thought I would be appreciated as a much-needed resource, and treated as a valued guest. To some extent this is true, but many people only see me as the hated American. Mr. Young told me that many of the teachers (was he talking about all of them or only about the English department?) didn't want an American teacher in their school.

The second-grade English textbook includes dialogues that deal with differences and misunderstandings between the American and Korean cultures. I decided to do a lesson on "The Ugly American." I asked the girls to tell me "all the bad things about Americans." "What do you say about Americans?" I asked. I could see they were shocked that I was actually trying to elicit these things from them. Sometimes it took a while before they could get into it. But their attention was riveted, and girls who didn't have the English huddled with those who did so the charges could be conveyed. I wrote their answers on the blackboard. I never defended my country; on the contrary, I would often say, "Yes, that's a problem in America," or "Yes, that's true."

I presented this lesson in all eleven of my second-grade classes. At the beginning of the week, I intermittently glanced to the back of the room to check the face of my Korean coteacher for a reaction. Initially confusion, worry, and discomfort all registered there, but I also detected curiosity and even excitement. To my relief, no objections were raised; they assisted with the lesson attentively and unobtrusively. I was surprised—I thought they might stop me the way the principal stepped in when I was planning my housewarming. The candor evoked by the lesson is directly opposed to the way Koreans normally behave toward foreigners. Apparently their eagerness to vent their feelings—the students directly, the teachers vicariously—overpowered their reserve.

Here's the list that appeared on the blackboard:

> They have big noses.
> They're fat.
> They're fuzzy (have too much hair on their bodies).
> They don't like black people.
> They kiss too much. They kiss everywhere. They kiss in the streets.
> They say "I love you" too much.
> They think they are the best because they are Americans.
> They have a sex problem.
> They fight a lot.
> They have too many guns.
> They have a special smell. (This, of course, is not a compliment and I'm told the distinctive odor is the result of eating dairy products.)
> They're rude to older people.
> Dinner is too long. (Americans sit and talk during and after meals. Koreans eat quickly and leave.)
> They eat too much meat.
> There are gangs.
> There's too much divorce.
> Men love men and women love women.
> There is heroin.
> There are many poor people.
> They don't like Asians.
> They waste things.
> They're selfish.

Some girls who particularly liked me squirmed impatiently in their seats during this exercise. They were visibly embarrassed, and insisted on listing good things about Americans:

> They're rich.
> They're tall.
> They're handsome.
> They're kind.
> They have many different-colored eyes.
> They have different hair colors.
> They're free.
> They love dogs and cats.
> They live in big houses.
> They have parties.
> Halloween.
> School is easier.
> English is the language of the world.
> It's a big country.
> It's a beautiful country.
> They always smile.
> There are kind gentlemen.
> There are many glamorous women.
> They speak English well.

After Korea got its loan from the IMF, these two were added:

> They save many things.
> They are wise.

Entry 10
Wonju, Fall 1996

    The windows of my home are large and look out over the street. To the left I can see the school yard. Beneath my apartment are two stores that are very popular with the students. Neither is any larger than my living room. The newer one (on the first floor of my building) is owned and operated by my landlord and his wife. The other is directly across the way. They're both packed with school supplies, junk food, and trinkets in unnaturally bright colors. Tiny stuffed penguins, rabbits, and bears that the girls like to attach to their backpacks dangle from the ceiling. Students crowd in before and after school, at lunchtime, and even during the ten minutes between classes. There are no trash containers in the area and wrappers, cups, and soft drink cans are tossed onto the sidewalks. The entire neighborhood is littered with paper, plastic, and garbage.

    The three-story cement building I live in is the best-looking one around, and the most recent addition to the neighborhood. The stairway has quickly become dirty and sprinkled with glossy shreds of food wrappers left by students attending the academy below me. The cement balcony shared by my apartment and my neighbor's looks unfinished, but I'm sure is as complete as it will ever be. The surface is rough and uneven. It's covered with dust, debris, and a certain amount of what looks like soil. I swept it assiduously not long after I arrived, piling the dirt in a corner.

    Sweeping is not an easy task in Korea. I have yet to see a push broom here. All sweeping is done with wispy, short-handled brooms that require you to bend over to use them. They're inefficient and back abusing. Still, whole streets are swept with them. I see Korean soldiers at the expansive entranceways to their army bases flicking away at the dust and stones, making progress inch by inch. The girls clean the long driveways surrounding the school as well as the interior rooms and halls this way. They wield their brooms with listless resignation.

Every day, toward the end of the day, desultory, exhausted students perform their cleaning tasks at school. Girls drag wet mops behind them up and down the stairs and along the floors. While I sit at my desk, someone slowly and not very effectively wipes the dust off any exposed area in front of me. Someone else sweeps underneath as I push myself out of the way on my wheeled chair. I allow myself to merge with the lazy current of their trancelike movements.

My neighborhood contains mostly single-family homes. Some are fairly large brick houses with the usual flat roofs that provide a place to hang laundry and store huge ceramic jars full of kimchi—the national dish of fermented cabbage, red peppers, and garlic that accompanies every meal. Other homes are old, cramped, low constructions whose peeling exteriors reveal their plaster-and-lathe walls. There are also some "villas" or small apartment buildings only a few stories high. Small neighborhood businesses such as grocery stores, butcher shops, restaurants, hair salons, music academies, and dry cleaners are interspersed among the houses. The streets are narrow asphalt, shared by both pedestrians and vehicles. Cars and trucks often squeeze by each other with only an inch or two between. Other than during the twice-daily rush hours, the streets are fairly quiet. Brick walls that butt up against the road surround the larger houses and from the glimpses I get through the gates, most of the ground inside is paved or covered with stones. Gardens and flowers are rare and draw my hungry attention.

Koreans don't seem to wash windows, so buildings often look empty or abandoned when they aren't. There are plenty of thriving businesses hidden behind smeared glass in this country.

The overall effect, especially with winter coming on, is grim, gray, and dirty. When I walk through these streets to go to the bakery or post office, there's a gritty feeling in my mouth, as if the cinders I see beside the road are inside me. I hold my breath as I pass through intermittent pockets of sewer gas. (Handling sewage well seems to be one of the hallmarks of a developed country.) Occasionally my nose tells me there's a cache of rotting garbage nearby, or the vomit of last night's drunk returning home.

People keep repeating to me that the air is clean in this province, and I keep nodding in agreement. But there are persistent gray-blue thread-like particles that coat the surfaces in my apartment only a day after I dust. Everyone says the water is clean too, but drinking tap water is unthinkable. Many people get their drinking water from nearby springs that have their sources in the mostly uninhabited mountains. I buy bottled water.

....

As of today I have a pass to be admitted to the nearby American military base—Camp Seward—anytime I want. The commander encouraged me to apply and volunteered to be my sponsor. (There's an implicit understanding that American civilians in Korea want a refuge, and that the base will provide it.) He's thirty-seven years old, which seems young to hold that position. His wife is the one whom I recently replaced as an English conversation teacher at my school.

I now use the curving, hilly, tree-lined roads on the base for my daily run. There's almost no traffic and the green, the cleanliness, the order of the base are so welcome. There are leafy private places for practicing T'ai Chi. I can't shop at the PX, but I can use the snack bar and the library, and hope to use the outdoor pool when hot weather returns.

It's ironic that the most peaceful place here for me is an army base. The only connection I had with the military in the past was when I protested against the war in Vietnam. Standing face to face with National Guardsmen, their eyes hidden behind gas masks, their guns raised, was the closest I had come to a man in uniform. The base is really a foreign country within a foreign country as far as I'm concerned. But I hear English spoken there; and there are books, magazines, and newspapers in English; and I have contact with familiar Western products and food, even if they aren't the things I customarily eat or use at home.

Without going into the questionable reasons for the U.S. military's first arrival in this country, and the political machinations that spawned it, I'm impressed with the necessity of their being here *now*. The North Korean government is irrational, unpredictable, belligerent, and well armed.

Ever since my arrival there has been feverish political tension. Only two weeks after I got here, a stranded North Korean submarine was discovered off the coast of this province. Some of its crew apparently committed suicide soon after they reached land. The others skillfully concealed themselves in the mountains and killed more than a dozen South Korean civilians before being killed or captured themselves. Almost two months have passed and one is still unaccounted for. As we native English teachers toured this province by bus during orientation, we entertained ourselves by spotting South Korean soldiers crouched behind bushes on the hills overlooking the highway. Their faces blackened, branches attached to their helmets, they peered out at us along their gun barrels. The bus stopped for several roadblocks while vehicles were searched. There was an eerie unreality about it all, especially the big, cold, sinister gun hanging at the side of the soldier who boarded the bus. I wasn't sure how to react, wondered how nervous I should be. The Koreans eagerly downplayed the whole incident, but I got a whiff of their fear. I thought a bunch of Westerners might make good hostages.

Entry 11
Wonju, Fall 1996

After a lull of a couple weeks, my obsession with Mr. Young stormed back. I don't sleep well for all the heart-pounding fantasies. Our desks in the teachers' room are beside each other, and I'm acutely conscious of his absence or presence.

A group of teachers had dinner together at a restaurant close to the school last week. I watched Mr. Young across from me drinking too many glasses of soju. Ignoring the fact that I'm not interested in men who drink excessively, I entertained myself with a fantasy of jumping on him right there, in front of the principal and everyone else. After the dinner I decided to do some shopping at a nearby grocery store before walking home. I was standing at the checkout counter with my purchases when he walked by. It was the fulfillment of a scenario that I'd been formulating in my head while gathering potatoes in the produce section.

"Are you shopping?" he asked.
"Yes," I answered. "What are you doing here?"
"I must buy toys for my children."
"Oh."

I paid for my groceries, looked up, and he was gone. Deciding to match what I perceived as his boldness—a tentative overture—I went looking for him in some of the other shops that occupied the same large open space, but couldn't find him. Most of the businesses were darkened and closed. I wondered where he had expected to find toys at that time of night. Disappointment and relief clashed with each other. I knew my tone of voice had been uncaring and dismissive, and I felt guilty about that. In a way I was betraying myself by denying the power of the emotion I feel toward him. But I'm afraid of too much contact and the entanglement it might lead to. I have always said I would never become involved with a married man—no matter how strongly I felt about him. I don't remember ever being this tempted before.

But that's the nature of passion, isn't it? It obliterates everything else, especially memory.

I laugh as I think about this episode. We're two strangers. But that only feeds the fantasy. Getting involved with him would be a stupid thing to do. I've done stupid things before, disastrous things (for me), that came out of this sort of heat. Maybe it's just my loneliness in disguise. The fantasy seems real and solid enough at the time—it definitely has its physical component. And I think in this case it's shared by its object. Is some of this coming to me from him?

I feel a deep sadness, too, when I think about the futility of it. Such a waste of ardor. Sometimes I resent it as a distraction and interference in my life. The fact that it cannot be satisfied or consummated, the fact that I have decided not even to express it verbally is a hard thing. I'm equally distressed when I envision myself as someone who could be immune to all this. That is death.

I'm okay at the moment—not writhing internally with frustration or plagued with unfulfillable fantasies. Not depressed. Not exhausted. It's the best I can hope for in my current life. I clamber up a jagged slope and hope to avoid plummeting back down into my own abyss or meeting with the tusks of the wild boar on the trail. Just continuing is good enough right now.

....

My apartment fills up and becomes more of a home. I enjoy my evenings of Korean and English mutual teaching with Ae-ja and Bo-ra. Ho Young-kun, an English teacher at the school, has joined us a couple times. I've also just been introduced to Yu Pil-lung, a science teacher at a different school. At thirty-two, she's another "old miss." She says she wants to be my "special friend." I like her soft voice—I'm drawn to anything soothing. She's an interesting person who has traveled internationally.

....

Today was a typical day at school. I arrived at 7:45, ready for my 8:00 class in English conversation. I checked the door of the classroom—the music room—and discovered it was locked, so I went to the General Affairs Office to get the key. (This office is a depressing hole of a room with sullen, surly denizens.) There's a board on the wall with all the room keys hanging on it. I knew what I was looking for—knew the name in Korean. One of the room's occupants came up to me and (for the first time ever) decided to help, unbidden. I asked for the key in Korean, and he handed me a key marked with a different name. I thought I recognized it as the conference room key, but decided to give it a try, thinking maybe I was mistaken. I got to the classroom and quickly ascertained it was the wrong key. Before I could get away, the music teacher came by, grabbed the key from my hand, informed me it was the wrong one, and led me back to General Affairs. There he gave me the proper key. Our mutual ignorance of each other's language made it impossible for me to explain to him what had happened. Nor could I communicate with the man who had foisted the wrong key on me in the first place. I was embarrassed and irritated by the rigmarole I had to go through just to get into a room. They must think I'm an idiot. The room in which I teach this early class has changed several times, and there is almost always some glitch.

I installed my materials and myself in the room, then waited until 8:15. Two students showed up and they were first graders, not the second graders I was supposed to be teaching according to the new schedule that began today. I sent them back to their homeroom then left and locked the door, returning the key to its board.

After I got back to my desk, I decided to run to my apartment to get a magazine I wanted to use for visuals. I came across Mr. Young in the driveway, and told him no students had shown up for my class. He said oh, that was probably because second graders have standardized tests today and they have to use the time to study. No apology, no expression of regret that I had not been informed and had been inconvenienced. I pretended to take it breezily, and changed the subject. If anyone is supposed to keep me apprised of this sort of schedule change it's Mr. Young.

I try to roll with the punches, allow for the language problem and cultural differences. But it pisses me off.

I was also supposed to teach a conversation class for the English teachers today. By now I knew there were schedule changes as a result of the second-grade tests, but I figured the teachers couldn't all be occupied as monitors. Still, class was cancelled for the third week in a row. Mr. Lee came to my desk, pulled up a chair, and talked with me during the entire forty-five minute period. I didn't realize until he left that he had "attended class." I hadn't understood his first words to me as he sat down. Later I realized they were, "Emerson, I'm present." I was grateful for the conversation—he related a story about a minor traffic accident he had some years ago. This was the fulfillment of an assignment I'd given at the first meeting of the teachers' English conversation class: tell us a brief story about something that happened to you. Sometimes I'm just so glad that someone speaks to me. He's becoming a friend.

Mr. Lee is thirty-two years old. He's a very slight and delicately made man. His facial features are fine and a little arch. His high forehead embarrasses him because his hairline is apparently receding. I admire his long thin fingers. He dresses meticulously, fashionably, and expensively. I perceive him as a woman. He's very serious about learning English and regards my presence in the school as an opportunity.

It's evident to me that the English teachers are reluctant to attend my class because they don't want to expose the limits of their conversational skills to their colleagues. Every now and then I get a sly question from one of them about the level of another's English. They're quick to pick up on any reference I make to misunderstandings that occur between another teacher and me. I try not to take their nonattendance personally. I'm sorry we don't have a class because talking to people who can express themselves at all in English is a treat for me. I was happy to prepare lessons.

I'd like to sit in on some of the English classes, but the teachers don't want me observing them. Through a mix-up in the schedule, I did appear in one of the first-grade classes, and (probably because the teacher was too polite to ask me to leave) was there for the whole hour. If I didn't understand some Korean, I wouldn't have known it was an English class. Occasionally an English word sailed by my ear, but recognition was always delayed because of the heavy accent. The government wants their teachers to teach in English, but few are skilled enough or brave enough for that.

A few days ago I asked the secretary in the teachers' room to type up my schedule for me. I gave her my handwritten version in Korean. She did it very quickly, and handed it to me just as I was about to go to a class. I had to put off proofreading it until later. When I got back, Mr. Young was standing over the schedule on my desk. He pointed out to me that I couldn't teach during lunch. The secretary had moved Monday's schedule down one space so it looked as if I had a class in that time slot. Her mistake, not mine. But Mr. Young seemed to be assuming I didn't know the Korean word for "lunch" and had put my class there out of ignorance. I picked up my hand-written schedule and checked to see if I had made the same error. I was hoping that he could see there was no class in the lunchtime hour on that one. I restrained myself from blurting it out. It was a petty thing, and it seemed unreasonable that I should have to justify myself or blame the secretary for making a simple typo.

I often feel uneasy and tense at school, the object of constant observation and discussion, yet excluded by the language barrier. I know some of the teachers regret not being able to talk to me—they've expressed this through Mr. Young.

I feel so relieved to get into my apartment at the end of the day. And at lunchtime. My own space, a place to relax. Unfortunately I haven't been relaxed enough to sleep well. Reality invades my dreams with grinding banality. Or I have bona fide nightmares or just plain bad dreams.

I had *one* tender dream. It occurred the night of Mr. Young's and my meeting in the grocery store: I was lying in bed, feeling very separate from him. I saw that we were literally separated by a series of single beds placed alongside each other. One set of covers spanned all the beds, so I could reach across to him. As I did so, he did the same. I felt his arm; he drew me to him. We kissed passionately, a lovely, lingering kiss. Then he turned away from me on to his side and curled into a fetal position. I understood that he wanted comforting and protection. I curved myself against his back and gladly provided it.

    This attraction must present difficulties and conflicts for him, too. But if we are all the people in our dreams (and I believe we are) then his gesture expresses what *I* want too.

Entry 12
Wonju, Fall 1996

There's a British couple in Wonju. They arrived in Korea when I did—as part of the same program—and we went through the three weeks of orientation together. Of the 250 native teachers that I mixed with during that time, Charlotte and Percival Hamilton were the last people I would have chosen to be put into the same town with. They ooze hatred of Americans. On the bus tours of notable Korean sites, their continual whispered or unwhispered comments about bloody Americans rankled me. I was transported back to grade school each time Charlotte actually cupped her hand to hiss into Percival's ear while fixing her eye on the object of her indignation.

They feel England's loss of status in the world keenly. The brash, crass, illiterate Americans are taking over. While the Hamiltons were rubbing elbows with a motley group of native English teachers, much more than half of whom were U.S. citizens, they behaved as if they were under constant and immediate attack by me and my compatriots. They had only to know my nationality in order to have a fully formed opinion of me. Canadians, New Zealanders, Australians, and other Brits were accepted immediately and jovially as friends—or was it allies? Americans were just as quickly identified as the enemy.

The Hamiltons were quite proud of the international travel they had done and were eager to inform everyone about it. I assumed their vitriol had its source in firsthand experience and asked Percival what parts of the U.S. they had visited. "We've never been," he said. I was momentarily stunned, and actually stopped in midgesture as I was slinging my daypack over my shoulder. His curt, defensive tone of voice told me in those three words that the contradiction was as blatant to him as it was to me. How much contact, I wonder, have they actually had with Americans? I'm working hard to refute the Ugly American stereotype with the Koreans, but I disdain apologizing for my country to the Hamiltons, who I feel should be more sophisticated.

Charlotte is a big woman—about five foot seven, large-featured, and very heavy. She looks especially outsized in this country, and must feel it acutely. Her face has "good bone structure" and gracefully arched eyebrows over wide brown eyes. Her brown hair is straight and extends below her shoulders. She frequently equips her face with a cheerful look and her voice with a chirrup in order to belie her thoughts and intentions. Charlotte uses this breezy façade while denigrating nearby Koreans to fellow native English speakers. She's more confident than I that the Koreans can't understand her words. Even if she's right, I wonder if they understand *her*.

Essentially a sour, angry woman who is quick to take offense, Charlotte suspected the Koreans of all sorts of treachery, even as early as the orientation period. Now, when she tells me about the teachers and conditions at her school, her voice drips with sarcasm and contempt. She has refused to teach extra conversation lessons. (Mr. Young has made sure I'm paid well for these, but she would receive no pay.) Charlotte says she complains frequently about the lack of planning and last-minute changes in her teaching schedule. She relates dialogue that takes place between herself and some of the Korean teachers she works with, and I'm surprised she could be so candid and confrontational. I wonder how much of it is true. The grade school memories return again: I suspect she's like my eight-year-old friends who told stories about all sorts of brazen back talk they gave teachers when there were no witnesses. I never believed them. Likewise, I think Charlotte is embellishing and letting off steam.

Percival is also large and revels in his height in this part of the world. At six foot four he can carry the extra weight he has without its being obvious. A beard and mustache further set him apart; his hair is dark and longish, his features strong and regular. His smile is marred by a gap behind his right incisor. He's dependent on cigarettes and I often find myself trailing behind in his smoke as we walk the crowded streets of downtown Wonju in search of a movie on a Saturday night. (I hate the smell of cigarettes and exposure to it instantly irritates me.) Percival often has a sly, boyish, mischievous look on his face, and really does get a gleam in his eye when he's up to something. They're both capable of being quite funny, thank god.

Neither of them seems to be especially accomplished at anything or passionate about a vocation or avocation, unless it's traveling and collecting souvenirs to send home. I'm getting gradual intimations that Charlotte doesn't enjoy the globetrotting as much as Percival. She says she hates the hot, sticky weather in tropical countries, and would like to resettle in England soon. But I can tell she's determined to hang onto her man, so she follows him. I was surprised to learn that neither has a college degree. That was supposed to be a requirement for people in this program, but they're not the only ones who were accepted without one.

I first attracted Charlotte's ire (directly) when I was studying Korean on the bus during our orientation tours. I once ventured to be helpful by telling her which was the men's room and which the women's, pointing out the Korean signs and pronouncing them for her. She glared at me and snapped, "Oh, and I'm supposed to know that, am I?" More recently she has declared herself incapable of learning a foreign language. Sometimes she says it's congenital, other times she blames it on the poor teaching methods of her instructors.

Charlotte is indignant if anyone asks her age. She has plenty of opportunities to puff up about this issue in Korea. Many Western teachers like to build whole lessons around "touchy subjects" that Westerners feel are inappropriate in conversations with mere acquaintances. ("Are you married?" "What's your religion?" "How old are you?" "How many children do you have?") The point of the lesson is to teach people of other cultures to restrain themselves from invading our privacy as soon as we're introduced. I'm tired of answering these questions myself, but I chalk it up to natural curiosity, reveal as much as I choose to, and have never blanched at revealing my age to anyone. I figure it's part of my job—Koreans need to learn about our personal lives to some extent. They need flesh-and-blood examples, not Hollywood or TV sitcom characters. To

Charlotte's dismay, documents listing all the native English teachers in the province are freely distributed and there's a column for age as well as address and phone number. She's thirty-eight. Percival is a couple years younger.

While I was practicing T'ai Chi yesterday I was thinking that she will probably outlive me. Although I delight in many more things than she does and am proficient at and can participate in many more things than she can, she is better equipped to survive. She looks for unhappiness and is not disappointed. I look for happiness and am. The kind of hostility that Charlotte carries with her is its own punishment—it fires in both directions at once. So why is it that people like her seem to thrive and live such long lives?

Under normal social circumstances, I would have nothing to do with the Hamiltons, nor they with me. But as it is, they're the only show in town. I regard them as better than nothing. Despite our mutual reservations, the three of us meet once every week or two. We've been thrown together, and offer the closest thing to normal conversation available here. If I want to vent my frustration after a week of school, I have to do it with them. Even though there are two of them and must use each other for this purpose, they seem to view me similarly. We do have to ask each other to repeat things at times. More often I am the one requesting to hear something again—either they speak too quickly for me or I don't understand their idioms. Charlotte and Percival really enjoy asking me to clarify something—they like to get the point across that they don't understand me because I'm diverging from their one true English.

On another plane, the usual delicate situation exists between the Hamiltons and me—any decent-looking woman will have a hard time being accepted as a friend to most couples. I thought the fact that I'm ten years older than Charlotte might make things easier. But my being thin and fit is enough in itself to make her hate me. And Percival clearly likes me, enjoys talking to me, and despite his contempt for Americans, calls me regularly. Our conversations are prolonged discussions about work and the travails of living in Korea. I talk to him on the phone far more than I do to his wife. He's the one who initiates the invitations to dinners or movies. I hold back in this area, unless I'm feeling utterly desperate for company. Charlotte is uncomfortable with my existence, and I know this. I adopt my long-established, prepared behavior with them: (1) focus my conversation on the female even if the male is the more interesting of the two; (2) make frequent eye contact with the female in a three-way discussion, and (3) avoid any actions or words that could be considered remotely flirtatious. Charlotte is an eager, often verbose talker, so the first requirement is easily met. Eventually Charlotte and Percival will "have it out" about me. My presence may even temporarily shore up their marriage as any outside threat can make a group more cohesive. Charlotte will gradually see that I'm not attracted to her man, and think it serves him right. If I'm lucky, things will smooth out and I will not be denied access to their company. This precarious dynamic makes becoming friends a slow and, at times, impossible process.

Last night (Saturday) I took the bus downtown and met them in front of a bookstore on Main Street. (Koreans generally don't give names to streets. In English, this central road is referred to as A Street or Main Street.) After a quick discussion about where we wanted to have dinner—Korean? Western? KFC?—we walked to a pizza restaurant. I have almost no social life, and was looking forward to this outing—to eating Western food and talking to Westerners for a change.

Charlotte and I sat on one side of the booth and Percival on the other. Percival, as usual, jumped in to do the ordering, speaking in English and pointing to pictures of items on the menu. Why does he not defer to me? He knows I've been studying Korean and can read and order in the waitress's language. I assume it would embarrass him—a woman, demonstrating superior knowledge. As it is, he embarrasses me. The process did not go smoothly.

As soon as the waitress was a few feet away, Charlotte said, "Well I'm sorry, but there's no hope for these people. You'd think they could understand the *pointing* to the pictures even if they can't understand English."

Percival barely acknowledged his wife's comment, adjusted himself on his seat, and folded his hands in front of him on the table. "This is quite civilized. Some good, hearty pizza, a sufficiently violent American movie, and then we'll pop by Baskin Robbins." The gleam entered his eye with the mention of ice cream. He says he's trying to lose weight.

The Yankee hater wants an American dinner, American movie, and American ice cream. No sense in even thinking about it, let alone bringing it to his attention. All I wanted from this evening was—at least briefly—a taste of home. It wasn't just the food that I was hungry for. I was starved for stimulating conversation. Already I was feeling let down, and chided myself for harboring such naïve expectations.

Then Percival went on to say, "We're working on describing people in my conversation classes now, and I must tell you, Margy, that my second graders spent almost an entire hour discussing the color of your hair. No one can decide if it's white, gray, silver, or blonde."

I felt both uncomfortable and a little flattered. My hair color has been a topic of discussion for two decades. At the age of twenty-eight I got out of bed one morning, looked into the mirror, and saw a flash of light. My hair had flopped over to the left, revealing a white patch at the right temple. I remembered my father told me his hair started turning silver at the same age. Over the years, strangers have come up to me and commented admiringly, or asked if it's natural. The Korean teachers at school want to know if mine is a common hair color in America. A psychic told me at least fifteen years ago that it was turning white because I would be a teacher, and people would be more likely to pay attention to what I said if I looked older. Twenty-eight was also the time of my second divorce, and a long period of loneliness and anger (mostly at myself for having married him). I thought stress was a factor in the accelerated whitening of my hair, and in the back of my mind were the stories about people's hair turning white over night from fright. Several women have told me that people pay a lot to get hair color like mine. I told them I paid a lot too.

"I'm not sure what it looks like," I answered Percival honestly. "I've never had much of an outside image of myself. If someone needs to pick me out of a crowd, I tell them to look for my white hair."

Charlotte settled it: "It's gray."

The subject switched to last week's school life, and we shared some ideas for lessons. I was glad we didn't spend the whole time complaining.

The pizza arrived in an iron skillet. Charlotte pushed it toward me with a gesture of letting me go first. I thanked her and used the spatula to put a slice onto my plate. As I did so, it occurred to me that the more gracious thing to do would have been to serve the others first, and I said this out loud.

Charlotte didn't miss an opportunity. "Don't worry, you're an American. It's only natural that you would take the first slice."

There was a pause while this latest barb sank into my tired body. Percival looked up under his eyebrows to see how I would react. Mentally, I slumped. Maybe I did physically too. It has been a long several months of weathering these sorts of attacks from the Hamiltons, and coping with the insecurities and resentments of the Koreans too. I said nothing, and of course I regret now that I didn't lash out at Charlotte. I guess I was too sad and too exhausted to respond. She was being unfair, and we all knew it.

We proceeded to eat our pizza in silence. Charlotte finally thought of something to talk about, and, ratcheting up her cheerfulness a couple notches, aimed her comments at me in an effort to compensate. I was completely deflated, and only wanted to escape their presence. I wondered if I would go to the movie with them. I didn't want to leave the pizza.

I did trail along to the movie. The sound was blasted way too loud, as always. The Koreans like it that way. The dialogue becomes unintelligible at that volume, but it doesn't matter because they're reading the subtitles. I settle for watching explosion-riddled Hollywood movies here. Little else is available. At least I skipped the Baskin Robbins. By the time I boarded the bus to go home, I felt thoroughly assaulted—by the movie and the Hamiltons. Dazed and depressed, I reached the life raft of my apartment. That was my night out.

....

This morning I went to a *mok yok t'ang* (public bathhouse) for the first time. I was very happy to learn about the place. It's in my neighborhood, just a few minutes' walk. It's clean, the walls and floor are tiled, and the employees are friendly. Ae-ja walked me through it yesterday so I would know the procedure. When I undressed in the locker room, four or five other women were there too. As I walked naked toward the door of the bath area, every woman stopped what she was doing, turned to face me, and stood utterly still in order to watch as I left the room. Nothing subtle or surreptitious about it. What did they think I would look like? How many breasts did they think I would have?

I took a shower, then sat in the searingly hot sauna for as long as I could stand it—about ten minutes. Afterward I dunked myself in the eight-foot-square cold tub, submerging completely for a stroke or two and savoring the longed-for sensation of swimming. Next I floated and made waves with my arms in the hot tub. I told one of the two masseuses that I wanted a massage. I guess Sunday is the wrong day for this—I had to wait around, dabbling in the hot and cold tubs for forty-five minutes before it was my turn. Nearby, mothers scrubbed their passive children while sitting on low plastic stools in front of rows of waist-high showers; women vigorously soaped each other's backs with nylon wash cloths. After a few minutes, I no longer caught people staring. They had gotten used to me.

There are bathhouses like this in every Korean neighborhood, and this is still the place where many Koreans come to get clean. Bathrooms in the older apartments and houses are often cramped and not equipped with tubs or showerheads. The more modern homes are different. Some wealthier Koreans still come for the massages, saunas, and hot and cold tubs. Others cringe when I mention the bathhouses. They seem ashamed of them, as relics of an older, poorer Korea. And they have become more modest. Teachers assume that I would not want my students to see me naked. I'm not willing to worry about it. Like I said, I'm from California.

When the time came, I got on one of the massage tables that were set up in a corner of the bath area. The masseuse started vigorously scouring my body with a nylon mitt. She was dressed in a bra and underpants—the whole area is too hot and steamy for clothes. The scrubbing of my body went on…and on. The skin rolled off. Periodically the masseuse poured warm water over me to wash away the grayish oblong pellets. She scoured and rinsed, scoured and rinsed. It was anything but relaxing. I kept myself braced to withstand the discomfort that gradated into pain at times. I'm used to gentle oil massages in a quiet room with soothing music. After about twenty minutes, she applied hot towels to my face and body. This "wrapping" was very comforting. Then she applied some sort of cucumber goop to my face. At this point my skin started stinging—especially my neck and shoulders, and gradually my back. I tried to ignore it, but it finally became alarming. I sat up and told her I needed to take a shower. First she resisted the idea, then agreed. I was given some shampoo to wash my hair, and she indicated the massage was over. The other masseuse, who was older, seemed fairly concerned. She came over and studied the reddened skin on my chest and back. In the brighter light of the locker room, I could see that I was breaking out in red, prickling splotches. I couldn't yet see the raised welts of the hives I suspected. I think the older masseuse, who followed me into the locker room and helped me apply lotion to my skin, thought I was reacting to the cucumber face pack. It was a possibility. But by the time I got home and could really take a look at myself, I saw many small welts mixed with the red rash on my chest, back, and neck—nothing on my face. I recognized hives from a few past encounters. They're the result of a stress overload. In this case it was the heat of the sauna and hot tub alternated with sudden immersion in cold water. Also the painful, cathartic massage. Everything was coming out through my skin. By the end of my time on the massage table, I felt like crying. I feel sorry for the masseuses. I don't think it was really anything they did or any product they used. I was probably just cleansing, releasing some of the stress, anger, frustration, and confusion of my first several months in Korea. In a few hours, the rash was barely visible. I'll wait a while before venturing back to the bathhouse. Perhaps I'll skip the massage.

Entry 13
Wonju, Winter 1996-1997

It's down into the teens over night, and often stays below freezing during the day. We've had a few inches of snow so far. Living in northern California for eleven years, I'd forgotten what real winter is.

....

It seemed auspicious to be going to a country with the *T'ai Chi* symbol in the middle of its flag. (Koreans call it *Tae Guk*, Americans call it "yin-yang.") This symbol has been in my thoughts for two decades while I've practiced and studied T'ai Chi. (The full name of this slow motion internal art rooted in martial principles is *T'ai Chi Ch'uan*, meaning the physical exercise rooted in the philosophy of T'ai Chi.) I've read about the 2000-year-old design, discussed it with others, and watched it work in my practice and in my life.

Elegant and striking, it's been appropriated for commercial purposes by numerous businesses in the East and the West. It's also succinct and profound. The more I learn about it, the more complex it becomes. I'm gradually seeing it at the core of every particle of my existence.

My Chinese T'ai Chi teacher defined it as "the universe" (T'ai) "and beyond" (Chi). Some translate it as "Supreme Ultimate" or "Grand Terminus." The fact that it's a circle before anything else suggests wholeness, completeness. Its division into two halves of contrasting color suggests a fundamental polarity. The *S* curve through the middle gives the impression of continuous revolving movement—a straight line would convey a static state. Appearing in the fullest part of each side is the seed of its counterpart, a reminder that when things advance as far as they can in one direction, they begin to reverse. Most people associate T'ai Chi with harmony, meaning peacefulness. Maybe this is wishful thinking. They don't want to acknowledge the tension that exists between the two forces, the constant tug and pull that's inherent in the universe and in our lives. Maybe we need to expand our idea of harmony. One thing I've learned from practicing T'ai Chi is that balance is not a static state. It requires constant adjustment.

A Korean lecturer in the orientation program said that Korean values stress harmony in society. I don't see harmony here. I see repression. These are two different conditions, although they may look the same if all you see is the unruffled surface. My T'ai Chi teacher said that one way to define "harmony" in English words is "go your own way." But Korean life is the opposite of go your own way. Following one's own path inevitably leads to individuality, even eccentricity. These qualities are hammered down as quickly as they pop up.

Every day at school I watch all the various soft round pegs being pounded into a few hard square holes. If someone learns differently, develops at a different rate, or is talented in some area not currently recognized as valid, they are discarded, their potential wasted. Many of my peers in America would have been ignored or crushed in the Korean system, and some of these people are the brightest, most talented and productive people I know.

Outside of school the family is a life sentence. Its inflexible bonds and rigid structure keep the lid on. The family is the rebar in the cement of tradition. It perpetuates power for the males, especially elder males. Yet, in a country where weakness is contemptible, and there are no laws to protect the weak (no dependable justice system) the family is a refuge. Koreans have a choice between the stultifying protection of the family and defenseless vulnerability outside of it.

Mr. Lee once said to me that a difference between East and West is that the East emphasizes inner values while the West is preoccupied with outer—material—values. I can't argue with his assessment of the West, but I observe the same thing, maybe even more rampant, in Korea. Money, status, and position seem to be the overweening goals—this is their definition of success. Personal fulfillment, the nurturing of talents and proclivities, "following your bliss"—none of this enters into it. Both children and adults are frantic, frenzied, and chronically overworked in their pursuit of financial advantage. Where are their artists and poets? One of my best students told me that she liked to draw and paint, but had to give it up when she entered middle school. She's intellectually gifted—that means she must focus on the four academic subjects: math, science, English, and Korean. Everything is measured in tests and competitions from the very beginning—even art and music. Their zeal gets results—they develop excellent skills.

I have a Korean-American friend in Seoul. She grew up in Korea, finished high school here, then went to the United States for college, and has essentially lived there for the last thirty years, along with half her extended family. Now she's come back to Korea to teach English. Twenty-five percent of her high school class is living in America.

My friend William was stunned when a Korean woman he'd taken out on a few chaste dates walked into his bedroom, took off her clothes, lay down on his bed, and said, "I want to have your children." I noted he didn't say definitely that he'd managed to resist, but accepting her offer would mean he intended marriage and taking her back to the U.S. with him. This, he realized, was her motive. He moved to Seoul recently—to escape the consequences?

Why do so many Koreans want to go to America? Is it just for material advancement? That's what they strive for here. The same Korean lecturer who said that the East offers harmony summed up what the West has to offer as "efficiency." Is that really what Koreans see in the West? I don't believe all those emigrants are trading harmony for efficiency.

The Koreans I talk to are convinced they can't change the nature of their society—its rigidity, its disregard for the beauty in individuals and in the environment. Parents dread sending their children to middle school because that's where the six-year-long forced march to the university begins. The mother of one of my better students is an English teacher at a different school. Along with her husband and daughter, she visited New Zealand last year. "Everything is so fresh and clean there," she sighs. "Nothing is fresh and clean here." But emigration requires more money than they have. And her husband, who does not speak English, is reluctant to try it.

This is a country with bad growing pains. It's a messy transition—I guess most of them are. What was Korea like before? Was its internal life any different?

I'm disillusioned. The T'ai Chi symbol on the flag, the talk about harmony misled me. I know from living in my own country that cultures often don't exemplify their ideals. Maybe this is why we take outsiders and their messages more seriously than our own. We know the flaws in our own societies, and every day we see the imperfect application of our stated precepts. Some of the Western reverence for Asian culture is "the prophets in their own land" syndrome: anything exotic is better, even transcendent. It's wishful thinking—the hope that we will be rescued by a superior, external entity that knows the secrets that have eluded us. Perhaps it takes an outside culture to recognize and extract the best from another culture—and really put it to use.

....

A strange thing happened today. I've been sick with a cold and persistent cough for more than two weeks now. I have not stayed home from school because that's not done here. Everyone goes to school even if they're at death's door and spewing their diseases in everyone else's face. It's part of being diligent. My attraction for Mr. Young has been at a low ebb. Nonetheless, while I was preparing lessons at my desk, I slipped into some heavy daydreaming. Fantasia: I'm younger, he's unmarried, and so on. Mr. Young came up to me and showed me a passage from what appeared to be a textbook: "Like a boy of nineteen, my grandfather had love on his mind." He asked me to explain it to him. Given what I had just been indulging in, the sentence touched an exposed nerve. Change the gender and it could have been written about me. The subject matter was surprising—it sounded a little racy for a Korean schoolbook. My initial "hit" was that this was a signal from Mr. Young about his own feelings. And just as quickly I rejected the possibility of acknowledging this or responding in kind. I launched into an explanation, concentrating on the idiom, "on his mind," assuming, or pretending to assume, that was what he was unclear about. I said it meant you were always thinking about the same thing. He looked at me and said, "By himself?" This scared me. I shied away, letting it slide by unanswered while I rattled on with an example about a student's being worried over a test and thinking, thinking, thinking about it: it's on her mind. He looked at me again, said "I understand," and left.

I was impressed with his nerve and grateful to him for broaching the subject, even though I refused to enter into it with him. His indirect method protected him and provided an escape route.

I don't know or trust Mr. Young. (I don't understand or trust Korean men.) I later wondered if he has been reading my feelings, and was teasing me. If I admitted any special feeling for him beyond friendship, would he immediately broadcast that to everyone? My feelings toward him are ambivalent. He has not treated me consistently—sometimes he seems warm and helpful, other times cold and abrupt. And I know I can be infatuated with the wrong person just as I can with the right one.

I've often thought that just being able to say "I love you" once would release the pressure in my heart. But I think that's a Pandora's box that ought to stay shut. I like the idea that there really is part of me that's not reachable or touchable—that I can and do have some privacy, even with all my transparency. I don't think he really knows any more about me than I do about him. I don't need to make any admissions. Neither of us does.

This last incident reminds me of the time we were on a third-grade trip to Lotte World—the indoor amusement park in Seoul. He talked about riding the train, but never stated it as an invitation. "How about riding the train?" he said. I thought he was asking me if I thought it would be a fun thing to do, or if I would ride the train by myself during the course of the afternoon, not if I wanted to ride it with him. He had just made a point of not sitting next to me on the bus by rearranging boxes of snacks for the girls, so I doubted that he would want to sit beside me on the train ride. All the other teachers were standing around at the time, and I would have been embarrassed to go off with him alone. As the teachers split up, I walked away with a couple of women English teachers. One of them, Mrs. Ho, explained that I hadn't understood him. She was amused at Mr. Young's expense, openly laughed at him. If nothing else, his English had been inadequate to express what he wanted. I hated contributing to his humiliation. When I next ran into him, I apologized and told him I didn't know he was inviting me to go with him. He said simply, "Why?" We stood there and looked at each other for a few moments, then he changed the subject to some shopping we both wanted to do while in Seoul. At times he seems bold, but he's never direct.

  He noticed that I bought water at the school snack bar the other day, and seemed concerned that I was spending money on water. He told me about a spring only one kilometer from the school. That was good to know, I replied—I could walk there. A few minutes later he came to me and said Mr. Han, a math teacher, had volunteered to drive me there. I walked home to get a few water bottles, and the three of us went to the spring in Mr. Han's car. What was that about? What do people think is going on between us? Do we require an escort? A month ago Mr. Young would have taken me there by himself.

  The girls ask me if I like Mr. Young. When I say yes, they giggle and make woo-woo sounds.

  Yu Pil-lung comes to my house to trade language lessons on Tuesday and Thursday evenings. She tells me she likes to listen to love stories, and wants to hear all of mine. I select one (being careful that it's the same one I told Mr. Young), and say that's all I've got. In a complete non sequitur, she makes a point of teaching me the Korean word for secret: *bi mil.* Does she introduce the subject because she thinks I have one? Now I'm wondering if she's fishing—trying to become my confidante in order to pry out information. Does she suspect something between Mr. Young and me? Maybe she wants to discover whether I'm sexually experienced—whether I'm a virgin—as I believe she is. I ask her to tell me one of her love stories. It takes place on a trip to India. She becomes friends with another member of her tour group—an Indian man. When they are alone one evening in her hotel room (I'm surprised he's gotten that far), he tells her he thinks she's sexy. First she makes him sit down in a chair. Then she replies, "Why do you say that? That's not why I want you to like me. I want you to like me for other reasons." I can read on her face that this is at best only partially true, but I believe this is the extent of their intimacy. They promise to write, but neither does. She seems to think that even that would be improper. Or maybe she would never be the first. End of story. I tell her there's nothing wrong with being both sexy and smart, knowing she will infer implications for my life, my behavior. I realize any tidbit she learns about me will be flashed to half of Wonju by the next day—my opinions on sex, my love story. She talks with teachers at my school and with Ae-ja. Everyone is connected here. If nothing else, I'm a catalyst for communication.

Entry 14
Wonju, Winter 1996-1997

Last Tuesday Mr. Young came to school and his face was literally stony—gray and rigid—as if he were just managing to contain some explosive force. He was completely uncommunicative. His movements were brusque, and his eyes seemed to be focused inward. Was he sick? In pain? Furious? There was no good opportunity to ask him. The next day he didn't come to school in the morning, and I felt anxious and sad. He arrived later—at about 3:30 or 4:00—looking his old self. I was relieved to learn that the earlier part of the day had been spent accompanying the third-grade students to their high school entrance exams. Either there was no disaster, I concluded, or it had passed quickly.

The following day he told me he will leave our school in late February, at the end of the school year. He laughed while explaining that he and his wife will trade schools—his wife will come here and he will go to hers. I was stunned and confused by his gaiety. He was giggling, gesticulating, widening his eyes at me as if communicating some great, hilarious irony. And I was supposed to be in on the joke. I wasn't capable of responding other than to acknowledge the information. I went to my class feeling wounded, bereft, and on the verge of tears.

Later that day, the students made lunch for some of the teachers. He waited for me to return from a class and walked with me to the home economics room. I had had a chance to recover. Doing my best to sound wholesomely cheerful, I told him I would really miss him, and would prefer that he stay at our school. He said if he stayed he would have been put in charge of the third grade and wouldn't have had time to assist me. (Just the week before he told me he would teach first or second grade next year and would have *more* time for me.) As it is, he has recommended to the principal that Mr. Lee take over as my guide teacher. During lunch he spoke to other English teachers in English, saying he was glad to move to the other school because the faculty there is younger. I'm sensitive about our age difference, so this stung me. And it was confusing because the English teachers at our school are, with one exception, in their early thirties. To me, that's young. But he has to deal with much more than the English department, including a very strict and rigid principal who is within a few years of retirement.

Is this a case of Big Brother intervening to head off any sticky problems? Also last week, one of the physical education teachers sat down across from me at a dinner and proceeded to talk to the teacher on my right about Mr. Young and me. I recognized the names, but couldn't follow anything else. This kind of rude behavior is starting to make me feel paranoid. And why is his wife coming to this school? What's more, Mr. Young knows about this move fully two months before any other teachers know where they'll be working next year. Normally these decisions are put off until a week before the start of the new school year.

At first I saw this as a blow that would be difficult to recover from. Now I see it as a blessing. The distraction of Mr. Young's presence, the self-consciousness, the expending of psychic energy—gone. Mr. Lee would be a good replacement. No attraction there. In many ways he has been able to be a better friend to me, and probably speaks better English. But there is that part of me that craves its love object, as well as excitement and emotional involvement. We've been attracted and we've denied each other. We've never spoken candidly about our feelings. Is that good or bad? We're too far apart—in age, culture, interests, and probably personality. (Neither of us knows what the other's personality *is*.) If we wanted to be together at all, it would have to be a secret, temporary affair. But that isn't possible here—how could it be kept secret?

From the beginning I saw myself as a potential predator, an experienced Western woman capable of wreaking destruction in his life if I encouraged anything between us. Now I'm wondering if it wasn't also the other way around. I'm the one away from home, without friends, in a strange culture where I don't speak the language. We are both vulnerable. Maybe we are simultaneously predator and prey.

Even though I know our staying away from each other is the right thing to do in the eyes of society and in the interest of his family (not to mention in the interest of at least *my* job), there's a part of me that feels it violates nature. I suppose that's the tireless, never-say-die procreative part.

....

School will be officially recessed between Christmas and mid-February. It isn't quite the end of the semester—the semester finishes in late February. Classes are scheduled to avoid the coldest and hottest months. But during the better part of each of these breaks "supplemental" lessons are set up that are mandatory for students and teachers. My contract states I have only four weeks' vacation. So the school is supposed to use me to teach conversation lessons even during times when Korean teachers are free. Fortunately these lessons involve only a couple hours of teaching each day. In January I will teach a two-week workshop for elementary school teachers in Chunchon. That will be full time, and very demanding. But I'll be paid incredibly well—about $3,000.

Entry 15
Wonju, Winter 1996-1997

    Charlotte and Percival and I took the bus to Seoul last weekend—an easy hour and a half ride. (The buses in Korea are clean and comfortable and run frequently.) We rode a taxi from the bus station to Itaewon, a favorite shopping district for tourists with lots of Western brand-name clothing at cheap prices. Many of these things are made in Korea, thus the shipping costs are eliminated. I bought tights and sweatshirts to keep me warm at home, a winter coat, and some hiking boots made of Gore-Tex. At least that's what it says on the boots. I hear you have to look out for knockoffs. I think I'm done finding the clothes I need for winter. I bought two good wool pantsuits in Wonju that I wear to school (they're a few steps up from the clay-smeared overalls that I was used to wearing in my studio). Charlotte and Percival bought very little in Itaewon. They have a hard time finding things in their sizes. Again, Percival takes pleasure in this fact, whereas it's a source of embarrassment for Charlotte. They did scout out antiques—Percival collects clocks, so they turned a number of these over in their hands. And they scrutinized ponderous chests of drawers with ornate brass fittings.

    I enjoyed the day, with one major drawback. Percival doesn't like Korean food, and is irresistibly drawn to junk food. We had breakfast at Wendy's, lunch at Burger King, and dinner at McDonald's. Or, rather, they did. I ate a small breakfast—it seemed harmless—and didn't eat for the rest of the day. Before getting on the bus for the trip home, I bought roasted chestnuts and a bag of tangerines from a street vendor. If I ever spend the day with the Hamiltons again, I'll insist on getting a decent meal.

    Late in the day, we were looking through a series of stores in an underground shopping area by the bus station. This particular section of the mall specialized in Christmas decorations. Charlotte asked if I intended to get a tree. When I said no, they both seemed startled by my lack of enthusiasm for the holiday. I soon realized that by "tree" they meant artificial tree, as they set about selecting one. I was getting punchy by that time, and my mouth was escaping my control. I teased them for wanting a fake tree. This had a much greater effect on them than I expected. They didn't buy one (at least not then), and I fear I dampened their Christmas spirit.

I don't know what I'll do for the holidays this year. Officially I have only one day off. The head teacher, Mr. Shin, has invited me to go to a Christmas Eve service with him at The Full Gospel Church.

Many of the Christians here, including Mr. Shin, are fundamentalists. They ask what religion I am as soon as they're introduced to me. On my second day at school, one of the English teachers offered me a copy of the New Testament.

"Do you need this?" he asked.

"No, thank you. I'm not a Christian."

"You aren't?"

"I'm not."

Korean zeal and Christian fundamentalism mesh readily. They're a good fit, or a bad one. I don't like the result—it's one form of repression layered on top of another.

I'm hiding out from the usual American Christmas frenzy. It was too busy, too scattered, and too expensive for me. In a country that's only twenty-five percent Christian (the rest are mostly either Buddhist or don't claim any religion), I'm getting a vacation from the holidays. I'll send some cards to friends and family.

Entry 16
Portland, Winter 1998-1999

There's a gray and gentle rain outside. It's Christmas day in Portland. I'm grateful to be here. I like this classic old apartment with its wood floors, white walls, and hot, clanking radiators.

Last night my sister and brother and their families came for dinner. I took the whole day to clean house, wrap gifts, and cook. Several days before, I decorated the apartment with pine boughs, silvery garland, and shiny red and blue ribbons. I've designated the pathos plant hanging in the dining area window as my Christmas tree. White cotton snowflakes made of tatting—bought from a woman in Illinois twenty years ago—hang from its leaf stems. A few delicate, clear glass ornaments dangle there also—birds in flight, bells, a star. Every candleholder and candle I own is placed high and low throughout the living and dining rooms. (When my mother died fifteen years ago, we four children split her brass and glass antique candleholder collection, and I came away with ten.)

All of us contributed food, and we had a delicious meal—from the black olives in the relish tray to the pumpkin crisp. We adhered to our family tradition of exchanging gifts after dinner. Later we walked along the Twenty-third Avenue shops, a consumer's paradise, stopping in front of windows to critique the brightly lit merchandise. It was a proper Christmas Eve. Today we'll do it again at the home of my brother-in-law's father. Evidently my two-year hiatus was enough to renew my appetite.

Entry 17
Wonju, Winter 1996-1997

    I had to get away from Wonju over Christmas. I desperately needed a change—some relief from the combined tedium and anxiety of school. The teaching is challenging and interesting at times, but doesn't inspire me. (One of the disadvantages of having made my living in the past doing what I most wanted to do is that anything less is boring.) I applied for a week off. Even when school is not in session, I have to get permission from the principal and vice principal to leave town. It's the same for all teachers. The administration wants to know where you are at all times.

    Seoul, with its historic sites, shopping, and movies that will either never come to Wonju or will arrive six months late, was my natural destination. Having been there before on day trips, I'm familiar with the subway system and don't have any trouble getting around. Twice in the past I've met my Korean-American friend Min-hi. We visited historic sites, perused the upscale department stores, indulged in Korean noodles and dumplings, and caught a French movie.

    Min-hi and I met during orientation and instantly liked each other. Her eyebrows, the clarity of her forehead, and maybe something about her mouth reminded me of my eldest sister. That endeared her to me. She's a thoughtful person, and she's my age. After thirty years in the U.S., most of them spent teaching English to Korean immigrant children in the public schools, she's returned to Korea to do similar work. Our friendship is based solely on mutual first impressions fleshed out by a couple late-evening conversations when we roomed together during the native English teachers' site-seeing tour. The younger ones were out looking for nightlife. Already in our pajamas, Min-hi lounged on the couch and I lay on my sleeping mat on the floor. We were strangers who felt an affinity for each other, and our talk consisted of vague, ginger self-disclosure about our histories, our experiences with men. We laughed at ourselves and each other.

Min-hi's English is still not altogether fluent. Listening seems to be her biggest problem. I have to speak slowly, simply, and clearly. Complex sentences go right by her. Often I need to repeat myself. This is frustrating because I long for the customary conversation with a friend in which ideas, observations, and jokes can be traded rapidly, with no comprehension difficulties. Still, I'm eager to spend time with her.

She was assigned to teach in Seoul. I went to Wonju. We've kept in touch with occasional phone calls and our meetings in downtown Seoul. Now I wanted to invite myself to be her houseguest for a few days before Christmas. After that, I thought I'd finish out the week in a hotel. I assumed Min-hi would have plans for Christmas with her family.

Living in a foreign country can compress the friendship-developing time. Of course I need Min-hi much more than she needs me. She's back in her home country, surrounded by her home language, and living in the same city with some of her dearest family. There are also the old friends from high school to look up. Still, I can tell that I offer her something none of the others do. Maybe it's just conversation with a peer—an American woman her age. (She has been at least partially Americanized.) I surmounted my shyness and proposed the visit. She seemed happy to have me come.

Min-hi lives on the eleventh floor of a fifteen-story apartment building in a new and fast-growing suburb of Seoul. The apartment complex is vast and laid out to include green areas, playgrounds, and wide brick paths for pedestrians and bicyclists. I can run and practice T'ai Chi in the mornings. Min-hi's much older sister lives only ten minutes away by foot. The two of them are like mother and daughter. One of Min-hi's nieces, the daughter of this sister, is about thirty-five years old and frequently visits Min-hi. They're good friends, and Min-hi dotes on the two little daughters of this niece as if they were her own.

On one of my visits to Seoul we toured Kyongbokkung, a palace that was intermittently Korea's seat of government for over two hundred years. The image of Min-hi, strolling on the sunlit grounds, smiling and relaxed, sticks with me. It was as if her lungs could finally fill out again. She was home, and I felt happy for her. I can't imagine preferring Korea over the United States, but everyone has their soil of origin, the place where they were first molded, and their contours will never be received by any other landscape so well and comfortably.

My soil of origin—outside of Pittsburgh, Pennsylvania—could be gray, grim, and cindery like my Wonju neighborhood. The air, our homes, our very interiors were polluted by the tireless smokestacks of the steel mills. But there were country roads in fall, the swimming pool in summer, drive-in theaters, friends, boyfriends—any love I have of life had its start there. I got out, and don't want to go back, but have never felt such a thorough sense of home and belonging since then. I understand the Korean ambivalence: they want their freedom and a better material life, but they have to leave home to get it.

One of Min-hi's high school friends, Ho Kyu-yeon, invited us to lunch. We met at a department store, then Ho Kyu-yeon drove us to a traditional Korean restaurant whose vast windows looked out on a human-made waterfall. Luxuriant green plants sprung from rocks and around the pond at the base of the rolling white water.

Min-hi's friend married a man who is an executive with one of the big auto companies. She is lovely and perfectly tended—hair, skin, makeup, nails, and clothes. I was glad I'd worn my black wool suit.

Min-hi is a sophisticated dresser and I think she wishes I would dress up more often. My usual jeans and T-shirts make me look kidlike next to her. Despite my appropriate clothing that day, I was self-conscious about a mysterious redness and swelling around my eyes.

Ho Kyu-yeon's husband's business made it necessary for them to live in London for ten years. I don't know how fluent she became there, but since then her English has evidently drifted down into the lower recesses of her mind, and she has difficulty retrieving it. Most of the time she and Min-hi chattered on in Korean. I was content to doze in the car or daydream in the restaurant.

Ho Kyu-yeon's marriage has provided her with wealth, position, respectability, and—most of all—a sense of ease. But who knows what the quality of that marriage has been. As we left the restaurant with its gleaming wooden walls and elegant brush paintings, we passed a series of alcoves. Inside one, several drunken businessmen were sitting cross-legged around a table strewn with glasses, bottles, and the usual myriad plates of food. Two beautiful young hostesses dressed in brilliantly colored *hanbok* (traditional long dresses) entered the alcove. One of the men reached over and closed the sliding door behind them. Ho Kyu-yeon noticed I was watching and gave me an embarrassed smile that confirmed my wonderings. It was the only fraying I saw in her satiny façade. She paid for all three of us, and we left.

Min-hi and I are easy companions. I'm learning about her previous life in America. As the youngest in the family, it was her lot to live with and care for her widowed mother. About two years ago, her mother died of Parkinson's disease. Min-hi says she also suffered from a long-term mental illness. (Alzheimer's?) Her mother was paranoid about Min-hi's leaving home. It was difficult for her to travel and even temporarily escape the unrelenting burden. Sometimes Min-hi's sister would come from Korea to briefly take her place. Her mother didn't want Min-hi to marry at all, but her main concern was that she not marry an American, meaning a non-Korean.

Now Min-hi is free, living alone for the first time in her fifty years. She still relies on family for most of her social contact. She has dinner with her sister and brother-in-law virtually every evening. They are dear to her, but barely contemporaries and not people she can talk to. Her nieces and nephews in both Korea and the U.S. have always occupied much of her time and thought. She wanted (wants) to marry. She always hoped to have children of her own.

I feel her confusion over how she arrived at this age with a life so partially lived. And the future not looking too promising: at fifty, a woman in Korea *or* the U.S. becomes discounted and invisible to much of the population. Min-hi is a devout Catholic. A crucifix, rosary, and portraits of Jesus and Mary hang on her walls. This is her solace, but it makes me wince. It's the kidnapped victim identifying with her kidnappers. It only assures her continued imprisonment.

We looked at her mother's life—someone who lived in a permanent state of petulant unhappiness. I said to Min-hi that I had only recently come to terms with the fact that it is possible to fail, to have a failed life. A glance from her disclosed that this remark had penetrated deeply. Another thread materialized between us, adding to our connection.

Despite my secularism, I always expected to emerge sometime into the light, into a period of fulfillment, contentment, and—I blush at the thought—freedom from constant money worries. Min-hi's mother never emerged from her tunnel. Will Min-hi emerge from hers or I from mine? Okay, I know that life is really a series of tunnels and emergences. I suppose I could "end up" (die) when I'm in a tunnel or when I'm out. The roll of the dice. Talking to Min-hi about her life makes me feel fortunate. Although my life's not been easy, it has been full.

As it turned out, Min-hi invited me to stay through Christmas at her apartment. I spent only one night in a hotel in Seoul before returning to Wonju. I stayed in the Seoul Plaza, one of the most expensive ones. Min-hi came downtown with me and we both enjoyed the luxurious surroundings. Before she went back to her apartment, we watched a movie on TV. Later I soaked in the tub. That's one of my deprivations here—no bathtub. Long hot baths were a daily form of therapy for me in the U.S.

Entry 18
Wonju, Winter 1996-1997

    I first noticed a problem with my eyes two days after my visit to the bathhouse. I was at a dinner with a group of teachers, feeling exhilarated by the return of good health following my cold. My left eye was scratchy and foggy. Rubbing it didn't help. Finally Mr. Young gave me one of the damp towels everyone receives at the beginning of a meal, and told me to wipe my face and eyes. When I got home, I saw white pus coming out of the inside corner of that eye. The infection spread to the other eye within a day so that both were red and swollen. I thought my cold, after ravishing my sinuses and lungs, had found a new part of my body to attack. In the first few days, I had a hard time opening my eyes in the morning—the discharge had dried and sealed them shut.

    While I was in Seoul, Min-hi went with me to a drugstore, and with her help I was able to describe the problem to a pharmacist. I told him I thought there were two possible causes—the bathhouse or the cold. He asked me if it was in both eyes and was there mucous. I said yes. He quickly fingered the bathhouse. (Was I now paying a price for my irresistible few strokes underwater in the cold tub?) The pharmacist gave me eye drops that brought immediate improvement. But a week and a half later the infection was still not completely gone. I started taking some antibiotic herbs that I brought with me from the U.S. My doctor (a doctor of oriental medicine) recommended them. The information on the package specifically mentioned conjunctivitis and the presence of pus, so I was hopeful.

    This has been a new and frightening experience for me. Perhaps I'm helpless to fight off these unfamiliar germs. And they're in my *eyes*. What if there's permanent damage? I have always avoided going to doctors, and especially want to avoid it in a foreign and less developed country. But I felt I had to go. I asked Ae-ja to accompany me to the eye doctor as an interpreter.

It was evident the man did a brisk business and saw this sort of thing routinely. I was beginning to understand the frequency with which I saw people walking around with eye patches. The examination took only a minute or two. Then I was sent on my way through a well-oiled process: first a shot in the rear, then a treatment with a sunlamp, and finally the dispensing of an array of pills and eye drops to last me a week. The doctor had no interest in discovering where I had contracted the infection. This apparently isn't seen as a public health issue, only an accepted hazard of the bathhouse. It's been many years since I've taken antibiotics. I didn't like taking them, but I also wanted this infection out of my eyes as quickly as possible. The treatment helped.

After a week I returned by myself to the doctor, having practiced the appropriate sentences in Korean as well as having prepared written notes and questions. Some of the redness was still there, so I went home with another black and blue spot on my rear end, as well as more pills and drops.

The return of my cold and a sinus infection combined with sick eyes and the effects of antibiotics have made me feel foggy, weak, and helpless. I've lost a lot of weight during this time. Food doesn't look appetizing, and the pills have a diuretic effect. My body is suffering in this country.

I discussed my conjunctivitis with Ho Young-kun, one of the most fluent among the English teachers at the school. This is a sore subject with Koreans. They don't like to think of their country as "dirty" or backward. They don't like the idea that their bathhouses are sources of diseases. She was defensive, and assured me, as had others, that I must have picked it up somewhere else. At some point I realized that she thought I was also implying that Korean germs are more virulent than American germs, and that's why I got this infection here and had never contracted it in the U.S. I tried to explain that it's a matter of not having developed an immunity over time, and that if I went from one part of America to the other, I would be likely to pick up some sort of illness. This was a fogging of the issue, but I hoped I could get away with it.

One of my favorite students—she's bright, lively, creative, and gentle—called me last Saturday evening. It was brave of her to initiate a phone conversation with me in English—I'm sure she rehearsed it. Gi-wan said she had had a dream about me the night before: I was very sick, so she and her best friend came to my apartment and made food for me. "It was not a good dream," she said. She had intuited my situation precisely. I was touched.

Entry 19
Wonju, Winter 1996-1997

We've all heard that Asians are very attentive to "saving face." Before living in Korea, I thought this was a way of showing sensitivity and consideration toward people, and that it applied to everyone. But after five months here, I think it should be termed "saving ass." Koreans will go to great pains, including taking unwarranted blame on themselves, in order to save the face of someone above them on the rigid ladder of position and authority. That person can hurt them, and will not hesitate to do so if contradicted or thwarted in any way. However, if someone occupies the same rung or a lower one, then not only is there no obligation to save that person any embarrassment, but opportunities to ridicule or denigrate are pounced on. I watch this dynamic in the teachers' room daily. It's one of the reasons I'm wary of trusting people here. Korea operates on a "might makes right" system. If someone has power, you try to ingratiate yourself. If someone is powerless, they're fair game. Mr. Young recently told me that Koreans are always trying to get ahead by pressing someone else down.

A teacher from another school came to one of my English conversation classes very flustered and angry. Just before leaving to come to my school, she said, she had been severely scolded by her principal for a mistake made by her supervisor. The supervisor was standing beside her at the time, listening attentively to the whole harangue, yet made no move to take the blame. The fact that this teacher would express her anger—and to a foreigner—shows that change is stirring.

So many people in this society are viewed with contempt, including anyone who makes a living with any sort of manual labor. I saw a short film prepared by the government that's being screened before the feature film in Korean movie theaters. It's about three high school boys. They make a pact to go to college together and become successful. Two of them follow through on the promise, but one starts hanging out with the wrong crowd, doesn't go to college, and becomes an auto mechanic. He's disgraced, and doomed to lead an unhappy life. Let that be a lesson to all those young men out there.

The problem is, too many people are graduating from college. The big Korean corporations don't have jobs for them all. They have to languish unemployed, take jobs that they feel are demeaning, or emigrate. One of the English teachers told me many people who go to college aren't really college material. But there's not an acceptable alternative. At this point there are very few vocational schools or junior colleges in Korea. Awareness is growing that this has to change.

....

It seems Mr. Shin, the head teacher, is smitten with me. His English is surprisingly good considering he's a social studies teacher, and he works hard to improve. He keeps language tapes in his car, and likes to practice with me at school. Mr. Shin has also been very patient and helpful in my attempts to learn Korean. He made sure I knew to call him *Kyo Mu Sansaeng Nim* which means, loosely, "Head Teacher Sir." Koreans refer to each other by their titles (sometimes preceded by a family name) and it's considered impolite to use given names except for children. Mr. Shin is shorter than I am, and decidedly homely. His teeth are disordered and confusing to look at; he has an occasional tic in one eye. He's playful at times with the other teachers, and laughs readily. I was amused to see him take both hands of another male teacher in his and swing them back and forth while they talked. (Touching between males is common and acceptable here whereas public touching between males and females is considered inappropriate.) Some weeks ago he pointedly told me we were the same age, and therefore could be friends. Did he mean it's not appropriate for Mr. Young and me because of the difference in our ages?

He invited me to dinner at his house, one of the few times a teacher has done this. Before going into the kitchen to eat, Mr. Shin, his wife, and I sat on the spacious chairless and couchless floor of the room they use for entertaining guests. Their bedding was stored in a cabinet.

Floor sitting is a problem for me. When Koreans sit, their knees flop naturally to the floor. But my knees are Western knees, and not used to flexing outward, so they poke upward when I sit in a cross-legged position, and soon start to ache. Sometimes I stay in this position, noting the gradual ossification of my legs, enduring the pain, and knowing how difficult it will be to unfold and stand up. Other times I periodically try different positions in a search for comfort: my legs straight out in front, both legs to one side, then the other. Or I'll start out sitting on my feet. This works until my feet begin to turn numb. When I sit like this everyone immediately urges me to change to cross-legged, assuming it's as comfortable for me as it is for them. By the end of a meal I have to get up very slowly while my legs painfully straighten. Sometimes floors are padded like the floor of my apartment; sometimes they're not. Usually, square cushions are piled in a corner for people to use if they want to. But these cushions are never thick enough for my needs. Most restaurants in Korea offer a choice of Western or Korean seating. My Korean companions will choose the floor over chairs any day.

On the wall of the room I sat in with the Shins is a decorative toilet paper holder with a roll of toilet paper in it. This sort of thing has taken some getting used to. Rolls of toilet paper also appear on most restaurant tables. They're on the desks at school—I was shocked to find a roll on my desk one morning. My delicate sensibilities were assaulted by this open display. Gradually I've gotten used to regarding this as tissue just like "Kleenex," and forgotten the usual narrow associations I had with it.

Mr. Shin's wife is very energetic, young looking, and has a good sense of humor. In addition, she's an excellent cook. They tease each other good-naturedly, and their relationship seems harmonious. While she was out of the room seeing to our dinner, Mr. Shin and I looked through some photographs, and he commented that his wife used to be pretty, but she isn't anymore. I think she's very attractive. She has gained some weight; otherwise she hasn't changed much. To criticize his wife's appearance like that! In worrying contrast, he often compliments me on how I look, and frequently praises my clothing.

Mr. Shin is persistent in coming up with ways for us to see each other. He called me from school on Thursday evening. He was on night duty, one of the many extra jobs teachers have. One male teacher is scheduled to be there all night as security. He stays in a room off the entrance hall that's provided with bedding, a TV, and a bathroom with a shower. Female teachers hold down the fort during the day when school is not in session. Mr. Shin informed me that there were "five pieces of letters" waiting for me. (My mail is delivered to the school.) I was too tired to take this alluring bait, and told him I would be in the next morning. He wanted to know when I was taking the bus to Chunchon the next day to teach my workshop. I told him 10:00. At about 8:00 the following morning he called to say that I now had "eight pieces of letters" and he would be driving to Chunchon at 10:00 to see his daughter at the university. I told him I had decided to leave later because I had to go to the bank first. Foiled again.

....

Mr. Young invited me to have dinner with him at a Chinese restaurant close to the school. He didn't say that his wife would be coming too. Korean men often fail to mention their wives—at all. I should have expected it when his wife arrived to pick us up in her car at the end of classes. I sat in the back with their two little girls, aged four and six. The older girl fingered my hair and earrings. Earrings, especially the dangly kind that I like to wear, are rare in Korea and associated with loose women. Her gentle touch almost put me to sleep.

When we got to the restaurant, we came to a table with six chairs, three on either side. Mr. Young's wife sat on one side between her two daughters. I slid in against the wall on the other side, assuming Mr. Young would want to have an empty chair between us. His parents' generation was brought up not to touch people of the opposite gender after the age of seven and did their best to pass this on. He sat down on the outer edge of the outer chair.

There was only one menu per side, and as we discussed our options, he held on to one side of the menu while I held the other. With my free hand I pointed to one of the dishes, then let my hand drop. Unintentionally, my finger brushed the tip of his finger. He emitted a quick, low moan as his body curved slightly inward.

The intense and hopeless yearning of that small sound, that almost imperceptible movement penetrated my body. I was surprised. To have such an effect.

I remember my first lover, thirty years ago. We sat in a brightly lit restaurant, our hands resting on a Formica-and-stainless-steel table. He stretched out one index finger; I met it with mine. We pressed the tips of our fingers together. He looked up at me with a sweet, ardent look, and the current flowed between us like a river. We smiled, then laughed, having just had sex on the restaurant table in plain view of everyone there.

Entry 20
Portland, Winter 1998-1999

    I'm proceeding, but without direction. My intellect is making the decisions and I'm obeying. I'm taking two graduate courses—nineteenth-century British women writers, and technical writing. I'm looking for T'ai Chi teaching jobs. School is getting in the way of my copyediting training, but I'm managing to keep that up too now. Soon I'll be ready to send out resumes and take the tests required by most publishers.

    I hate school. I have always loved learning, but the academic environment is fundamentally toxic to me. I remember looking at my students in Korea, lined up in their cramped desks, packed fifty to a room, with their heads uniformly bowed over their papers as they took the eighth of twelve final exams in three days. That's what I was thinking then: I hate school. What it does to people.

    It sounded like a great course—I read nineteenth-century British women writers for pleasure. I've read four of the six assigned books, three of them more than once. When I was in between books in Korea, I opened my copy of *Pride and Prejudice* to any page and started reading there. Having a chance to discuss this and other books and writers with people who appreciated them was tantalizing.

    I guess it was naïve of me to anticipate lively discussions and arguments. The professor is stiff and insecure. She's rude to students—often cuts people off in midsentence—their first sentence. She enjoys showcasing her knowledge of the subject and seems to be afraid that a student might offer up something she hasn't already thought of. Or that students may *think* she hasn't already thought of it. This professor is ready to retire, yet after several decades she has learned nothing about teaching. At the root of the problem are insecurity and an inability to relate to people.

    We are studying marvelous writing. It should be celebrated, read aloud, savored for its wit and insight and grace.

There's no joy in this class, no fun. Just a lot of pages to plow through and papers to be written on each book.

The literary criticism I read while preparing these papers is the product of an industry desperate to perpetuate itself. The writers grasp at subjects, shamelessly fantasizing, half inventing the foundations of their arguments. Their writing is deliberately dense in order to disguise the fact that an article filling dozens of pages could be condensed to a few unremarkable sentences. The professor has chosen to make copies of only one critical essay to distribute to the class. I wonder what she's thinking, what is her motive, because this one is the worst of all. Is it another attempt to impress us with her intellectual powers? Only a few pages long, it takes me at least two hours to decipher it. English is not the author's first language. But that hasn't stopped her from adopting the most opaque academic jargon. I'm angry during the entire time that I'm reading. What is the author saying? That the industrialized world objectifies and stereotypes the people and cultures of the nonindustrialized world, and that nineteenth-century British literature reflects and reinforces this. Surprise!

I got a B on my first paper. In it I disagreed directly with both the professor and the writer of the introduction to Mary Shelley's *Frankenstein*. The other papers so far have been granted As.

If you take these papers seriously, they require a terrific amount of time. I wonder how many of the other students who are taking three or four courses manage to keep up. From the conversations I overhear before class, they're not doing too well. Lots of late papers, and already talk of incompletes.

Many teachers pile on the work as if their course is the only one. They need students to validate them by focusing exclusively on their course, while ignoring other courses (and other teachers). The students *expect* to live in a state of panic past the first couple weeks of the term. A teaching assistant who is taking the British women writers class told some of her friends that she warns her composition students they'll work their asses off in her class—harder than they have ever worked before. The abusee becomes the abuser.

At least the quarter system means that whatever the course, it will be over in ten weeks.

As for the technical writing class, I'm paying $900 to do something that I could do, should do, on my own. But I don't want to work on my own. I've done too much of that; I don't have the energy for it now. I like the contact with people, and the fact that someone else will read my writing and offer suggestions. I'm writing an article on studying T'ai Chi in Korea. It will have to substitute for work on my Korean narrative.

Tracy Dillon, the professor teaching the technical writing course, operates outside the usual academic pattern. He's interested in a real product, not just diversionary hoop jumping. He's trying to establish a new master's program in writing. It might be exactly the thing for me. The British women writers class has erased any illusions I may have had about pursuing a degree in English literature. I couldn't bear it.

I understand again why I left Duke, why I had to abandon the study of English literature and art history. Art and academics don't mix. Any attempt to apply such narrow, compartmentalized scrutiny to art only results in embarrassing absurdities. How lucky I was to be a potter for so long! When I left for Korea, I was questioning my long-ago decision to transfer from Duke to Ohio State where I could major in ceramics. I had never done that before—questioned past life decisions. Now, after some forays into other possibilities, I see they aren't—and weren't—possibilities after all. I've always gone the only way I could go, and I will have to continue on that path. It remains to be seen if a master's degree is part of it.

....

A dream of a group of people (a family?) They are offered tarantula soup. It's a pale, unhealthy, yellow-green color. Only one accepts it—the large male. The women and children look on, wonder why he is eating it, how sick he will get, and how long it will take him to become ill.

Another dream: a relative of mine gets married on Halloween. It's a doomed mismatch between male and female, and a ghastly parody of all the marriages coming up on Valentine's Day.

My life has been poisonous for a long time. I'm seesawing out of balance, the center cannot hold. My yang side has taken control over the last years, bullying its counterpart, beating it down.

So much bad stuff is stored in me that I've become my own alien environment. I have to vent it somehow.

People ridicule New Age music, but I need it. My heart immediately slows down when I hear it. It really does soothe the savage breast. I can rest; I can work. One of my tapes ends with "Amazing Grace." (New Age unabashedly draws from all sources.) I never realized how sad that song is. It released some of my tears. As in all genres, some of it is good, some mediocre, and some bad. Classical music is full of angst—almost all of it gets around to a frenzied state at some point. When I was a teenager, a friend's mother was seeing a psychiatrist to help her deal with anxiety. Among other things, the doctor prescribed Smetana's *The Moldau.* The music (the river) begins by gliding and rolling gently, but inevitably builds into a ferocious torrent. The prescription always mystified me. How could that piece do anything other than make her jumpier? Especially after hearing it once and knowing what was coming?

T'ai Chi helps too. For months I was alternating styles—one day I'd practice my original Wu style, and the next I'd practice the combined form (a modern amalgam of four styles) that I learned in Korea. But now I only practice Wu style. The forcefulness, the emphasis on the external in the combined form doesn't feed me. And maybe it reminds me too much of the abrasiveness of Korea and the ceaseless effort expended there. I require the easy circular flow and internal focus of my first style—it's still and quiet and opens me to the healing green around me—the grass, the trees. The trees. I recognize them as my cousins, the tall standing people who surround me and witness my practice. We absorb each other and I become a standing person too. Bit by bit, I breathe in the life around me and exhale my sadness.

I rent only funny movies. But they often turn out not to be funny. I can't stand the violence, the constant string of explosions in most movies. Nor can I handle watching the self-destructive, wasted lives. I'm full to overflowing with all that.

I was introduced to a couple who I thought might become friends. But their relationship is too tenuous. They live together, and at one moment talk as if they're planning a future together; the next moment they talk as if they're headed in completely different directions. He clearly likes me, enjoys talking to me. The friendship has fizzled.

A bad cold and sinus infection sap my energy. I don't sleep. I lead an emotionally impoverished life. Some days I talk to no one other than saying hello to grocery clerks or people at the Y. There is virtually no touching in my life.

I have lain awake nights during these last months pondering suicide. Life seems to be nothing but a struggle for survival, and survival alone is not enough. Death seems to offer the only escape, the only rest. If there were a graceful way to do it without traumatizing relatives and sending such a depressing message to my nieces and nephews, I've thought I would do it.

Paradoxically, at times I feel physically very strong. My swimming—especially butterfly—can feel transcendent. I've been running three days a week and swimming the other three. I practice T'ai Chi six days a week. And I'm stretching in the sauna at the Y. All of it is a form of release. A trip to the ocean with my sister and her family restored and enlivened me, even brought on a light menstrual period.

In the middle of the night last night, I gave up trying to sleep. I drew a bath and lit incense and a candle in the bathroom. With music in the background, and surrounded by sparkling white bubbles, I soaked. Then I dried myself and danced my own naked dance, drawing on my repertoire of T'ai Chi movements. Finally I fell asleep while reading Margaret Atwood. I have *some* resources.

In small increments I'm feeling more at home, gradually abandoning my siege mentality. For a few days I had a euphoric feeling. Was it the influence of the ocean? Or was it the St. Johnswort I've been taking for the last couple weeks? A well-timed beer, I've discovered, (just a fraction of a bottle) can work wonders. I sleep, I feel great the next day. But this works only once in a long while. Used any less sparingly, alcohol just compounds my problems.

I miss my women friends. I just watched Emmy Lou Harris, Linda Ronstadt, and Dolly Parton singing together on TV. They're women my age who are full, alive, and expressive. Emmy Lou has let her long hair go gray. Linda has put on a lot of weight. Dolly remains true to her wigs and false attachments. All three of them are beautiful. Their music and their obvious delight in singing as a trio elicited welcome tears.

When I was in my last months in Korea, I wrote a list and taped it to the inside of my armoire where no Koreans would see it. I don't remember exactly what was on it then, but this is what's on it now:

> I'm an artist and I need to create.
> I need community and conversation.
> I need massages.
> I need cats.
> I need to get my hands back into clay.
> I need to write my Korean story.
> I need to make money.

The last has a nasty way of taking precedence and making all the others difficult. I've invested many hours in training myself for copyediting. Is it poisonous too? It's sedentary, tedious, uncreative work. I will begin teaching T'ai Chi for the community college and parks and rec beginning April 1.

Entry 21
Wonju, Winter 1996-1997

My friends are dropping away.

Bo-ra has stopped coming to the evening English-Korean language sessions at my apartment. She used to be so enthusiastic about our Tuesday and Thursday meetings with Ae-ja and Pil-lung. What happened to wanting to be my "special friend?" The cooling of her attitude took me by surprise.

She wants to go to grad school in the U.S. and has already been admitted to a theological school, but the INS won't let her in. A single woman like her is too high a risk—she might decide to get married and stay. I think she has determined that I'm in no position to aid her cause. Now she always has an excuse for not coming here, and doesn't bother to tell me ahead of time that she's not coming.

Pil-lung is in India for winter vacation, and I'm glad she's gone. We've planned numerous dinners together at my apartment. She has either shown up late (often having already eaten!) or she's called at the last minute to say she can't come. It's hard for me to believe that this can be explained by "cultural differences." No other Korean has behaved this way. One time I specifically told her not to come because I was very tired and needed to prepare for my workshop in Chunchon. She came anyway. I had the feeling she was checking up on me. Did she expect to find Mr. Young under the bed?

Ae-ja is very busy with her kids, but we still get together occasionally, and she's always ready to help when I need it. I'm trying to get in touch with a friend of hers who goes by the name of Isabel. She has taught Korean to soldiers at the U.S. Army base. I want to arrange some formal, paid-for lessons.

All these people know each other and I feel their cumulative eyes on me, watching, evaluating, discussing, comparing notes. Min-hi is the only person I trust.

I've been giving a lot of thought to my solitude. Why am I alone? What are the effects? Is it healthful or unhealthful? Is it timely and useful? I do crave floating time, staring-into-space time. How will I fare if I extend this for a second year? How will I do through the rest of this year?

I bought two tapes the other day—Julian Bream with John Williams, and Kitaro. I play them on the tiny tape recorder that I bought for playing language tapes. I'm amazed at the pleasant, calming effect. As my friend the dulcimer maker once said, "Music helps." So now I know I need a decent tape player. Maybe I'll start to really listen to music again, use it as a release and comfort. It's been years since I sat and listened to music. I used to do that all the time. I craved it—it spoke my emotions. Either I stopped having time for it or it became more convenient to keep my emotions unspoken. Did I give up?

I wonder about happiness. I can remember times. Will it be in my life again?

....

Mr. Shin invited me to dinner yesterday (Saturday) at 4:00. I bought some fruit on the way home from Chunchon because I was expecting to have dinner at his house again. It's customary to show up with a gift when invited to dinner at someone's home—fruit or flowers are most common. He called my apartment at about twenty minutes of four and arranged to meet me downtown in front of one of the bookstores. I thought perhaps he would accompany me to his home because I had had a hard time finding it the last time. Or he and his wife and I would go to a restaurant. We met, and there was no wife. As we walked down the street, I asked him twice, "Where is your wife?" before he told me she had gone to her father's birthday celebration in a nearby town. He said he thought the two of us could have dinner by ourselves, but it was early for dinner, so would I like to go to a *norebang?* Norebang is the Korean version of karaoke. I said no thank you.

My only personal experience with norebang was with Shi-eun when I was living with her family. She asked if I wanted to go to one with her on a Sunday afternoon. I agreed, not knowing that she worked there for three hours on Sundays and I was expected to stay for the duration. It was a small business on the second floor of a building across from her father's shop. There was a counter out in front and three small, somewhat run-down booths. Only a few customers drifted in. Shi-eun and I sang in one of the booths for a long while—until I reached a saturation point. She loves to sing, and has a sweet, supple voice. I like to sing too, but I was embarrassed by the videos that played behind the lines of lyrics: women in bikinis reclining side-by-side in lounge chairs and slowly running their fingers up each other's legs toward their crotches. Shi-eun didn't react at all to soft-core sex scenes like this; they didn't distract her from the Mariah Carey, Elvis Presley, or John Denver songs. It was bad enough enduring this with one of my students. I was not going to be trapped in a small room with Mr. Shin and forced to watch that sort of thing.

 Mr. Shin suggested a movie. I said no, I thought we could have tea or dinner together and then I would go home. He asked if I would watch TV that night. I said I would probably read.

 This all felt like too much of a date to me. In America, a married man's inviting a woman out for dinner, a movie, or karaoke on a Saturday night definitely would look like a date—especially to his wife. Koreans can be sort of innocent and childlike when it comes to relations between men and women, so maybe it isn't like that for Mr. Shin. On the other hand, there's the tradition of men having mistresses. Probably I'm the naïve one.

 He told me several times over the course of the evening that he wanted to think of me as a good friend. I told him we *were* good friends. I do like him. He struggles to speak English and patiently helps me with my Korean. He is a good man generally—a head teacher who's unusually compassionate toward the students and the teachers. And a typically Korean man with inadequate regard for his wife. Interesting that he would be so bold. Mr. Young would never have behaved this way. Maybe Mr. Shin wants people to see us in public together so they will think there's something between us. Of course we ran into girls from our school. They smiled and made their woo-woo sounds even as we stopped and politely said hello to each other.

....

    I was standing outside the school the other day, watching my breath condense and drift away in the frigid morning air. It was entrancing, soothing, sensual. I was watching my breath. A meditation. It came to me that smoking is a breathing exercise, just like Ch'i Kung or T'ai Chi or Yoga. That's got to be one of its appeals. Humans naturally seek a form of meditation.

Entry 22
Wonju, Winter 1996-1997

The two-week workshop for teachers at Chunchon is finally over. It wore me out—inventing all those lessons, teaching up to eight hours a day, six days a week, commuting by bus, and braving the ice and snow. The students were the best part—lively and appreciative. One class gave me a string of pale green beads made of a jade mined only around Chunchon. It's supposed to have healing properties. There's a long (and questionable) history of students' giving presents to teachers in Korea. But I was delighted, even though it did seem extravagant.

I'm just about over my cough, and the eye infection really seems to be gone. I was feeling almost euphoric last night when a headache started coming on. I took an aspirin for it this morning before teaching a two-hour conversation class at my middle school. The pill jazzed me, but the headache burned through. I need that necklace.

The classes I'm teaching now are supplementary lessons that I'm required to teach. The other teachers are on vacation, and the girls normally would be too. I wonder if the girls resent these extra classes. I've decided to teach the first hour at school and the second hour at my apartment. It's a treat for the students, and it gives us a little break as we move from one place to the other. I make hot chocolate and have snacks like cookies and fruit. Today I taught them two songs from a Bette Midler tape: "Chapel of Love," and " The Rose." I think they enjoyed it, but I'm not sure. They're acting shy and reserved.

My apartment is cold; I can see my breath in the morning when I get up. The heating coils in the floor are barely producing detectable heat in only a few spots, so the girls keep their coats on and cover their legs with the carpet. I light incense before I leave for school so that the sewer gas smell in my apartment is masked when I return with the girls. I'm embarrassed by these problems, as if they're my fault. I'm working on my landlord to get the heating fixed.

....

I've had my first Korean lesson with Isabel (she uses this English name with her conversation students). I'm afraid she's used to teaching the soldiers who have no background in the language at all, and are just learning to count and read signs on stores or on the road. I can tell she's going to have to make up lessons for me as she goes along. But her English is so good, I can't help but think she'll be an effective teacher. Our plan is to meet on Sunday afternoons; I'll get an hour and a half of Korean, and she'll get an hour and a half of English.

Isabel is fifty-seven years old. She's hardy and energetic, physically solid and sturdy. She lives in a comfortable apartment with her grown son, Ho-chang. I have not yet discovered her marital situation. While working on her master's degree in English education, she's teaching conversation classes in various places in the city.

I hope Isabel will be a friend and occasional companion. She wants to take me swimming at a resort about twenty minutes outside of Wonju (how I would love to get into the water again!) and to a bathhouse she uses regularly. With her help as a translator, I may be able to get a massage that isn't too painful.

Through Isabel I met an American who's a civilian employee—an airplane mechanic—at the army base. Jess is a fiftyish African-American who's well over six feet tall and hefty. Having recently lost weight by running and eating less, he has also lost the adjective "fat." He showed me the "before" photo of himself. He comes from Georgia, and has a thick southern accent. I've noticed the Koreans can't detect this, and also don't seem to notice his nonstandard grammar. English is difficult enough without having to differentiate among regional variations. Unlike me, Jess makes no attempt to enunciate more clearly, slow his speech, or simplify his language when he talks to Koreans. Yet people seem to understand him—or pretend they do. Jess's and my backgrounds are completely different, but he's a gentle man, and I enjoy talking with him. Mostly we compare notes on Korea. He's starved for companionship just as most of us Westerners are. Korea gives internationals a keen appreciation for friendship. Jess has had the same experience with Korean friends that I've had. Some people were extremely attentive to him for weeks—they picked him up to take him to their church on Sunday mornings, and frequently included him in other church events. Then they disappeared, simply stopped calling him, and he has no idea why. Jess met Isabel when he took a Korean language class at the base. In his spare time he runs the ceramics studio there. At one time he had a ceramics shop in the U.S. If he could make it pay better, he'd like to go back to that way of earning a living.

Isabel's son Ho-chang and his girlfriend Bo-mi are avidly producing and painting mold-made pieces under Jess's instruction. They both do original hand-built work as well, and Ho-chang shows real talent as a sculptor. They've already completed their master's degrees—Ho-chang in anthropology and Bo-mi in biochemistry. Now they want to go to school in the U.S.

Jess bought small speakers for me (with my money) at the PX in Seoul. They work well with my pocket-sized tape deck. It was nice of him; he seems genuinely eager to go out of his way to help friends.

Ae-ja, who also met Jess through Isabel, gets together with him for English lessons. I've noticed she has more time to see him than she does to see me. She seems jealous of Jess's other women friends, and talks freely about her husband's suspicions regarding him. I get the idea she promotes this, maybe to get her husband's attention. He's only in Wonju from Saturday evening to early Monday morning—during the week he lives in a rural town where he teaches high school math. His first priority on arriving home is to get together with his male friends.

There are several other Korean women from Isabel's English conversation classes who have gotten to know Jess—Isabel regularly invites him to her classes as a native English speaker. I've had lunch at Jess's apartment a few times with this group, including Ae-ja. All the women at these Saturday lunches are in their thirties and forties and married with the exception of one "old miss" who happily flirts with him and makes sure he sits next to her. We played Monopoly after lunch—Jess and his lady friends are avid participants and the women have had no trouble assimilating the rules despite their beginner's-level English.

Jess is married, but he's giving a lot of thought to how he can financially manage a divorce when his tour is over in three months. His wife wants his continued support although she has a "good job" and their several children are grown. He has talked with me about his marriage—his unashamed infidelities as well as his wife's. Here in Korea he seems to be settling for an abstinent existence. He doesn't want to go the usual route of hiring a "housekeeper" who does more than keep house and hopes to be taken back to America at the end of the tour. He makes hinting comments about an attraction to me. I slough them off; he's married and I'm not attracted.

....

Mr. Young and I went to the school accounting office to take care of some business today. A man who works there came up to us grinning and jabbering in Korean, making hand signals for my benefit indicating that Mr. Young and I were close (and was he saying more than that?). I did my usual nodding and smiling. Now that Mr. Young is leaving, it seems everyone is free to talk openly about our friendship. Maybe they're getting loquacious out of relief—Mr. Young's leaving will return things to their proper order. I doubt it. What will they have to talk about? Maybe they're just relishing the upheaval—an overt eruption (the job switching) verifying a long-suspected subterranean buildup of dangerous forces. Their very own soap opera.

Mr. Young is dear to me, but the illusions are fading, and along with them the aura of lust and romance. Still, some kernel in him resonates with a kernel in me. I think that's been the source of our attraction. This resonance has penetrated multiple outer layers of flapping discord. I've experienced this before. My deepest center touches someone else's deepest center despite the barriers created by our mismatched lives and the "clothing" of our personalities. We may not even be sexually compatible.

Twenty years after a brief and totally untenable affair, I still dream of a man. I wonder if he dreams of me.

....

Last Saturday I went to Mr. Lee's wedding. I rode to Hongchon, about one hour's drive, in the back of Mr. Young's car with two male teachers. I was barely spoken to. Almost as soon as we arrived, Mr. Young and some other men went down into the basement where the food and drink were being served. They skipped the ceremony.

The wedding hall was garlanded with artificial pink flowers and plastic greenery. The mothers-in-law graced it with their fluttering hanbok—one in vivid pink, the other in glowing blue. By the time the ceremony began, all one hundred fifty seats were taken and the remaining space was crowded with standing people. This was a Western wedding, as most are now. When the bride walked down the aisle with her father, people started to laugh and giggle. What was funny? Either it was more of the Korean ridicule, or I missed something. Mr. Lee was very serious, waiting up there in front of the altar. The bride and groom bowed to each set of parents who were seated on couches on either side of the aisle at the front of the hall. This bowing, which takes place again at the end, is a critical part of the ritual, and is an acknowledgment of the primacy of the parents in these people's lives. Mr. Lee and his bride then bowed to each other. Their heads almost touched; maybe they bumped heads. In any case, this set off another round of giggling from the onlookers.

This was a civil ceremony with a gray-suited man officiating. He spoke into a microphone, but it was soon impossible to hear him over all the talking and commotion in the audience. Children ran around unrestrained, squealing as they twisted away from each other. Adults didn't bother to whisper their conversations.

I was reminded of the arts festival put on by the students in November. While all these extremely talented and carefully prepared girls performed on their big night, virtually the entire audience (mostly students) was in motion and talking loudly to each other about subjects unrelated to what was on stage. And what was on stage was fantastic. What is this about? An attempt to deprecate people? To trivialize people's accomplishments? Is it the crabs-in-the-bucket syndrome? (One crab starts to escape—to separate itself or distinguish itself—and the others pull it back down.) I don't get it.

The wedding lasted fifteen minutes at most. The bride and groom repeated their bows and headed back down the aisle. A knot of students (Mr. Lee's wife is also a teacher) set off streamers and sprays of confetti directly in their faces. Mr. Lee scrunched up his face and bore it. His wife kept her head down as she had from the beginning. Neither looked amused. They went off to have their pictures taken.

The guests went downstairs to the dreary-looking hall where lunch was being served with typical hustle and clatter. I sat with several other teachers from my school, and within fifteen minutes we were done eating and ready to head home.

Marriage and family are so important in Korea. I expected the wedding to be a sacred event, and much more solemn and drawn out. I couldn't help but contrast the noisy perfunctoriness with all the hushed emotion and carefully chosen words of recent weddings I've attended in the U.S. This was pure practicality, and everyone assured me all Korean weddings are like this.

As for gifts, it's customary to bring cash in a white envelope. In the foyer of the wedding hall there were two tables with two men sitting behind each. They took the envelopes, opened them, counted the money, and wrote the names of the guests in a ledger. I assume the amount of the contribution was recorded too. I brought handmade teacups with saucers wrapped in a box with a card attached. Mr. Young made sure my name was also written on the outside of the box. I only saw one other nonmonetary gift.

I had a very informative talk with a friend of Mr. Lee's while we waited for the ceremony to begin. He's also an English teacher, and surprisingly fluent, so the conversation went smoothly. He told me that most people give twenty thousand won (twenty-five dollars) at a wedding. Then he went on to tell me that he and Mr. Lee and some other male friends went out drinking the night before. He and his buddy got really drunk. When they returned to their hotel room, they fell into their beds and forgot to lock the door. Someone came in during the night and stole a considerable amount of money from his wallet. This sort of thing is not uncommon, he said, and cautioned me to always lock my hotel room door. From the time I first arrived in Korea, I've noticed the multiple locks on doors and windows, as well as the prevalence of bars on windows. I've wondered if they were necessary. I guess they are. The man had a hangover in addition to having lost his money. Still, he was quite cheerful.

Mr. Lee's hair was cut very short, evidently part of his grooming for this special day. I thought he looked shorn. The saying "lambs to slaughter" sprung to mind. His first name, Gye-man, sounds a lot like "gay man," which is what I thought he was from the time I first met him. But according to Korean officials there are no gay people in this country. I'm sure Mr. Lee has never questioned this government line. At thirty-two, he is only three years beyond the customary age for a man's marrying.

He's such a delicately made man—graceful and small, I love to look at his long, narrow fingers. His bride is larger than he with heavy features.

He's a dedicated English teacher who works hard to increase his skills. His classes are often fun for him and me, as well as for the students. His are the only classes in which I play a secondary role. We actually do something resembling "team teaching." It's a welcome break for me—I just show up and do what he tells me to do. I know he doesn't want to relinquish control of his classes. Unlike most teachers, he's confident enough of his English to be willing to converse with me in front of the girls.

My conversation students tell me he is not well liked because he hits hard and often. Sometimes there are bruises. He has not hit a student in my presence. Maybe he hates or at least deeply resents women. He and I discussed a particularly violent American movie about a serial killer of young, beautiful women. Mr. Lee told me what a wonderful relief and release he felt after watching that sort of movie.

....

I rode home from the wedding with a group of female teachers, then walked over to the school to get a book. An English teacher, Shin So-ra, was there on duty. (Two teachers stay in school all day every day during vacation.) She's someone I enjoy talking with, and I'm sorry she's leaving our school in March. She's a lovely woman, about thirty-six. I refused her offer of a cup of coffee only because I can't drink caffeine, but I sat by the gas heater with her under the pretense of needing to warm up. She was clearly eager for company and I sensed a rare opportunity—a Korean wanted to *talk* to me. I might learn something; I might be a little less in the dark.

Shin So-ra and I sat together for more than an hour and a half. I talked about myself as little as possible, concentrating on asking questions and refraining from filling the pauses—I knew that if I allowed her enough time to collect her thoughts and turn them into English, she would eventually resume talking. The subject of the wedding led into telling me how she met her husband.

It was an ordinary arranged meeting at a coffee shop with the go-between (a professional who arranges matches), the two mothers, and the couple. The matchmaker left immediately after the introductions. The mothers sat at a separate table and discussed their families, especially the two grown children who were with them that day. The couple sat at their own table and discussed their families, their educations, and their life histories. Shin So-ra said she didn't like him very much at first, and thought he didn't especially like her. But the mothers were enthusiastic. His mother called her mother after the meeting and said, "The virgin is good! Let's marry them." Her son overheard this and followed up on the relationship. He drove seven hours from Wonju to Taebek in order to see her. His willingness to do this repeatedly impressed her. Two years later they were married, at nearly perfect ages. Shin So-ra was twenty-six when she met him. Any older and her shelf life would have begun to expire—she would have become an "old miss." She knew it was time to marry. He was twenty-eight when they met, so his clock was ticking too.

I asked her, "And did you fall in love?" She gave me a half-hearted yes, and said she loves him now. I think she felt she had to say that.

Shin So-ra's resentful now because he only showed her his good qualities during courtship and waited to reveal his negative traits later. She said she's happy but wants more freedom, and is "fighting" with her husband's shortcomings. (I wondered about the "happy.") She has a seven-year-old and a new baby, so her whole life is housework, kids, and school. Her husband, an M.D., takes Thursday evenings to go out with the boys, play billiards, and get drunk. He comes home at midnight or later. She asked him for her own night off. He laughingly agreed and asked her what she intended to do on that evening. She said she would sit on their apartment balcony—just to have some time for herself. Later she invited a friend to meet her on Tuesday evenings; the friend said she didn't have time. Shin So-ra told me she thought about going to a movie by herself, but she's afraid of the men at night. I said she could call me. She didn't respond to that; probably she wouldn't want to be associated with a loose-moraled American.

We talked about the importance of having women friends. Korean life, she said, is a very "narrow way." I talked a little about American life, some of the pitfalls of all that freedom, all those choices. I also said I was comfortable in my home country, and felt confined as a single woman in Korea.

At one point Shin So-ra said marriage is…is…(she searched for the word) "endurance." I remembered saying to a friend in the U.S. that marriage is a matter of how much shit you can put up with for how long. She agreed with me. She's still married. I left my husband soon after making that remark.

I've wondered if Koreans missed freedom. How can you miss something you've never had? I think Shin So-ra has some illusions about freedom as a panacea. Her complaint about her husband's withholding his bad side can happen anywhere. It can take years to get to know someone, and then they change. Often married couples don't really come to understand each other until they go through a divorce. She said she thought men and women should have a chance to get to know each other without always having marriage in mind, because it skews things. But things are always skewed between men and women. Sexuality alone manages to accomplish that. At the same time, I've always liked my freedom to date—to initiate and end relationships, to take emotional risks, and to not have to regard every relationship as a possible lifetime commitment. Freedom can come at a high price, but it's worth it.

....

I didn't mention this before. I had dinner at Mr. Young's house in late fall. After we ate, I wasn't sure if I were expected to leave immediately or if I should stay a while as Americans would do. It turned out that it was time for Mr. Young's favorite drama on TV, so that decided it. I sat on one end of the couch and drew pictures with the seven-year-old daughter. Mr. Young sat on the floor, leaning up against the other end of the couch. After Mr. Young's wife did the dishes, she sat on the floor and snuggled up against her husband. The next time I looked over that way, I saw he had pulled himself away from her and was sitting further forward with his arms gripped compactly around his knees. He had left nothing for his wife to hold on to. I felt he wanted to separate himself from her, and that it was because of my presence. I had two reactions—I was gratified, as if he were being loyal to me; at the same time, I experienced the pain and embarrassment of her rejection.

A scene from a few years ago materialized in my head. A lover and I were having dinner at the house of some friends. There were at least eight of us at the table. One woman was new in town—a very bright and attractive teacher who had just been hired at the university. My lover was obviously fascinated. At one point, while he was sitting forward, I put my hand on his back. He instantly sat back, making it necessary for me to remove my hand. It was the same dance, and it hurt.

That's the trouble with being this age and having so much life experience. It gives you compassion and can be very inhibiting. Do I finally stop acting altogether? When I appeared at school to go to Mr. Lee's wedding, Mr. Shin offered me a ride in his car. I accepted. But Mr. Young blew into the teachers' room at the minute we were all supposed to depart and said to me, "Let's go!" I said, "In your car?" He said yes. I quickly told Mr. Shin what I was doing, then turned and left. I felt sorry for Mr. Shin and a little dishonest. What would Jane Austen's heroine have done in my place? She would have informed Mr. Young that she had already agreed to go in Mr. Shin's carriage, while deeply regretting having to do so. But I'm attracted to Mr. Young, not to Mr. Shin. Sometimes it's refreshing to be selfish without always thinking about someone else's feelings.

....

Two of my favorite conversation students came to my apartment at about 1:30 on Friday. They're best friends. Gi-wan is the one who had the dream about cooking for me when I was sick. She's taller than I and not especially pretty. A complex network of wires covers her teeth. Yet her intelligence, sensitivity, and self-confidence give her an overriding grace. Yun-mi is small and exquisitely made. She freely admits to *kong ju byeong* or "princess syndrome," and revels in the fact that eyes are often drawn to her. Both are excellent students, but it comes easier for Gi-wan. She's the one who will grow, year by year, into being a wholly beautiful person.

They called earlier to ask if they could take me to lunch. I had already eaten and asked them (actually they invited themselves) to go downtown with me while I did some shopping. Before we left from my apartment, I went into the bathroom. When I came out, Gi-wan and Yun-mi were walking out of my office, discussing Tae Guk Kwon. They had been looking around in there and had spotted the business card of a man recommended to me as a teacher. Probably they perused everything else too. I had notes for my last journal entry under a letter to my accountant. I can't leave anything lying around.

I'm developing a strong love for the girls I teach, and even for those I don't. It's a distinct physical sensation, occupying and enlarging my heart. This despite the fact that teaching conversation classes during the winter break has been onerous. They're only two hours a day, but teaching without a text means preparing new lessons every day—it's time consuming and makes my brain tired. During class, it can be a real strain to get the girls to talk.

Yesterday was the twelfth day—the last class. Six of my students took me to lunch at a fancy Western restaurant downtown, and insisted I order the most expensive meal. Of course that meant the entree with the most meat, something I eat very little of. I suggested the pizza or spaghetti, but they wouldn't go for that. Once I got the idea that this was my present, and the finances had already been worked out, I ordered the "surf and turf" for 20,000 won (over twenty-three dollars). They got the pork cutlets at 6,000 won and pitched in 10,0000 won each. It wasn't a bad Western meal. Instead of a bowl of rice, there was a plate of rice on the side. And ice-cream sundaes for dessert. I'm sure Koreans feel the same way about American attempts to cook Korean food—it just isn't the real thing.

Before going to lunch, we had a good last class. I had compiled a list of fifty words that Koreans have adopted from English. I asked the girls to check my *Hangul* (Korean writing) and add any more they could think of. I now have over a hundred and fifty. It was fun. I'll make a good lesson out of this list. I want to impress on the students that many of the words aren't even English—we've borrowed them from French, Italian, German, Spanish, and so on (spaghetti, banana, koala, Los Angeles, Hyundai). All countries trade words with other countries. Maybe the girls will feel less invaded by the English language.

I've been conscientious about gathering and polishing my conversation lessons, although I still have a lot of work and organizing to do.

....

A dream-hallucination: I felt the bed shaking as it so often did when my cats scratched themselves at night. It was so real. I felt and heard Tigger walk to the edge of the bed and clump down onto the floor. I followed her, pulling some of the bedclothes off the bed as I got up. The room was not my current room. I looked around. It was so real, so physical. Yet it also had the familiar feel of a hallucination. I knew Tigger should not be there, and it was as if a ghost were present. I wanted to emerge from this quasi-reality but couldn't break out. Tigger yowled, her mouth wide open. I told her I knew, I understood.

Later the same night. I looked up and saw a hand drooping over my head. I was terrified, but pulled on it anyway. A whole arm appeared, then another arm attached to the first where the shoulder would normally be, like two link sausages. They plopped down onto the bed. I wrapped them around me in an embrace. It was scant comfort. There was no body. Nobody.

Sounds dreadful, doesn't it? I think these nightmares are partly a product of my not eating well lately. Too much fatty meat or too much sugar; maybe the Hershey's kisses I had the night before. Comfort food. My constitution is delicate.

When people ask if I get lonely, I say "Sometimes." Everyone gets lonely sometimes. Married people can be lonelier than single people. At this moment, I don't feel lonely. I'm impressed with how much I like my time alone, especially when I don't have to prepare lessons. I've wondered recently how I would manage if I ever did find someone I wanted to live with again. My dearest pursuits require quiet and solitude.

Entry 23
Wonju, Winter 1996-1997

This is day number 157—almost half a year since my last period. Maybe this is it. I'm reading Germaine Greer's *The Change*. It's a book of generalizations, as any such book must be. As I read, I do a mental check of my own experience and that of my friends and find us diverging from her conclusions. Every individual is different. Greer's voice in *The Change* is the same that I run up against in most feminist books—angry, complaining, self-righteous. It's all warranted, but tiresome just the same.

I am aging, but I'm not sure what age I am. Inner youth does remain while the outside moves on; the exterior surprises when met in the mirror. All my recent illnesses are taking their toll. My eldest sister once said (when we were well into our adult lives) that our mother still thought of herself as a young girl. She said it indignantly, as if Mum were trying to poach on her territory. I defended her, saying that believing she was still young was a good thing. What could be wrong with it?

One of the effects of my infatuation with Mr. Young is that for the first time in my life, I've been embarrassed by my age. The pure sexuality of the attraction turned the spotlight on my body. I'm in good shape, but I'm forty-eight, not thirty-eight or twenty-eight. Yet my hormones have responded no less intensely than they did twenty or thirty years ago. I've felt off balance and at a disadvantage. This episode has hit me like any natural disaster, flooding my life and demanding my attention, then receding, leaving a shallow residue that I know will wash away in time.

What a rare gift (it didn't used to be so rare) such intense passion is, and what a pity to have to pass it up. It requires a person to trigger it. I feel sorry for Mr. Young too—for the frustration I sense in him.

....

Spring vacation dates were in flux right up until this week, when it's supposed to begin. Teachers who are changing schools at the beginning of the new year (two weeks from now, on the first of March) still don't know what school they'll be assigned to. Some will have to move to a different town, either with or without their families. Mr. Young is the only exception, having known for a long time that he's trading schools with his wife. After the teachers get to their schools, they'll be told what grade they're teaching. No one objects to this; no one complains.

I've been wondering lately how well Koreans communicate with each other. Isabel didn't understand all the words in Hangul on the thermostat in my apartment. Mrs. Ho couldn't decipher all the labels on the controls of my washing machine. Does poor communication feed into all the planning and scheduling problems?

Graduation ceremonies were held outside today. The girls stood on the dirt playground in freezing wind for at least an hour, wearing only their polyester uniforms and turtleneck sweaters. It was the ordinary suffering in the ordinary silence. Out of a graduating class of five hundred, three hundred fifty had perfect attendance records for the entire three years of middle school. That means their bodies were in class, but not necessarily their minds.

The teachers went to lunch afterwards. I didn't want to wait around for the eventual loading into cars and the departure. I wasn't feeling well and have had a couple of recent lunches with teachers, so I ducked out and went home. Closed up in my apartment, I slept, studied Korean, and read. I like that I took care of myself for once instead of doing what the school planned for my "off" hours. Not that I would be missed. Their meals are so rushed, merely an opportunity for ingesting food.

My conversation students want to continue classes when school resumes. We'll meet at my apartment at 3:30 for one hour. They claim they learn better at my home. I think they just like the novelty, but of course they're bound to learn better than they would in that dreary, unending school. I prefer having class at home too, although it means more work for me. I have to make sure my place is presentable, and that refreshments are on hand. It's well worth it—I won't have to go back to school after class and watch the hands of the clock trudge their way to five before I can leave.

....

I'm making plans to go to Hong Kong for five days before school starts again—I want to see it before China takes over. I'm hoping Min-hi can go with me. She's been sick with a bad flu, and has tests scheduled this week to investigate a lump in her breast. She's scared and depressed. A trip would do her good.

I got a fax from an elementary school teacher who was one of my students at the Chunchon workshop. He wanted to know if I'd received a copy of a New Age tape he'd sent me. It was one I'd heard in his car when he gave me rides back to Wonju after several class days. I immediately faxed him back with my belated thanks and filled out the note with some chatter about my plans for Hong Kong. He called me the same day at school and told me he wanted to go with me. He said he was interested in the electronic equipment available there. I was taken by surprise, and didn't want to hurt his feelings by abruptly refusing, so I told him I would have to discuss it with Min-hi. I knew she would likely not be going, but my first thought was that I could use her complete unfamiliarity with him as an excuse for not including him. Moments later I realized I didn't need an excuse. I didn't want to travel with him; his request was presumptuous, and probably very disrespectful coming from a Korean. He seemed like a nice person, but traveling with a man as a friend can be problematical in America. I have no idea if it's even possible in this country. He had put me in an awkward position, and I resented it.

The next day I went to lunch with Mrs. Ho and told her all about it. She pursed her lips angrily at the man's impertinence and flatly told me to refuse. I knew that with this single telling, word would spread like wildfire. As a matter of fact, it was a little game I played with the teachers—tossing meat into a river just to watch the piranhas' feeding frenzy. I thought I'd give them something to talk about for a week or so.

After my lunch with Mrs. Ho, I went shopping in the neighborhood for small gifts to give the teachers who would be transferring to other schools. I returned within an hour and immediately went to the vice principal's desk to apply for permission to be out of town for the next week. He speaks almost no English, but he laughingly said, "A romance vacation!" I said, "What?" (I wasn't even sure I'd understood the words through his accent.) Then I thought he meant Hong Kong was a romantic place. I shrugged good-humoredly and said, "I don't know." Then it dawned on me that he had already gotten the word. They must have some paranormal communication system.

I tried to call the man back to tell him it wouldn't work for him to go to Hong Kong with me. I never did reach him. Maybe he was deported.

Entry 24
Wonju, Winter 1996-1997

Min-hi decided not to go to Hong Kong. I missed her company, but thoroughly enjoyed myself anyway. Such a fascinating and varied city. A jumble of buildings and lights completely supplant nature—create an alternate world of cement, steel, and pulsing neon. A short trip to the far side of Hong Kong Island delivered me to lush greenery fringed with calm beaches. I squeezed in as many of the tourist imperatives as I could, sampled the native food, and sought out—and found—real Western food as well. I bought silks for American friends and family, and found clothes for myself at Selfridge's, a British department store, and at Gap. The one formal tour I chose was a historical one that explored Kowloon, a part of the Chinese peninsula. I navigated the rest of the city on my own. The Kowloon hostel where I stayed provided everything I needed, including my own bathroom and as much peace as is available in that environment. I was surprised to discover that it's truly a Chinese city, not a British city. Most of its people are looking forward to officially becoming a part of China again.

The name of a kiosk at the bus terminal in Seoul: "Terminal Snack."

The trip energized me, gave me back some of my self, some of my internal balance. It gave me privacy and a welcome anonymity. I rediscovered my love of adventure and curiosity about the world. I resolved to plan more short trips for myself while in Korea. A changed person arrived back in Wonju, and I wanted to hold on to my newly uplifted, positive perspective.

....

I taught five classes today, my normal load. This year I'll teach the second graders by myself, and the first graders with the help (or at least the presence) of Korean English teachers. I prefer having a Korean teacher in the room for all the classes—the students can get explanations in Korean when they need them, and the teachers benefit from having to listen to and talk with a native speaker. But they say they're overloaded and need me to take on more of the burden.

I learned I really have had an effect on the students. I was asked to introduce myself to the third graders at the end of the school year, and almost all of them had a very difficult time understanding and speaking to me. The first and second graders that I had contact with over the last semester comprehend much more of what I say, and respond.

....

During one of the first classes I taught in Korea, second graders were asking what I thought of their country. Among other things, I mentioned the strong family ties that I thought existed here. I said Koreans take care of each other. One student interjected, "No, they don't!" Now I agree. They live within families, but often no real consideration is given to individual personalities and their needs. Children and their particular talents are sacrificed to the draconian educational system. Parents routinely live apart. Exhausted mothers and fathers send one or more of their children to live with grandparents for months at a time—often in towns that are hours away. The children at home spend their time in day care centers or at schools and academies. People push and shove (literally) and rush. There's no graciousness around me here. That's a deprivation I feel deeply.

Isabel told me the story of her family. When she was eight, her mother took her and her six-year-old brother, one in each hand, to what she called "a nice place." She admonished them not to call her "Mother" when they got there. The place turned out to be an American-run orphanage. She dropped off her children and left.

Isabel assumed her mother intended to return for them. While the Korean War ran its course, they had a chance to be adopted by an American family, but Isabel refused, confidently expecting her mother. At the end of the war, family members came to collect their children. Finally only she and her brother were left. So at the age of twelve, with her brother in tow, she set off to find their mother.

"It was a very scary experience." Until then, Isabel had only been as far as the church down the road from the orphanage. It took her a week to locate her mother in Cheongju, about forty miles away. A baby was strapped to her mother's back, and Isabel simply accepted that she had a sister, not understanding this meant her mother had been with a man.

Isabel says she knows now that her mother didn't want her and her brother, but she didn't realize it at the time. She and her brother went to work to earn money; their mother drank it. Isabel got no further than elementary school.

At thirty, she met her husband in a calligraphy class. She didn't fall in love, but he did. They lived together for three months, then he left on a ship. I'm not clear what kind of work he does—engineer, merchant marine, business? Isabel is vague about this. His work takes him all around the world, to places like Spain and Fiji. He returns every three years. He has always supported Isabel and Ho-chang, their son. They've lived in one of the three apartments he owns, and have been permitted to use the rent from the others when needed.

In 1992 the three of them went to Kangnung on the eastern coast for a vacation. They were in a restaurant surrounded by honeymooners. Ho-chang, who was twenty-two at the time, asked her what was the sweetest memory from her marriage. She thought for a while and said, "If I could, I would erase it all, except for having you." That brought the conversation—and the vacation—to an end. Ho-chang told her she should not stay married for him; he encouraged her to get a divorce. Her husband knew he had not been a good husband, and didn't fight it. She got her divorce, which freed her not only from her husband, but also from his demanding parents. She had always disliked them, and the marriage had indentured her to them as a housekeeper, cook, errand runner, and nurse for twenty-three years.

Isabel still sees her ex-husband when he's in the country. This year he paid off about six thousand dollars in debt that she had accumulated, mostly to pay for Ho-chang's education. She continues to live in his apartment, and still has the option of using the rent from the others.

It sounds to me as if she's had a couple of lovers, including one while she was married—an American who was a civilian employee at Camp Seward who encouraged her to get an education. She took his advice and traveled to Seoul by bus every day to get her high school equivalency. Now she has a bachelor's and is starting on her master's in English education. Another boyfriend was a married American whose wife was back in the states—he rented one of her husband's apartments. Shyly, slyly she told me she went to bed with him sometimes. I said good for her. It's a relief to know she has gotten some comfort.

Isabel says only Americans have helped her, never Koreans. She and her brother were well fed and well clothed during the war, unlike so many other Korean children who suffered horribly. She likes Americans, and clearly doesn't feel too good about Koreans. She says ruefully that she waited too long to get a divorce and apparently feels marriage is no longer a possibility for her. She's probably right.

Entry 25
Wonju, Winter 1996-1997

My post-Hong Kong buoyancy sank under the weight of only a few days of school. I felt it slip from my hands, watched helplessly as it vanished into the murkiness of my life in Korea. Today was a truly horrible day. There has been a shift in the atmosphere with the leaving of my allies—Mr. Young, Mrs. Ho, Mr. Shin, and Shin so-ra. Other than Mr. Lee, they're the only people who talked to me.

The faculty member who has taken Mr. Shin's place as head teacher is someone who has been overtly hostile to me since my arrival at the school. Today he came up to my desk and rubbed his thumb and fingers together while running on in Korean. He was complaining that I was paid too much for my teaching in Chunchon. Mrs. Jong, a Korean language teacher who is friendly toward me, but doesn't speak much English, told him to stop. She sounded disgusted. This same man has been bringing pretty girls up to my desk and grunting, "Beautiful girl? Beautiful girl?"

"Yes, she's very beautiful." I nod and smile at the blushing student. Generally Koreans think Westerners are the standard of beauty. He's on the defensive and trying to counter this by getting a Westerner to acknowledge that Koreans can set their own standards. I'm lucky he and I are equally inept at each other's language. I'm sure this has spared me many insults.

Koreans *are* beautiful. When I look for the airport gate where a Korean airline flight is boarding, I can recognize it by the extraordinary number of good-looking people standing in line.

I realize now that Mr. Young was running interference for me. Suddenly I'm taking the brunt. He recommended that Mr. Lee be my new guide teacher. Mr. Lee was glad to fill that role, and I was glad to have him do it. Instead, the principal assigned my nemesis, Mr. Won. Mr. Lee says he will be helping, which is good because his English is far better than Mr. Won's.

Mr. Won is tall and thin, a nice-looking man in his thirties who has many talents. I'm told he's a computer whiz, plays the guitar, and is an accomplished tennis player. He's married with a twelve-year-old son. His wife is a full-time homemaker, something unusual in his generation. A fundamentalist Christian and rigid traditionalist, Mr. Won strictly obeys any directives that come from the administration. He seems eager to advance. Several times he's told me that he majored in German in college, but the school needs English teachers, so he's teaching a subject that he did not prepare for. With me, he's very shy and soft-spoken; he avoids talking to me at all because he lacks confidence in his English. Although I've taught classes with him in the room for a whole semester, he has never once said anything positive to me or shown any appreciation for my work.

This semester, against my will and better judgment, I'm teaching the second graders by myself. They're divided into A, B, and C classes by ability. The A classes are a breeze to teach, the B classes vary but are mostly difficult and unpleasant; the C class (thankfully there's only one) is a complete loss. Many of the girls in the C class would be in special education in the U.S.

I had a B class today that got entirely out of control—there was a constant murmuring in the room that frequently erupted into full-blown conversations and the trading of notes, combs, and materials for other classes. What do I do? Fifty girls, many of them dwarfing the chairs designed for the preceding generation of less well-nourished children. They know I won't hit them. I raised my voice to quiet them, actually heard myself scream. That only worked momentarily. I made some girls stand at the back of the room. Whenever I turned away from them, they continued their shenanigans with their friends, long distance. I was ready to burst into tears by the end. I'll have to start ejecting some of them. Maybe *I'll* leave.

I ran into Mr. Won in the hall. As he has many times, he told me some students say they can't understand me. I was ready this time.

"What do you want me to do?" I asked. He looked confused and repeated his statement. I repeated mine.

"I think you must explain the meaning of the sentences in the textbook in easy English."

"Any English is too difficult for some students."

At least he conceded this. He said he thought things would improve and it was good for the girls to have a chance to listen to me.

In the past I accepted Mr. Won's criticisms; acted as if I humbly welcomed them and considered them valid. No more. Of course students don't always understand me. Of course some complain—they're children. One day he took a poll in class to discover how many students could follow my English. I know he expected the opposite response. Only two or three students in the back of the room held up their hands to say they couldn't grasp what I was saying. I noticed the others looking around, catching each other's eyes with a look of solidarity on their faces. I had the impression this had been a topic of discussion in the class when I was not there, and most students had determined to take a stand against Mr. Won and in my favor. I have tried hard to get along with him. I've massaged his ego by seeking his help with computer problems (I can tell he likes that). I think it's time for him to contribute something.

I had lunch today with the *haksaeng kwa* (the student department) which is my designated niche in the school organization. I reluctantly sat beside Mrs. Yu, a pretty, bustling woman in her thirties, and one of the English teachers I work with. She's respected and liked by her students, and I admire her as a teacher, but she has never initiated any conversation with me beyond what is necessary for class. I mustered my positivity and told her what a great class I thought her homeroom was. She turned her eyes to me and I felt—as well as saw in them—an oozing malevolence. A cloud of freezing air poured out of her.

Where did all that hostility come from? Surely it couldn't have been bred solely by the eight hours she said she spent translating my "Impressions of Korea." I know that between school and parenting she's overworked and that she has chronic pain from a lower-back problem. She must have deeply resented the extra assignment. But that one offense couldn't be enough to generate anger on this level. I remembered an incident at one of the farewell dinners for the teachers who were leaving at the end of the school year. Mr. Young was moving from table to table, saying his good-byes. He squatted down beside me. I noticed the disapproval in Mrs. Yu's face as she leaned away from him. The soju had made him voluble and smiley and a little loose-tongued. He swatted me on the shoulder (a Korean gesture of endearment) and started talking about how I would miss him, which I cheerfully agreed to. I think she especially objected to the swat. Is that it—whatever she thinks went on or is going on between him and me?

My allies are gone. Mr. Lee is my only hope. To almost all the others I'm a burden and a threat.

There's another English teacher, Mrs. Song, who is a sweet person, but I only make her uncomfortable because she's so unsure of her English. Mrs. Jong, who told the head teacher to stop harassing me about how much money I made, speaks very little English. She's the one who introduced me to Yu Pil-lung, and since the friendship between Pil-lung and me has cooled, perhaps Mrs. Jong's attitude will change too.

The school is in chaos. This is nearly the end of the second week and my teaching schedule wasn't finalized until Wednesday. There is still no plan for English conversation classes. The teachers are overwhelmed with the busywork of record keeping. There are too many students and too many long hours. People are exhausted already.

Adding to all this cacophony are the way-too-loud jangling bells that jolt us into moving from one place to another. Eight periods with ten-minute breaks between. Like cattle prods, these buzzers shove me along sixteen times a day.

....

I had lunch at Jess's last Saturday. The ladies were there, also Isabel's son, Ho-chang and his girlfriend, Bo-mi. Jess baked potatoes in his microwave and grilled steaks and burgers. We spooned cheese sauce and sour cream onto the split-open potatoes. Jess prepared frozen mixed vegetables and cucumbers with onions in a vinegar sauce. This was the most Western meal

I've had here. Jess buys his groceries at the U.S. Army base near Seoul, so he can get all sorts of things I haven't seen since I arrived. Ho-chang inhaled a huge steak and a hamburger. Many Koreans think that eating a thick steak is the essence of American success. It's the influence of our soldiers and the 1950s American diet. Come to think of it, the menus at the army base's restaurant and snack bar haven't evolved much.

Next weekend I'll make a spaghetti dinner for Jess, Isabel, Mr. Lee, and his wife. I gave Jess a shopping list for the ingredients.

During the lunch I listened to another sad story about a daughter in middle school who is in a constant state of exhaustion. The woman said many Korean parents send their children abroad to school in order to escape this system, but it's too expensive for her—about three thousand dollars a month.

I discovered something very interesting about Ho-chang. He never went to the after-school hogwons when he was in middle or high school. He discussed it with a teacher who agreed he could study on his own at home. Of his classmates, he's the only one who did this. Ho-chang said he didn't do all that much studying at home—he watched TV, fooled around, and looked at his books when he felt like it. Yet he has always excelled in school. Others may not have fared as well as Ho-chang did without the hogwons—he relishes learning and is self-motivated. But it shows that logging more hours after school in the academies doesn't necessarily improve a student's performance. Koreans aren't familiar with the law of diminishing returns.

....

Min-hi's lump was malignant. Tests show no other cancer in her body. She told me this is her second experience with breast cancer; the first lump was removed in 1992. Now she's deciding whether to undergo another year of being poisoned with chemotherapy. The first time it completely incapacitated her, and the insult added to injury was that she lost all her hair, eyebrows included. Her niece's advice is to forego the chemo this time and live her life—it didn't prevent the cancer from returning. I urged her to take advantage of oriental medicine alternatives available here. But that sort of thing seems beyond her. She has turned herself over to the conventional medical system and relinquished any initiative of her own. Already she's looking at wigs.

During one of our phone conversations, Min-hi said something about my not liking Korea. I didn't deny it, but I shifted the subject slightly by saying the two things Westerners I knew (including myself) objected to most about Korea were the pushing and shoving and the lack of planning. She said she would make a list of everything that bothered her about Americans.

I haven't talked about the pushing and shoving. It happens in the street, in the stores, and in the hallways at school. Koreans are adept with their elbows—especially the hunched and shriveled old ladies. Maybe it's most noticeable when it's *their* sharp elbows that have so much unexpected power behind them as they forge past me to get off the bus. I have to be aggressive just to hold my place in this country. If I put my backpack down on the ground while paying for oranges, someone will step on it. While walking to my desk in the teachers' room, Mrs. Yu shoved me in the back to make me walk faster. (An outlet for her anger?) Getting knocked around like this was a shock at first. Then I learned to use my elbows too.

Driving is the same way. Anything less than aggressive driving in Korea is dangerous. Everyone expects you to push your car in front, to try to be the first to cross an intersection. Traffic lights are considered optional. Pedestrians have no right-of-way. The girls pile up at the corner, waiting to cross the narrow street in front of the school gate while a teacher waves on the cars and trucks until an opening appears. Cars must not be stopped. It's part of the "might makes right" culture.

Koreans are justly famous for always being in a hurry. When we native speakers were picked up at the hotel in Chunchon to be taken to our assigned towns for the first time, it was like a contest or a race. Our guide teachers (in my case Mr. Young) grabbed our suitcases, sprinted to their cars, threw the baggage into the trunk, and took off. There were no exceptions to this startling behavior. Were they afraid of being late for lunch with the school officials? Mr. Young and I arrived at the restaurant in Wonju in plenty of time. It was my initial introduction to the perpetual Korean rush.

....

An English teacher from another school told me she gets to work at 7:10 A.M. Her first class is at 7:40. She teaches twenty-nine hours a week, the same as I do, which is an unusually heavy load. Her older daughter, a senior in high school, goes to a hogwon every evening and has to be picked up at 11:20 at night. She and her daughter and husband (a lieutenant colonel in the Korean Army) don't get to bed until midnight or later. Then up early to start the grind again. She looked into immigrating to New Zealand, but could not find work there.

I'm starting to think in terms of spending the next year in Singapore or Spain. I have a friend teaching English in Singapore. She called recently. She's refreshingly matter-of-fact in evaluating countries and teaching positions. I've been so entangled in day-to-day coping, trying to make my stay here successful. And in making and saving money. I forget there are other possibilities out there, perhaps less onerous ones. Singapore is alluring because it's a rich, clean, cosmopolitan city. I'm tired of poverty and dinginess.

Entry 26
Portland, Spring 1999

I first noticed the blurred vision when I got out of my car in Eugene. I had stopped for lunch on my way to Arcata. The winter quarter was over at school, and I was taking several days to catch up with friends at my former home. I thought maybe my eyes were slow to adjust from the long-distance focus of driving to the middle-distance focus of walking. But when I walked back to my car after lunch, there was no improvement.

This faltering of my eyesight scared me but I was quick to rationalize. My vision had always deteriorated when I was tired or under stress. I was worn out after completing two grad school courses, one of which meant six books to read and six papers in ten weeks. And I was tense with the anticipation of seeing friends, something I had not yet acquired in Portland, other than my family. Humboldt County was my home for eleven years before I left for Korea. This trip could only do me good.

By the time I reached Crescent City, eighty miles north of Arcata, I was feeling extraordinarily thirsty. I bought a quart bottle of water and drank it almost nonstop.

As soon as I got to the home of friends, we started trading news. I learned that Philip had recently contracted type-2 diabetes. He was working in a town several states away from Arcata when he called home and told Diane that he had been feeling deeply fatigued. When he got back to Arcata, he was diagnosed. His M.D. started him on a treatment plan that included medication targeting his liver, as well as diet and exercise. He's not the typical type-2 diabetic—he's slim and has always eaten much more healthily than the average American.

Philip has a contraption for measuring blood sugar. One morning before breakfast he pricked my finger and held it so a drop of blood fell on the narrow test strip clipped to the machine. He wanted to show me how it worked. In seconds, the digital number "304" appeared on the screen. That's three times higher than it should be, he informed me.

The conventional way to deal with such an extreme situation, Philip said, would be to put me into the hospital until a normal blood sugar level could be achieved—with drugs. I would never even consider this approach. How could I achieve a normal blood sugar level in such an abnormal situation? I would be inert in bed when I'm usually running, swimming, or doing T'ai Chi; and I'd be eating hospital food that's a fraction as healthful as my normal diet. I tried calling the man who had been my physician in Arcata—a doctor of oriental medicine—but he was out of town. I'd have to consult with him by phone and E-mail (as I had in Korea) after getting back to Portland.

This has to have been triggered by stress. The frustration and disillusionment that made me give up my former life in Arcata, two years of isolation in an alien country, then the pressure of deciding where and how to materialize a new life back in the U.S. Add to this the upheaval of menopause. My body is predisposed to manifest illness through diabetes—type 1 runs in my family.

I see now that the symptoms of diabetes have been coming on over the last month. It started with trembling hands (this isn't uncommon with me, but it's more marked than usual) and trembling legs while holding the low stances of T'ai Chi. For the last two and a half weeks, I've felt as if all the ch'i leaked out of me. My running has lost its spring, and by now I no longer have the energy to run at all. Over the last week I've had excessive thirst and urination to match, excessive hunger, and blurred middle and distance vision. My close-up vision has improved—a diabetic perc that results from swelling in the eyes.

I'm reading books on nutritional healing, looking for dietary recommendations. My diet over the last twenty years has already been the sort prescribed by the books—partly the result of an intensive period of natural healing that I embarked on twenty years ago.

In 1978 a PAP test showed that I had a precancerous condition—carcinoma in situ—and the doctors were adamant that I should have surgery. An overwhelming intuition told me that was not the way to go. I read both the conventional and alternative literature on my problem. If nothing else, it was evident that I had time. I used the shotgun method of alternative treatments—everything that made sense to me. This included changing to a vegetarian diet, using vitamins, herbs, colors, sitting meditation, and T'ai Chi. That's how I got started with T'ai Chi. Lots of teachers have had a life-saving, life-changing experience with it. Then they become teachers, they become fanatics like me. In two years the carcinoma in situ had disappeared. Natural healing is true healing, not just the masking of symptoms, and it takes time, persistence, and patience.

A fringe benefit of my T'ai Chi practice was that I started wearing my shoes out evenly. My left leg is slightly shorter than my right, and this resulted in an uneven footfall when I walked or ran, especially if I was tired. At the end of two years, my body had somehow balanced itself out. I know T'ai Chi didn't grow my leg any longer, but it did remake my posture so that a balance was achieved in spite of my lack of symmetry. I save money on shoes.

My diet has been less pristine since that time, but mostly I permanently incorporated all the diet and lifestyle changes made while I was in healing mode. My time in Korea has to be counted as an exception. It seems I'm in for a new round of healing. I didn't expect this; I thought I'd done my bit.

I'll be making some changes, mostly cutting out refined sugar and other sweeteners, although as an adult I've not been a candy eater or one who craves sweets. I get plenty of exercise, but I've been spending too-long periods of time stationary while reading and writing. Stress levels are diminishing with the spring break and only one course next quarter. However, I'll start teaching T'ai Chi several hours a week— for the community college and volunteering at my nephew's middle school.

I guess this is a breakdown. At least I can function, albeit through a thick soup of lethargy, clouded sight, and waves of depression. For now, the only thing I know to do is keep on with the things I'm doing and hope I can hold out until I get into a more nurturing life situation.

....

I bit on a job offer I learned about through a professor at school. Maybe I was the only person to show any interest; the publisher got back to me very quickly saying I had the job. I'll be writing a history of the Portland Police Bureau for their so-called yearbook. The last one was published seventeen years ago. My employer is a publishing company in Paducah, Kentucky that specializes in military and police histories. They have a contract with the Portland Police Bureau to put together the new book. I'll be paid ten dollars a page, and I have no idea whether this is adequate or inadequate. I have no way of knowing how much time it will take.

Even though the last yearbook was published in 1983, the written history stopped at 1951. The writers (a retired police officer and his wife) decided it would be best not to cover any more because too many of the people involved are still living. That indicates something about the level of corruption and frequency of scandals in the department. I'll edit and rewrite the existing history, then research and write the history of the last fifty years, focusing on new programs. This will not be muckraking. It will be friendly account from the department's point of view. This is not an area of life I'd normally be involved with, but it's writing. And I can be intellectually interested in virtually anything.

I've received five replies to my seven query letters about my article on studying T'ai Chi in Korea. All are enthusiastic. I'll send it first to the magazine that would get me the most exposure in the T'ai Chi world, although I know the publisher didn't like my last book. He thought it was too personal. I've written to my teacher in Korea to get model releases for the photos that I'll be including with the article.

I was perusing the magazines at Powell's Books the other day when I noticed my name on the masthead of *Qi Journal*. I thought, "What a coincidence! Someone else has my name." Then I realized they had published my review of Stephanie Hoppe's book *Sharp Spear, Crystal Mirror: Martial Arts in Women's Lives*. No notification, no payment. But it's free advertising for Stephanie, and an addition to my resume.

I got an A in my literature course. By the middle of the quarter, the professor's attitude toward me had changed. She was not only acting as if she liked me, but as if she wanted me to like her. She initiated conversations with me and another grad student I often lingered with after class. These were not conversations, really—just disjointed monologues designed to impress us with her scholarliness. Probably she was asserting her alpha position. My estimation of her hasn't changed. Three times a week I sat there in her class and wound up until I was ready to burst with my impressions and opinions. But she wasn't interested, and there were too many people in the class for all of us to express ourselves anyway. It was a combined grad and undergrad course—there were at least twenty-five students.

The best thing to come of the course was my introduction to Olive Schreiner. I was stunned by *The Story of an African Farm.* Why haven't I read her before? Why hasn't everybody? Her writing is groundbreaking, way ahead of its time. She writes in pure allegory and shockingly stark reality, and then mixes them. Her writing is spare, yet anything but sedate. It's the unhindered overflow of a boiling subconscious. Sentence fragments, repeated words and phrases, italics, exuberant exclamation points—Schreiner uses words, grammar, and punctuation like an expressionistic painter uses colors. She writes uninhibitedly about sex and pregnancy outside of marriage, desire without love, the blurring of gender identity, sadism, and the relative merits of fleeting passion versus long-term love. These things are not just discussed, they're experienced by her characters. The usual return to conventional mores by the end of the book doesn't happen.

All this in a novel written by a woman barely out of her teens in 1880 South Africa. It's a wonder it was published at all.

What most people would consider handicaps was the source of Schreiner's breakthroughs. She grew up unrestrained and isolated in the South African bush, without a formal education. She was hypersensitive, brilliant, and intense, and her separateness threw her back on herself. Her life was books, nature, and vast stretches of uninterrupted time. Luckily she escaped literary "sophistication" and simply looked inward to make her art.

She's remembered mainly as a feminist and crusader for workers' rights. Why is her artistic leap passed over? Are people unable to swallow this gigantic, inventive contribution because it comes from a woman? Is a world that worships males too threatened, too frightened by female creativity?

Her biographers say she grew old and rigid quickly. Her many battles took their toll. As she says in *The Story of an African Farm:* "All things on earth have their price; and for truth we pay the dearest. We barter it for love and sympathy. The road to honour is paved with thorns; but on the path to truth, at every step you set your foot down on your heart."

....

I've been manic in the last few weeks, and very tired at the same time. But right now it's a quiet Sunday morning and my dining room table looks quite nice with the holly bush outside the open window, daffodils in one of my vases, the curling pathos hanging above, and an assortment of high and low candle holders.

Before going to bed, I've been doing acupressure on myself aimed at treating menopausal symptoms and strengthening the heart. It helps me sleep, and comforting dreams have blossomed. In one, many thriving plants were hanging from the ceiling of my bedroom.

My cats continue to visit me in my dreams. Do I visit them in theirs? Do they remember? The flower garden, the wooden walk I sat on, so hot in the summer sun that they had to lie down in my shade.

"Dreams?" I liked having him ask me that when we woke in the morning. Dreams? he would say, and I'd think and we'd both tell. Quiet, intimate conversation. A chance to let stuff out into the air, float up so we could take a look at it. If I were loved by someone, I don't think I would feel so old, would feel better looking. Oh well. I hardly have the energy for that stuff. Men don't move me the way they used to.

I splurged and got a massage at the Y when I returned from Arcata. I have to find a way to be able to afford a weekly massage. I can't live without touch.

If life begins at forty, I'm only ten years old.

Entry 27
Portland, Spring 1999

And there's always diabetes as metaphor—a hunger strike on the cellular level. If you're going to continue to feed us this poison, we're going to stop eating. Frustrating as my life was before Korea, at least the clay, the T'ai Chi, the writing fed my soul, even if they didn't provide physical security. Giving up all these things as well as my cats, my friends, my kind and appreciative students; placing myself in an alien and often hostile environment for two years was a recipe for starvation. I brought myself to this state. My body and my soul want to die.

My Arcata physician suspects I picked up some organisms in Korea and that getting rid of them will help me do better. He recommends homeopathic remedies that help drain the pancreas as a good first step for diabetes.

He also recommended someone I could see in Portland. I've had several appointments with Marilyn, a woman who does acupuncture and has a naturopathic approach, although she's not a doctor of naturopathic medicine. She practices with her husband who *is* an N.D., and I'm assured by their receptionist that they consult with each other on all their patients. Marilyn thinks my problem isn't serious; I just need to "tonify." She says my kidneys are weak, and I'm suffering from a kidney-yin deficiency and what amounts to premature aging. Is she looking to my hair color for that last diagnosis?

Is the aging premature? Maybe my biological clock is set to stop at about fifty. My father's did. At the very least, my alarm has gone off.

Marilyn is a beautiful woman somewhere in her forties, tall and with the clear face, the bright eyes of well-rested health. She dresses in striking colors; her clothes are expensive and fit perfectly. She's intelligent, but she does not project warmth. Yet at this point I'm eager to clutch at any flotation device. I drag myself into her office and drag myself out. My eyes, my whole face feel heavy and sagging. If Marilyn is the picture of health, I'm the picture of unhealth.

I'm shaky and my heart pounds. My fatigue is concentrated in my legs—the muscles twitch all day long, and I wake up with cramps. When I put my hand on the contracted muscle, it feels like wood instead of human flesh. I have a sore throat most mornings. Sometimes I'm thirsty and have dry mouth. My vision remains blurred and my eyes ache with the strain of focusing on faces, blackboards, and street signs. When I close my eyes, or turn off the lights in a room, or sometimes after long periods of reading, writing, or work at the computer, narrow white blurbs skirt the edges of my eyes, rising from bottom to top. I think of lava lamps.

....

I was lying in bed, trying to come up with a good fantasy. I imagined getting a massage every day in my home. Then I turned it into a nightmare: A man posing as a massage therapist (I would never choose a male therapist) broke into my home. I'm good at this—inventing frightening scenarios and playing them out in my head is nothing new for me. But I believe I've never been this destitute of hopeful dreams.

My depression is so deep. I'm afraid of it, afraid of the future. I cling to life, ferret out hope, scratch for wispy roots that I can wrap my fingers around and anchor myself to, however tenuously or temporarily. Charlotte Bronte understands how people can live on—a sort of half-life, half-death. I think most people's lives are this way. Bronte writes my life in *Shirley* and *Villette*. Especially *Villette*—the life of a single woman teacher in a country not her own. I probably shouldn't be reading her now.

My female and male, yin and yang sides are wrestling with each other. I need the male side to get me through this hard time, to provide materially and practically: do jobs for money, slog through a master's degree. But my female side—the artist, writer, daydreamer—is protesting and getting beaten up.

Marilyn gave me something for depression—a form of gold—after I told her I consider suicide. It hasn't kicked in yet.

She put me on a ridiculous number of homeopathic and herbal drugs, most of which cannot be taken with food and also must be separated from each other. When do I get to eat, I asked her. Doesn't she know I'm starving? My appetite is limitless; I eat voluminous amounts of food at each meal and snack whenever I can. Quarts of water vie for space with all the burritos, salads, rice, polenta, apples, and cantaloupe. By evening my stomach is stretched taut and walking is uncomfortable. I sometimes wish I could lie flat on my back, slit open my torso and limbs, and have cool water poured continuously over me. Until I'm finally full, fully satisfied. Despite all the food, I lost nine pounds over the last three weeks; I'm down to a hundred and six.

Marilyn doesn't like my many questions about the supplements. (The alternative health practitioners are becoming just like the conventional ones.) Nor does she pay much attention to my explanations of how I got sick. The influence of my life circumstances—past, current, and future—is quickly tossed off.

She says to meditate and spend a lot of time with blue: blue water filling my entire abdominal cavity, focusing on the kidneys and adrenals. I'm supposed to smile at them. What Marilyn doesn't understand is that I need someone else to smile at them. I need help.

Entry 28
Portland, Spring 1999

My first T'ai Chi class for the community college attracted thirty-five people. There's plenty of interest out there, and a need for teachers. I was elated after that class; I felt I had come home and was in my element again. T'ai Chi holds real meaning for me; it enlivens me. The classes are a captive audience while I talk about subjects that fascinate me. And I always learn from students. After twenty years of practice and ten years of teaching, I feel sure that I have something to offer—if I can just hold up.

I do my best to pretend that I'm well, to project an energetic state despite my fatigue and weakness. I wonder if the students can detect illness in my face. I feel hypocritical at times, teaching what is, among other things, a healing art while I'm so sick. Usually T'ai Chi teachers look younger than their age. I'm afraid I look older than my age now. I rev myself up for each class, and put positive thoughts into my head. Afterwards I drive home, blanching at the coronas around the headlights and streetlights, concentrating intensely on the road, the yellow lines, the white lines.

I'll add teaching hours this summer—at the community college, at the Nike campus, and possibly at a community center close to my apartment. Because I'm paid well per hour, I may be able to put together a minimal living. I never could have achieved this with my T'ai Chi teaching in Humboldt County.

I'm feeling better. Eating protein seems to help—tofu, nuts, seeds, beans, fish (mostly salmon), chicken, and turkey. No refined sugar. No other sweeteners either. I've discovered I can make a great apple pie with no sweetener—just three gala and three pippin apples. I could add some Granny Smith to get the tartness that I like.

My energy level inches upward, sometimes two steps forward and one step back. T'ai Chi feels more solid; running still isn't an option. My stomach accepts food better; it used to flutter nervously and raise my heart rate as if it didn't know what to do with the stuff I sent down there. Thirst is intermittent, as is dry mouth and dry eyes. My eyes don't have to work so hard and don't hurt while trying to focus. Middle and distance eyesight seem almost back to normal except for slippages when I'm under extra stress. Spring greens, plum blossoms, magnolias, azaleas, sweet fragrances, and the occasional blue sky all help.

I've been using tape to check the glucose in my urine. It's sky high—registering in the 1000 range. Normal is 70 to 180. I need a more precise, reliable way to test, or forget it altogether.

The results of tests Marilyn ordered came back. Only at my insistence did these include a fasting blood sugar and another one two hours after eating breakfast. The first was 335, the second 447. Marilyn finally—after five weeks—woke up to my situation. "Okay," she admitted. "You're diabetic." She altered my tea and some of my supplements.

The tea I brew comes from Chinese herbs and roots that are supposed to treat diabetic symptoms and build the yin (kidney/water/life) force. The homeopathic remedies I'm taking are for the liver, pancreas, blood, and possible organisms picked up in Korea.

Marilyn, I can tell, is in completely unfamiliar territory. My reading has already put me ahead of her with regard to symptoms and possible treatments for diabetes. I wanted to feel enthusiastic about her, largely because a person I trust recommended her. I'm steadily losing confidence.

I've spent about a thousand dollars on office visits and supplements in the last five weeks. The slightest mention of a symptom brings on a new pill. She prescribed a bottle of adrenal supplements that gave me the jitters. I've never done speed, but maybe this is the way it feels: having to wrap my arms around myself, hold myself together physically and restrain myself during conversations. Adrenal stimulation is the last thing I want now—they need a rest. I used two pills out of fifty. What do I do with the remainder, the other thirty-eight dollars' worth?

Stress is the source of my problem. Money is the source of much of my stress. I've noticed health practitioners often don't get this: For uninsured people like me, or for insured people whose coverage doesn't include holistic care, physicians become part of the problem. They wonder why people don't come to them more regularly. Marilyn instructed the receptionist to take ten dollars off my bill after I told her about the effect of the adrenal supplements. I actually thanked her.

....

    I'm making progress on the Portland Police Bureau history—finished editing and rewriting the text on the first hundred years, and I'll start researching the last fifty years this week.
    The technical editing course is going well. I'm gaining skills through my internship with a local environmental engineering firm. It's another opportunity to get together with people—I'm so starved for simple human contact.
    Last night I had dinner with one of the students interning with me. A welcome friendship is developing.
    I was asked to talk about T'ai Chi at an employee health fair in a hospital. It felt like a very long four-hour effort, even though relatively few people came up to my table to ask questions. Besides fighting fatigue, I was almost constantly hungry and thirsty—a blatant stress response, I've noticed, at this point in my life. Several massage therapists were there, and I managed to slip in a ten-minute back and neck massage toward the end of the fair. It precipitated a decision: Somehow I will get a massage every week. It's part of my path to recovery. When I lived in Humboldt County and made my living as a potter, I traded pots for massages, almost on a weekly basis. Now I don't have anything to trade with, except possibly T'ai Chi lessons. I have to find some way to afford massage.
    I'm beginning to feel engaged with life, more hopeful, not so lonely. There are only fleeting moments of depression. I don't want to die. Can I communicate this to my kamikaze cells—rescind my past directive—and convince them to end their hunger strike before it's too late?

....

My dreams keep retelling the story of my yang side bullying and coercing my yin side. The male side is stuffing me into shapes that don't accommodate who I am. My dreams were strangely silent toward the end of my time in Korea and when I first returned home. Are these the dreams I didn't have then? Are they the responses I buried so deeply that I couldn't hear or see them? Are they being released now like bubbles letting go of their undersea surfaces, floating to the air where they can open? Are they telling me about what I was doing during that dreamless time in the past or do they apply now? Is what I'm doing now—preparing myself for editing and commercial writing, going to school—too small, too cramped for me? Should I drop it all and just do my T'ai Chi teaching and writing?

By the time I left for Korea, I had given up believing in dreams and intuitions. They had not led me into a life with any semblance of comfort or security. But now I can see that not believing in them leads to disaster. Following hopes and dreams and fantasies at least keeps me aligned with my nature. So I'm back. They're all I have.

Entry 29
Wonju, Spring 1997

It's a precious time: the moment of change when trees have a lacy translucent look and the greens are clean and delicate. Some streets are bound on either side by cherry trees laden with pink blossoms. They're breathtaking, but Koreans are ambivalent about this beauty that appears each spring—the trees were planted by the Japanese during their occupation of Korea between 1910 and 1945. We had our first thunderstorm last week. I missed these outbursts during the last eleven years in California. Korea needs more cleansing downpours.

I'm glad that with the beginning of this new school year, Mrs. Song has the desk next to mine in the teachers' room. She's one of the shy English teachers who have been afraid to talk to me. But apparently she decided to be brave—she requested to sit there. Mrs. Song told me that in her dreams she speaks English fluently. I told her that I speak Spanish fluently in mine. We laughed.

Before I arrived at her school she avoided speaking English because she was afraid of making mistakes. She isn't afraid anymore, and claims I'm responsible for the change. I so appreciate her kind words. I sympathize with her frustration with the English language—the more I study Korean, the harder it seems. The differences in sentence structure are almost impenetrable.

Mrs. Song is in her early thirties and looks girlish. She's slight and pretty; her round face is open and framed by shiny hair that's cut blunt and flattering. Her pale skin is textured by past and present battles with acne. That's why, she explained, she doesn't wear makeup. The naturalness of her face is one of the things I like about her—it's so unusual here. She's kind to the girls and they love her for it. They also are quick to take advantage of such a person. Mrs. Song says they push things further with her than they do with other teachers, and laugh at her when she scolds them. She promised herself while in college that she would never hit a student. But she carries her stick to class and has had to break her promise. There is not time for talking to parents and "hitting is fast."

Most Korean women, with the exception of elderly ones, are viewed by the world—and view the world—through a mask. Thick powder, plucked and drawn-in eyebrows, aggressive lip colors that startle me. I'm compelled to watch their full-lipped mouths as they speak, and sometimes can't attend to what they're saying. I relax and look into Mrs. Song's eyes when we talk.

Since coming to Korea, I've taken to wearing an unobtrusive, mauve-colored lipstick and filling in my eyebrows with an eyebrow pencil. It's been many years since I've done even this much. The clothes I've bought here are more feminine looking than my usual. I'm deliberately allowing myself to be swayed by the prevailing culture. I like living in a new place where I can make changes—experiment—without anyone around to remark that I've changed or make me feel self-conscious about it.

....

Mr. Young invited me to speak to his third-grade middle school English classes. I went there yesterday (Saturday) morning. The boys were cute and shy and very curious about me. Their inability to speak and listen to English is really surprising. They need a native speaker in their school. My first and second graders do much better.

I was interested to hear Mr. Young say that boys are easier to teach than girls. He says they're a lot less noisy and troublesome. Perhaps it has something to do with the other piece of information he gave me—that the teachers at his school do a lot of hitting. The boys are probably exhausted from the long hours, and afraid. One of the students asked me whether students are hit in America. I said teachers in most states are not allowed to hit students. The entire room gasped.

Mr. Young drove me home. He said he would return at 1:30 and take me to a traditional Korean restaurant for lunch. I wasn't surprised to see his wife and kids there when I walked out of my apartment building to meet him. I thought the lunch went well. She seemed placid and good-humored. I asked him to ask his wife how she likes having switched schools with him. He just laughed and said *he* thought it was a good change—he prefers his new location. She has not seemed happy at my school.

....

I got a letter from a friend going through a divorce. She believes her husband was stolen away from her by a conniving woman. She's incensed and her anger is aimed at the usurper. My friend has been married for at least fifteen years and has two boys, aged ten and thirteen. She seems to think her husband is relatively innocent—he only succumbed to an attractive woman's charms. Her story (she sent me a short story based on her experience) struck a nerve. I am now feeling, and have in the past felt powerful attractions for married men. I have never acted on them, except in two cases in which the men were already separated from their wives and did eventually divorce.

I confess I have questioned if that powerful emotion of falling in love doesn't transcend, or somehow exist with impunity outside of the imperatives of marriage and children. I know it's fed by hormones, but isn't sexual passion one of the joys of life? If you marry, do you have to forgo that overwhelming, transforming (okay, maybe temporarily) experience for the rest of your life? Do you have to deny it? I have done that at times. But I wonder. It's natural for humans to seek excitement. When it inundates you, do you have to let it wash past without drinking in any of it? Because I've been single most of my life, I've been able to ride that thrilling wave from time to time. I often wonder what long-term, faithful married life is like. It's a sacrifice.

....

Isabel asked if she could go to the U.S. with me when I have my summer vacation. I was taken by surprise; I didn't know we were that close. I recoil at the idea of taking part of Korea with me on my escape. I'll have to be able to vent freely. The fact that I have no home where I could accommodate her, that I'll be taking care of business, staying with friends, and only have two weeks are all excuses I can give. It seems awfully soon for her to be grabbing at me as a chance to get to the U.S.

I made my spaghetti dinner. The canned sauce and tomato paste came from Jess's kitchen when he cleared it out before the movers arrived. Isabel, Jess, and Mr. Lee were there. Mr. Lee's wife chickened out. He told me a week ago that she was very excited about coming. A few days later she told her husband that she was a little nervous. By the morning of the dinner she was feeling slightly sick. By late afternoon she was very sick. Most Koreans have virtually no experience with foreigners, and we intimidate them. I don't always realize what a challenge it is to associate with me. I was disappointed when Mr. Lee arrived alone. He did, however, bring some kimchi made by his wife and a beautiful miniature maple in honor of Arbor Day.

The dinner brought out a lot of squirreliness in Isabel. I told her I couldn't invite Ho-chang and Bo-mi this time because I couldn't accommodate more than five people—I don't have the space, the dinnerware, or the ingredients to make enough sauce. She assured me there was no need to invite them this time. Yet when I was at her apartment after going to the bathhouse, she said to Ho-chang, "Do you know where I'm going tonight? I'm going to Margaret's to eat spaghetti. Maybe you could drop by and ask, 'Do you have any spaghetti?' " I said the only thing I could say: by all means come—they would only have to bring plates and utensils. Having the grace to refuse, he said he had other plans. Isabel's words were baffling, beyond tactless, even antagonistic.

After everyone arrived for dinner, Isabel said, "Didn't you invite Mr. and Mrs. Hamilton too?" The tone of voice was—and is this all? This uninteresting group? She acted phonily cheerful all evening, saying nonsensical things, acting cute and prancing about as if she were a child on stage. While helping me clear the dishes before dessert, she said in a singsong voice: "Look at me. I'm helping Margaret with the dishes." Why was she so uncomfortable? Was she nervous about being around another English teacher? Was she showing off her ability with the language? When Isabel was ready to go, she indicated Mr. Lee and said, "Well, I have to leave. And he has to leave too." She left Jess out of her command. I wondered if she wanted Mr. Lee to go away with the picture of Jess and me there alone. Everyone, including Jess, left. What is this controlling behavior about? What undercurrents are flowing in this woman?

Isabel appeared at my door at 3:30 one Sunday afternoon and told me she wanted some food. She had been running around all day, was hungry, and didn't want to go home and eat alone. She knew I'd had students over earlier that day and expected I'd have food left over. I had only given my students cider and crackers. I pulled out what was in my refrigerator and cupboards, which were pretty slim pickings—a hard-boiled egg, sunflower seeds, and the cider. Isabel accepted these things unenthusiastically, making sure I knew that I had let her down. She didn't stay long. After answering a few questions I had about my Korean language textbook, she went on to the library to study.

Isabel once said that I should spend two years here, learn Korean, do my other traveling abroad, and then retire in Korea with her. I could make good money teaching English, she said. And "Koreans aren't so bad." Grow old in Korea with Isabel! What a thought!

It occurs to me that some of Isabel's behavior toward me might revolve around Jess. She and all his other Korean women fans are desperately concerned with whether Jess has a girlfriend, whether he's sleeping with anyone. Isabel makes leading comments; everyone suspects me. Maybe they all want to be his girlfriend, although I think most of them would be afraid to sleep with him. Isabel is always putting her hand on his thigh and leaving it there. Probably she would have gotten into bed with him if he had shown an interest. I get the idea they're all competing for Jess and a little angry at the newly arrived American competition. They may see me as having an unfair advantage because he and I share the same language and I am, they assume, a sexually liberated (loose) person.

Jess and I have gone out to dinner a couple times. Each time, we were sighted by the inevitable tittering students jumping to entertaining conclusions. Jess's lease was up on his apartment two weeks before he's scheduled to leave the country, so he's living in a new motel—a love motel—in the neighborhood. He described the room to me—the mirrors on the ceiling, the red plush bedspread—and invited me to come over and try it out. He told me he had been thinking about me a lot, and at least would be able to sleep better, having expressed his feelings. I treated his confession and his invitation lightly, sloughing them off. He has always talked about how lonely he is. Sometimes I have the impression he's appealing to my sympathy, hoping to wear me down before he leaves.

In two weeks he'll be home with his wife. Now there's an example of two people who have not denied their sexual attractions. It sounds as if she has had only one affair (that he knows about) whereas he's had several. Her straying was painful for him, as he knows his has been for her. He said he's been careful to be discreet, to never flaunt his relationships in front of his wife. But by now their marriage is in shreds, and who knows if the infidelity is a cause or an effect.

....

After six months here, I'm evaluating whether I will actually stay a second year. One year could be considered an interesting experience. But two years of this? My original intention was to save money and make myself more marketable by teaching in Korea for two years. The people at New World Teachers, where I got my certificate in teaching English as a second language, said you need two years' experience before going to Singapore. I've thought I would like to teach in Spain, too. It would give me a chance to use my eight years of studying Spanish and become bilingual.

I will have to have more to keep me here. This week Isabel will take me to my first Tae Guk Kwon (T'ai Chi) class and introduce me to the teacher. The *dojang* is open six days a week from 7:00 in the morning until 11:00 at night. For about ninety dollars a month I can go whenever I want. I'm not yet sure how the classes will work. I will also have Isabel call the potter in

Hoeng Song (about forty-five minutes away by bus) about brush painting lessons. If I can learn and practice things I really enjoy doing, then I won't feel my time here is wasted. The money isn't enough.

Within a month I should get a contract from the government. If I do stay, I want to remain in Wonju. As bad as things are at times, they're fairly good relative to the experiences of native English teachers in Seoul or other towns. There's no way I want to weather another homestay, locate another apartment, acquire the necessary household goods, and adjust to a new school and teachers.

I often think about the irony of my being here. I who am so health conscious and sensitive to bad food, ugly surroundings, and dirty air in a country that grows all its food on chemicals and has such a paucity of grass, gardens, and architecture. I dislike the doggedness and dryness of Korea. Am I not dogged and dry? Why would I flee to Korea, of all places? How can I satisfy my needs for rest and hydration here?

Well, I'm dead, right? So what exactly does that mean? Don't look for or expect happiness? Or does it mean I can take all the risks now, throw the future to the wind—I have nothing to lose. I had decided that taking care of myself financially was my first priority. I'm making progress there—I think I can save half of what I earn each year, about $12,000. But what a struggle my life is here! I'm especially disappointed right now because with the transfers of my allies to other schools, things just took a turn for the worse. I'd hoped things would get better with time; I'd always expected that. Where's some serendipitous good luck? Something to miraculously compensate for this dragging rocks over hard stones.

Running behind all this in my mind are my own self-doubts. Why haven't I gotten along better with people? Am I not outgoing and cheerful enough? Not enough sense of humor? Not strong enough? Thick-skinned enough? Not a resourceful enough teacher? I sure went into this with prodigious good will and energy. Flexibility, too, I think, and optimism.

While I'm ceaselessly exerting myself, what I really want is to be taken care of—loved, touched, soothed, and supported.

....

This week I'll begin teaching first-grade conversation classes in addition to the second-grade classes I already teach. At first I said no—repeatedly—to taking on more hours, but I finally gave in to seeing them three days a week, with the class limited to no more than twenty. Now I teach thirty-two hours a week. Too much. On Wednesday afternoon I'll start teaching middle school English teachers once a week. Thirty teachers from various Wonju schools are scheduled to attend the two-hour-long classes. It'll be a challenge, but interesting too. I reach out hopefully toward any opportunity for conversation. I'm sure some of the teachers will be able to actually speak English.

....

Mr. Lee told me about his "birth dream." Soon after marriage a man or a woman may have this. He dreamt of one very large rabbit. (Maybe it was really about himself—breeding like a big healthy rabbit.) A dream about one large mammal is supposed to signify the conception of a boy. A dream about many small animals, especially reptiles—snakes, lizards, and so on—indicates the conception of a girl. He said, "So I am very happy." It wouldn't occur to him what an insult this is to any woman. And come to think of it, rabbits are not usually classified as large mammals. Is this wishful thinking on his part?

I've had a few glimpses of Mr. Lee's anger. Last week during class, he stood over a couple girls seated at their desks, stiffened his spine, puffed himself up, and spat rapid, staccato words at them. From the other end of the room, and looking only at his back, I caught his fury—but only a fraction of what the students must have caught looking at his front. This kind of voice and physical bearing always carries with it the threat of barely contained force, of violence. I sensed it in my brother when I was a kid. It was in my father. You can feel if not see the fist being formed. How does a young, small girl in Korea's hierarchical society resist this? She doesn't. I caved into it once. As a little girl I pleaded with my brother not to hurt me as he charged and I backed up. I never did that again. I always stood my ground and refused to show fear, although he could easily have overcome me physically. Male bullying. Even slight, feminine-looking Mr. Lee can pull it off.

He and I had fun together at Dreamland when we accompanied the seventh graders on their field trip. We played a laser-shooting game inside a billowy room with spongy inflated floors, walls, and various tall cylinders to hide behind. We strapped on our laser-sensitive vests, grasped our long plastic guns with both hands, and entered the bubble. Mr. Lee and I stumbled from one end to another, screeching (I guess I did all the screeching), giggling, and shooting wildly. I haven't laughed like that since I arrived in Korea. It was good therapy.

I was also dragged onto some hair-raising rides by students. That wasn't good therapy. Later, Mr. Lee and I watched all the teams from ten homerooms perform their dance routines choreographed to popular songs. This was an important competition for the girls. Most of them had chosen the same couple of lengthy songs. Mr. Lee looked over at me and said, "What's the word for this? Torture?" "Yes," I said, "That's the word."

....

Friday after school I went to a dinner for the first-grade teachers. It was a gift from the well-to-do parents of a bright student—a common method in Korea of smoothing the way for their daughter or son. This was the second school-related dinner last week, and I was not eager to attend. Most of these meals are brief (less than an hour), so I was looking forward to getting home early. But the father is a pediatrician and half the kids in Wonju are sick now with colds and flu, so he was late. Long after we finished eating, the wife kept entreating us to stay "five minutes more" until he could get there. The dinner began at 6:00 and he didn't arrive until 8:30. At least the food was good—*pul gogi* (thin pieces of beef barbecued over charcoal stoves at the table and eaten wrapped in lettuce leaves with raw cloves of garlic), lots of spicy side dishes, and *naeng myeon* (cold noodles in a vinegary sauce) at the end of the meal. I finally got into a taxi with one of the teachers around 9:00. Three hours of listening to Korean all around me, straining to understand, not understanding much, and at the same time trying to keep my mouth turned up and act as if I were pleased to be there. This at the end of a long and draining work week.

I regard most of these after-school events as impositions. I wonder how the Korean teachers feel about them. They get very expensive meals that they wouldn't buy for themselves. But many are at least as weary as I am and have young children waiting for them at home. Mrs. Song often brings her sweet two-year-old son to dinners with her. The school owns the teachers twenty-four hours a day, every day. It's ironic that an institution devised to nurture and educate children keeps so many parents from being able to participate in the care and education of their sons and daughters.

....

There are three new English teachers this year. All three—two women and a man—have their desks in other teachers' rooms, smaller ones that are taking the overflow from the main one where I've been placed. The two women are friendly, although I hardly ever see them. After two months, I finally caught my first glimpse of the man when I had lunch with the English teachers. Even then I never really saw his whole face because he was at the other end of the table. I've asked to be introduced to him, but without result. He left so quickly at the end of the lunch, that I never did get a full view of his face. I wouldn't recognize him if I saw him. Does he avoid me because he has no confidence in his English? Does he resent Americans? At least the former has to be true.

The topic of discussion during the meal was the news they'd heard that morning—our principal had failed to inform them that they could apply to spend a month in Canada during one of this year's vacations. He decided they all must stay in Wonju and teach supplemental classes. The deadline has passed, therefore the decision is final. The teachers were furious and I definitely grasped that much without any translation. I wouldn't normally do this, but I insisted on being told in English what was going on. They looked at each other and were silent. I was relieved and grateful when one of the new women teachers translated.

My chest constricted as I listened. I felt personally thwarted, instantly both angered and depressed by this foolish, shortsighted, irreversible edict. The teachers don't even have a way to protest. If they want control over their lives, they will have to force change—take some risks, improvise. This is the kind of thing they have no experience with. Recently a bill was railroaded through congress by the ruling party (when the opposition party was not there) that stipulates there will be no teachers' unions. The one that exists was already illegal, and most teachers have been, with good reason, afraid to join. Union members lose their jobs.

Koreans are conditioned to passively swallow this kind of treatment. Percival gave me a good example of their trained submissiveness. He told me he got so exasperated with a student that he picked the boy up out of his seat, carried him to the window, and threatened to throw him out. Percival fully expected the boy to resist, but he never struggled or uttered a word. Percival thinks the boy would have let himself be lofted out into the air. Mr. Hamilton is known throughout Wonju and probably throughout Korea by now as the teacher who throws students out windows.

Entry 30
Wonju, Spring 1997

This quiet Sunday evening at home.

I went for a run in the morning along the curvy roads of the military base—my usual route to the top of a forested hill where the signs say no admittance beyond this point. I turned around beneath the watchtower containing a man with a long gun. Back at the bottom of the hill, behind the chapel, there's a flat area with scattered patches of frail-looking grass. The roots of the overhanging locust trees steal the moisture and nutrients for themselves. This is my favorite place to practice T'ai Chi. I like preceding my practice with a heart-pounding run, then gradually slowing inside and out as I make my way through the sequence. Until I'm still.

At one o'clock the members of my original conversation class came to my apartment to play *yut,* a board game usually played around Christmas. You roll sticks instead of dice. At three o'clock Isabel came to give me a Korean lesson. I timed it this way to chase the girls out. I love them, but they would stay all day if I let them. They'd turn on the TV and settle in.

....

"My son has died in my wife's body." This was Mr. Lee's way of telling me about the miscarriage. He was visibly depressed for several days last week, but seemed relatively cheerful by Friday. His wife required some sort of surgery as a result of the miscarriage, and wasn't allowed adequate time to recuperate before returning to school.

....

Mr. Young called me at school on Monday to say he'd be attending my conversation class for middle school English teachers. He asked how things were. My inclination was to complain, fish for sympathy, but I just said fine. I wasn't surprised when he didn't appear on Wednesday afternoon. He didn't attend a single meeting of last semester's conversation classes for English teachers. I think he's afraid his lack of fluency will be revealed. As I walked back to my desk after the class, I saw him in the hall outside the teachers' room. He came toward me smiling, hailing me with both arms high in the air. My reaction was mixed: I wanted to rush into those arms and hug him but I resented the showiness of his very un-Korean gesture in front of other people. He had arrived only a half hour before, he said, too late for the class. Other teachers returning from their classes stopped to say hello to him.

Mr. Won must have been right behind me, because as I walked through the door of the teachers' room, he said, "You know Yun Su-jin is Mr. Young's wife." "Yes of course," I answered. The stolid Christian keeping an eye on me. How dreary and meddlesome and self-righteous.

That settles my wonderings about what people think of my friendship with Mr. Young, the reason for his sudden departure, the arrival of his wife, and her coldness toward me. Who knows what part he played in sowing rumors—maybe he claims to, or has hinted at, having an affair with me. That's why I didn't like his display in the hall. I don't trust anyone here.

Yet seeing Mr. Young again brought a breath of life into me, lifted my spirits. I wonder how much his absence has contributed to my recent sadness. A sexual interest, a male source of energy is gone. The idea of him still excites me. The reality of him is less stimulating, and the reality of our circumstances leaves me cold.

On Friday a couple of female teachers were explosively angry with three girls. Mr. Young's wife was one of the teachers. She had them kneeling beside her desk for a long time, all the while berating them and prodding them with her stick. She repeatedly swatted one girl on the head with it. Finally she stood that girl up and gave her several vicious hits on the backs of the thighs. With each blow, Yun Su-jin drew her stick way back and threw her whole body into it. She paused between strikes to get her aim and gather strength. When it was over, the girl turned around and I saw her red-purple face straining to hold it in. She was groaning silently, holding her skirt against her legs, and curving forward with pain. She stood with the other girls for more lecture, still gripping her skirt. The fabric must have, at least at first, felt cool against her burning skin. Watching this, my heart felt as if it had received an electrical shock. And I was surprised that it was being done in front of me, the American. My presence had no inhibiting effect, as I think it has had on other teachers' use of physical violence against students. Later, Mr. Lee told me that the three had stolen another girl's backpack.

The next day Yun Su-jin showed up wearing a long black polyester outfit accessorized by a black ribbon around her neck. She has a pretty face, but is one of the few heavy Koreans I've seen. Given what I witnessed the day before, so much black made her look sinister—like a chubby Dragon Lady. Were the glamorous, uncharacteristic new clothes a gift from her husband to cheer her up?

When she sees me in the halls, she looks away or down, never saying hello. Even after the (I thought) friendly lunch. I feel sorry for her. She's unhappy at her new school, and she must be aware of the attraction her husband has felt for me. Does she believe we acted on it? Just knowing your spouse has been preoccupied with someone else is hurtful enough. The fury she unleashed on that poor girl—did it have more than one source?

....

The big news is that I started Tae Guk Kwon lessons. Isabel took me to the dojang and introduced me to the instructor, who speaks almost no English. Kim Byoung-chan is a boyish-looking man, like Mr. Young. I'm guessing he's about the same age too—in his midthirties. His hair flops down over his forehead, nearly brushing his glasses. He seems bright and very alert. I'm not sure what he thinks of this middle-aged Western woman among his all-male, almost all very young students. Isabel says it's "a feather in his cap" to have an American student.

I go to class three nights a week and practice by myself on the other four days. I'm obsessed. This is the way I felt when I was first learning my original Wu style from Kao Ching-hua in Illinois. Studying a new style of Tae Guk Kwon eases any doubts I've had about the value of being in Korea.

The form I'm learning is known as the Combined Forty-two Forms. It's a modern amalgam of the four major T'ai Chi styles—Chen, Wu, Yang, and Sun. The forty-two movements only take about six minutes to do, compared to the absolute minimum twenty minutes needed for the traditional long style that I've been practicing.

The Asian countries have adopted this new sequence as a standard for international competition. It's scored just like gymnastics—a person stands out there and goes through the form in front of judges who award him or her 9.3, 9.4, and so on. It's a more external, athletic art; the emphasis is not on the meditative content that I've cultivated in my own practice and teaching over the years. In my book *A Potter's Notes on T'ai Chi Ch'uan,* there's a chapter titled "Why T'ai Chi Will Never Become an Olympic Event." It shows my naïveté. As the games become more inclusive of non-Western sports, I'm sure it will be in there.

There's a short form of this new style with only twenty-four movements. My teacher says he'll show it to me after I learn the long one. I hope I can also get to some sword and staff.

Kim Byoung-chan is addressed *Kwan Jang Nim,* meaning "Captain," because he's the head of all three dojangs in Wonju where *Wushu* (Chinese martial arts) are taught. The plaques on his wall say that he's a sixth dan in Wushu and a fifth dan in Kung Fu. He graduated in phys ed from Seoul National University, Korea's most respected school.

I'm in awe of his skills. One evening I was practicing by myself in a corner of the dojang when I caught, out of the corner of my eye, something suspended above the ground. It was my teacher—airborne. I've seen plenty of martial arts, but I can't remember ever seeing such spring-loaded, perfectly directed energy. He's also incredibly flexible. The phrase "made of rubber" comes to mind. Are all the teachers here so proficient? Or did I just get lucky?

Kwan Jang Nim and his senior student—a man in his twenties—have put me through some rugged warm-ups including standing in a low horse stance with arms extended for long periods of time. I haven't given in yet, but it means tolerating searing pain in my thighs.

I'm one of two Tae Guk Kwon students. The other is a man about my age, a professor of Chinese studies at a local university. The form we're learning doesn't have the flowing circularity and inevitability of movement that I love in my traditional, ninety-seven-movement Wu style, but it's very powerful.

These classes are an extra motive for learning Korean. Today I got Isabel to help me with sentences I need for talking to Kwan Jang Nim about when and where he'll pick me up for class. (He picks up many of his students, and returns us to our homes after our training. Every evening, the streets of Wonju are clogged with vans and buses transporting students to their after-school classes.) Examples of other sentences I've learned: "Please show me that movement again," "I forgot." "I'm paying for May now," "What does this hand (foot, leg) do?" "It's difficult" (the pronunciation of which is aptly challenging in itself).

....

I was waiting for Kwan Jang Nim to pick me up in front of my apartment building after school Wednesday evening. Students—first graders who are still fascinated—quickly surrounded me. They were on break from their classes in the hogwon below my apartment. I asked them how late their classes ran; they said until nine o'clock. My automatic response (in Korean) was, "That's too bad." I was certain of my translation (sometime earlier I had asked a Korean friend how to say this) and the pronunciation isn't difficult. But after several repetitions, they still had no idea what I was saying. All of us were bewildered. I checked this out with Isabel today. She told me no Korean would think to express sympathy regarding a situation that is an accepted fact of life. Everyone here has strict, life-consuming obligations. That's all. It was the sentiment they didn't understand.

I didn't mention that while the teachers were gathered to have their picnic lunch at Dreamland, one of the male social studies teachers—the same one who complained about my making too much money for the workshop in Chunchon—came up to me, breathed whiskey into my face, and said in English, "What's my name?" I said I had forgotten. (We were introduced only once, soon after I arrived in Wonju.) He went on to say to me in Korean that when in America, you're supposed to speak English, and when in Korea, you're supposed to speak Korean. I agreed that it was good to study the language. The encounter ended there, but I was furious. I felt attacked, and unfairly. On the way home I told Mr. Lee about it. He sympathized with me, said the man had been rude, and blamed his behavior on the alcohol. I said that was no excuse. I'm sure Mr. Lee instantly spread the word: Emerson is angry. About a week later the same offensive teacher came up to me at my desk and started talking about Korean food and asking what I eat. I was able to respond in Korean. He knows almost no English. These are not friendly conversations. They're tests.

It's true I'm frustrated that I can't speak more Korean by now. After ten months of studying, and progressing well into the second-level conversation book, I still don't know how to say "and." There are three words for it, and I sort of understand them, but I'm not sure when to use which.

I'm trying to become independent in this country (I don't have much choice, which is good). Before going on errands—to the dry cleaner, hairdresser, or bank for instance—I study the vocabulary and sentences I'll need. Here in Korea, when I search my brain's foreign language section for a word, Spanish is still the first thing it hands me. Through junior high, high school, and college that's the language I studied. There is a vast gap between Eastern and Western languages; Spanish is a cinch compared to Korean.

I've accumulated a list of reasons (defensive rationalizations) why it's difficult for me to learn Korean:

Not much time or energy left over after teaching.

No formal classes available.

Koreans are just learning how to teach their language to non-Koreans.

Isabel's ability as a teacher is limited by her inability to explain grammar in English.

The English-Korean and Korean-English dictionaries are written for Koreans, and information about usage is in Korean. I come up with a useable word about fifty percent of the time, at best.

When I ask Koreans (like Mr. Lee) for a word, they often don't want to tell me what first comes to mind—the word most commonly used—because it's of Chinese or, worse, Japanese origin. They want to give me the pure Korean, which they sometimes can't remember. It's exasperatingly difficult to get a straight answer—to find out the word that Koreans use every day.

Koreans and Westerners don't express the same thoughts.

The difference in sentence structure goes way beyond subject-object-verb versus subject-verb-object.

The fact that I often don't have good feelings about many of the Koreans around me cuts into my incentive to learn their language. Part of that bad feeling comes from their naïveté about how hard it is for a Westerner to learn Korean. They don't extrapolate from their difficulty with English that it is equally difficult in the reverse. Even educated people actually think that because Korean is easy for them, it must be easy for foreigners too. I'm always salving their egos by saying how complex English is, and praising them for doing as well as they do. But a couple of times now, when someone has told me Korean is easy, I've countered by saying English is easy too—for *me.* This shocks them, and I catch the heat of their silently flaring tempers.

> Koreans are very bad at deciphering their own language when it's spoken with an accent. They have so little experience with this.
>
> They don't think to slow their speech or simplify their sentences in order to help me understand, as I do when I speak English with them. If I ask them to repeat something, they often just fall silent.
>
> I take some comfort in the fact that the world-traveling Mormons rate Korean the third most difficult language on the planet, behind Navajo and Finnish. Internationals in this country who attain fluency often become celebrities based solely on this accomplishment.

I resent being tested by Koreans on my language proficiency. It would never occur to me to treat them in this way. I work hard to make my spoken and written English as easy as possible for them to comprehend. I try not to embarrass anyone. The knowledge I've acquired of their language combined with my familiarity with how English is spoken here (sometimes called Konglish) increases my chances of being understood. I tailor my English for Koreans—I use and reuse the words, phrases, and sentences that they most commonly rely on. These are the ones stressed in their textbooks or picked up from American military personnel. Sometimes I speak in ways that would, in my own country, be considered incorrect. Every word goes through an editing process in my head before it comes out on a blackboard, on paper, or in speech. Speaking at normal speed, using normal vocabulary and sentence structure simply doesn't work. It's tiring, but anything less would amount to arrogance or ignorance or a lack of sincerity in wanting to communicate.

Charlotte and Percival are contemptuous of the way Koreans repeat the same mistakes in English grammar and pronunciation over and over again. If they'd study Korean, they'd discover that almost all these changes come from applying Korean grammar and pronunciation to English. It's a natural thing that people do when they're using a second language. English gets tweaked in all sorts of creative ways as it's filtered through different cultures and languages. No one—not even the Brits—has the one true English that everyone else must conform to. Get used to it.

I've noticed that humans have a natural tendency to pretend to understand language. We're ashamed of our ignorance, or we don't want to continually interrupt a conversation. We guess at meanings and these guesses often miss the mark.

I'm guilty. I have pretended to understand Korean, hoping to make myself look better. And I do my best to preserve the face of Koreans speaking English to me by acting as if I understand rather than shaming them in front of themselves or others. But there are times when I can't conceal my confusion. In the end, I have to be sure of certain information.

The importance of saving face in a rigidly hierarchical society exacerbates language problems. People in dominant positions don't want to reveal fallibility. Because they can't pass on what they're unwilling to clarify, the flow of information stops.

Isabel told me a story about one of her English professors who took part in a conference in the U.S. He had no trouble participating in the formal discussions. But as soon as the meetings concluded and the Americans started talking among themselves, it seemed to him as if they were speaking a different language. It no longer even sounded like English—the language he'd been studying and speaking for decades, and considered himself fluent in. "It was as if I'd had never studied it at all!" he told her.

The story demonstrates two things: The Americans customized their speech to make sure that internationals could understand them during the meetings; and even the most intense, long-term study of English doesn't guarantee that a Korean will grasp colloquial conversation at normal speed. It works both ways between the two languages.

....

Min-hi took two weeks and went to the U.S. to consult with doctors about the recurrence of her breast cancer. Fortunately they didn't prescribe chemotherapy this time. They've given her a new treatment—six months of hormones that they said will only make her gain weight. She's back in Seoul now, and feeling very sick and discouraged. The hormones are not agreeing with her as well as her doctors predicted. Her supervisor is giving her a hard time about having been away for two weeks. She refused to tell the school authorities why she was going—only said it was important and personal. She didn't want to jeopardize her job, but she also wanted some privacy, which is not an easy thing to come by in Korea. The supervisor is disrespectful and acts as if he thinks she went home for the fun of it. It's possible he's just curious and wants to pressure her into revealing her reason. I'll visit Min-hi in the next couple weeks. There's an international flower exhibition we want to see.

....

Jess is leaving Korea tomorrow. Daily lunches, dinners, and entertainment have been lavished on him by his Korean women friends over the last two weeks. I know they like him—he's a sweet person—but I also think they want to secure a place to stay when they visit America. They ask him how many bedrooms he has in his house. Isabel is planning to visit Jess in Georgia this summer. She says she will attend a language school in Florida for six weeks, and will be only three or four hours' drive away.

Jess told me Isabel took him to the home of one of her wealthy English language students. This woman and her husband own a hotel and bathhouse. As Isabel and Jess approached the door to the woman's house, she stepped out and asked them to wait there. She got her coat, came back out, and took them to a nearby restaurant for lunch. He had the clear impression that the woman saw he was African-American and didn't want him in her house.

He was right. Isabel told me later that the woman, who had been studying with her for years, wanted an American to practice conversation with. Isabel was offering Jess. Mrs. Choi's excuse for not accepting him was that she didn't want a man. Isabel then suggested a woman who's new here. I've met her and she's wonderfully bilingual—her mother is Korean, her father African-American. Mrs. Choi refused her too.

Isabel tried to get me to visit Mrs. Choi once a week. (I *have* been allowed into her house.) I said that not only did I not want more teaching, I also didn't like the idea that Mrs. Choi wouldn't permit my friend to enter her home. Isabel did some backpedaling and tried to make excuses. But she hasn't mentioned my visiting Mrs. Choi since. It could be the woman's husband who doesn't like Africans, and she can't go against his wishes. Or maybe it's both of them.

When I ask my students what they dislike about Americans, one of the first things they bring up is that Americans don't like blacks. I tell them some do and some don't. It's the same here.

....

I signed a contract to stay another year. Am I crazy? I feel unfinished here. I want more time to learn Tae Guk Kwon, make further inroads into the language, save money, and maybe take lessons in brush painting. I'll just have to hang in there with the teaching. We've had some days off and some interruptions in the schedule for midterms, so I feel better now. My second contract expires July 31, 1998. As long as North Korea doesn't interfere with my plans by lobbing missiles this way, I think I can last until then.

Entry 31
Wonju, Spring 1997

I'm essentially getting private lessons from Kwan Jang Nim. The special treatment makes me feel self-conscious—I'm afraid he's neglecting his other students while I'm there. It's a good thing I'm only going to class three nights a week. All the others attend five nights. And Kwan Jang Nim takes us lesser students home early at 8:30; the senior students stay until 10:30.

I like practicing by myself every other day. It gives me a chance to get used to new movements, figure them out. When I go back to class, I've made progress. This way I don't waste my teacher's time while he watches me bumble through the repetitions I need to grasp each new part of the sequence.

The Wushu students range in age from eight to eighteen. They seem friendly and respectful enough toward me; it's hard to tell what they think because they have no spoken English. At the end of my lesson, sometimes I watch while Kwan Jang Nim gives instruction and demonstrates for them before taking me home. I really enjoy this, although I can tell it's their turn to feel self-conscious. I think my teacher likes having an opportunity to show off a bit.

One evening last week he dropped me at the dojang, left his van running, came in, sprayed some air freshener around his office, then left to pick up more students. What was that about? Was it for me? I noticed last Friday that he had cleaned and rearranged his office. The trophies and plaques were more prominently displayed, and there were more than I remember seeing before.

I like him. At first I thought he was severe and humorless, but I'm starting to change my mind. He's a talented mimic—he entertains us by exaggerating all our clumsy mistakes. I guess it requires a thick skin on the part of his students, but it's hard to be indignant while I'm laughing. Kwan Jang Nim seems to enjoy the lessons and is remarkably patient, willing to go through the many demonstrations I require in order to get something.

I wish I could talk to him more. But maybe it's a good thing I can't. Learning physical movement from someone with a minimum of verbal explanation is an interesting way to learn. He corrects me by rearranging my limbs or showing me again. I can't explain or complain; I just have to observe and do. Gradually I'm catching on, but the movements will take a lot of refining. Sometimes he uses his English to assess my performance by saying, "Good. No very good."

One of the things I most appreciate about Kwan Jang Nim is that he slows his speech for me, repeats things, and says them in simple ways in order to accommodate my limited Korean. No one else does this for me.

His politeness extends to his driving, too. He never forces his way in front of anyone—always defers to other drivers. His reflexes are quick and accurate. I feel as safe with him as it's possible to feel on Korean city streets. Again, he's the exception.

I wonder if I can ever be flexible enough to do the leg lifts (higher and slower than the Wu style) properly. He told me to stretch three times a day. I'm able to fit in two stretching sessions—before and after school. On the days when I have class, I stretch at home before he picks me up, then again during warm-ups at the dojang. I'm not naturally flexible, and sometimes I think—especially at my age—it may be a losing battle. Frankly it's excruciating. It gets easier eventually, right?

Kwan Jang Nim said first he'll teach me the outside of Tae Guk Kwon, then he'll teach me the inside. Sounds good to me. He said (through Isabel) that I'll feel hot and cold sensations in my body as a result of the increased flow of ch'i. The hot flashes would be nothing new; a few cold ones would be welcome. He also informed me my wrists will be itchy. Itchy wrists? I almost laughed. Later I realized I'd experienced that already—while practicing at the base. I was furiously scratching my right wrist; it was a bright red. I thought something had bitten me, but couldn't find any marks. Then the left wrist started itching, not as severely. No evidence of a bite there either. The color faded from my wrists as quickly as it had come. Weird.

Last Wednesday evening I was the only student at the dojang. Were the other students between sessions? Preparing for midterms? I didn't like it. I've heard and read too much about martial arts instructors preying on women in the U.S. Should I be wary of this man? He presented me with a red satin Kung Fu uniform—normal attire for the dojang. Some of the other students wear purple, pink, or white satin. The uniforms are billowy, graceful, and striking, but bound to be hot and uncomfortable in the coming months. The youngest students (primary school age) wear purple cotton uniforms. I was hoping to get one of those someday. Kwan Jang Nim showed me the proper way to fold the uniform, then I had my lesson. On Friday evening, to my relief, everyone was back.

    I feel attracted to Kwan Jang Nim, and get inklings that he's attracted too. But then, I want everyone to be in love with me. Admire me if they're female, admire and love me if they're male. I guess the love part only applies to males I'm attracted to. It's Thomas Hardy's *The Beloved*. I see my love object in so many different, successive people. Maybe I'm just desperate for an outside source of energy. At this point, I would probably fall in love with any man who paid attention to me and whose looks I liked. This is nothing like the intensity of my feeling for Mr. Young, and I don't want it to get that way. I so admire Kwan Jang Nim's skill and his grace—in and out of the dojang. I "adore" him.

    I love the training. I've lost weight and gained muscle. This Spartan culture is going to whip me into shape—or do me in.

....

    Yesterday morning (Saturday), Isabel and I paid our usual weekly visit to the bathhouse by her apartment. We returned to her home for some breakfast followed by her English lesson. She's writing a paper on Jack Kerouac for one of her courses, so we looked at a biographical essay that's part of her research. It's way over her head—she *needs* help. I was feeling overwhelmed for her. All the idioms—"shipped out," "took it with a grain of salt," "a far cry," "in his element," "make ends meet." They take some explaining.

Like a dry sponge, I drink in Isabel's cozy three-room apartment—an established home, full of the accoutrements of living, everything well worn. There's a beautiful carved wooden ceiling. I want to lie on the floor and fall asleep. From what Isabel tells me, plenty of American soldiers she's brought home from her Korean conversation lessons at the base have done just that. After their cold, institutional dormitories, a real home must feel like nirvana. She seems to know what a relief it is for a foreigner to be admitted to her apartment, how exhausted we all are from never being able to entirely relax, never being "at home."

We finished the English lesson, then went downtown to a Chinese medicine store. I wanted to get some dong quai—one of the herbs I use to deal with my hot flashes and other menopausal symptoms. The woman behind the counter asked if I wished to be examined by the doctor (free of charge, assuming I buy some herbs). She said it only takes five minutes, so Isabel and I went into his office.

A man who was probably close to seventy, very wide and solid, sat behind a dark, highly polished desk. His hair was thin but jet-black. Probably he colors it as many Asian men do at his age. The room was spacious and richly furnished with antiques; framed brush paintings dotted the walls.

After Isabel explained why I had come, he reached for my wrist and I gave it to him. He felt my pulse, then took my blood pressure, which he said was a little low. Isabel and I sat down on couches that faced each other with a gleaming wooden coffee table between. We angled ourselves toward the doctor. Isabel translated for us as he asked about my symptoms.

A man appeared at the open door of the office, leaned against the satiny doorjamb, smirked, and settled in to listen. I signaled to Isabel that he made me uncomfortable (such an invasion of privacy!) but she shrugged and looked back at the doctor, stubbornly telling me with her body language to ignore the man. He stayed for almost the entire appointment while I fumed. Koreans judge women partly by their fertility (their purpose for existing). Being menopausal diminishes me in their eyes. I remembered the teacher in the women teacher's lounge telling me where they kept sanitary napkins and pointedly asking me, as she peered into my face, if I needed them. I said not right now.

The doctor told me that for 140,000 won (about $155) he'd give me a potion—the squeezings of various herbs—that would last about two weeks. I asked what happens after two weeks. He said most people need two or three treatments. So for about $465 I could get treated for mild menopausal symptoms for six weeks. Then what? Menopause is a long, drawn-out process. I respectfully declined. I bought a kilogram of dong quai for ten dollars. As we walked back to her car, Isabel said she thought he had given me a good price. She added that she took the treatments herself a few years ago. I asked if they had helped. She admitted they hadn't made much difference. My physician in the U.S. is a doctor of oriental medicine. I trust him; he has helped me; he's a lot less expensive.

....

I went on a clothes-shopping expedition to Seoul with two of Isabel's English conversation students. I've socialized with them before—mostly at Jess's. One is a twenty-nine-year-old single woman, the other is a woman my age with children. They're good humored and fun to be with. Their English is very limited which gives me a chance to practice my Korean, but makes communicating something of an effort.

What should have been a one-and-a-half-hour drive turned into four hours because we first dropped off something at Miss Kwan's brother's apartment in a suburb, then took a slow bus into town. One of the large buildings full of the best outlet stores closed shortly after we got there. They open in the wee hours of the morning and close at four o'clock in the afternoon.

The purpose of our trip was for me to find clothes for school, and my companions wanted to be sure I bought something. So I ended up buying (under pressure) a dress and a skirt. I regret both purchases now.

In the bargain districts, the clothes can be very nice, but you can't try anything on. The Korean sales people were extremely aggressive. They stuffed things into my shopping bag before I decided to buy them. They quickly brought the conversation to the point of discussing whether I would buy two or just one. Pushover that I am, I actually fell for this, coming away from the encounters feeling shrewd about holding the line at one. My companions joined in the sales pitch. They were in a hurry for me to complete my errand and get out of there.

Making our way through the crowded lanes outside, we passed an older woman who was bent over, sobbing, covering her face with her hands. Some people stood close by, trying to comfort her. A thief had just stolen her purse with her passport and 250,000 won ($300) in it. A few steps later the crowd was buzzing that it was 500,000 won.

We went back to Miss Kwan's brother's apartment on the bus and were invited to stay for dinner. After eating, I was roped into playing English teacher with the kids. Finally we headed home.

Phew! What a day! I came away from it wondering exactly what had happened. I wanted a simple trip to Seoul to buy clothes. Instead, I spent seven hours on the road, wasted money on clothes I don't like (not that it's the first time—I'm capable of doing that without anyone's help) and was shown off, I believe, as the American friend to someone's relatives. I often feel railroaded here. It sneaks up on me, and I'm not quick enough to respond. They seem like such nice people, and many of them are, but they all seem to have very forceful agendas of their own. I guess friendships *are* based on getting something from each other, but being an American in Korea exaggerates and distorts this.

....

I've gone swimming a few times now on Sundays with Isabel and Percival. Isabel drives us out to a golf resort in the country with a twenty-five-meter indoor pool.

I savor each twenty-minute car trip, sinking into my seat and letting the landscape slide by my half-open eyes. The drone of the engine and the presence of Isabel and Percival are strangely soothing. We follow a shallow but vigorous river dotted with flat stones that offer landings for narrow, long-limbed cranes. Starkly black and white magpies soar overhead. The green hills, the plowed fields, and the humble farmhouses are a relief from the concrete city. Here and there the earth is scraped bare as if construction is in progress. Sometimes I can tell they're building a road or a bridge, but often I can't see any reason for the digging. Sites seem long abandoned with no attempt to smooth the earth or help it heal. Torn edges of half-buried plastic flutter in the wake of the car.

The resort is for the executives in the *chaebol* (conglomerates like Daewoo, Hyundai, and Samsung) that rule Korean business and government. An undulating eighteen-hole golf course wraps around a huge, ornate clubhouse with banquet and meeting rooms, restaurants, hot tubs, saunas, and the pool. One side of the natatorium is solid windows with a view of rolling mountains.

Places like this pop up here and there—evidence of overflowing wealth for a select few. Korean society is topped with a thin layer of very rich people. This sparkling modern refuge of the elite is juxtaposed against the small, rickety homes that we pass on our way to it. Their mud and lath walls bow precariously under the weight of hundreds of years. Tethered goats or cows or ponies stand motionless in rugged yards of upturned dirt. Chickens wobble along the roadside.

Swimming helps. It stretches me out and relaxes me. I think it rid me of a stiff neck last week. I've spent a huge chunk of my life in water—working out when I was a teenaged competitor and since then for exercise and fun. I'm amphibious, and can't go for long without being in water.

One time, on the way to the resort, we met another car coming in the opposite direction on a single-lane road. Both cars stopped before coming alongside each other. There was a man and his wife in the other car. The man got out and gesticulated broadly to Isabel, demonstrating how she could squeeze her car by. His right wheels were already perched on the edge of the road. On either side of the pavement was a sheer drop-off of several feet—higher on our side than his. Any miscalculation could roll a car. Isabel froze. She didn't respond, didn't move, just stared straight forward. Percival and I were both saying it was impossible. The woman in the other car was as unmoving as Isabel. I told her to motion him to back up (not far behind him was a shoulder he could pull at least half his car onto, allowing us to pass). There was no indication from Isabel that she had even heard me. Percival weakly shook his head no toward the man. The man returned to his car and waited. After Isabel failed to do as he told her, he got back out and repeated the same gestures and instructions. Finally she backed up into a driveway that was several hundred yards behind us. She hadn't spoken one word. The man drove through. I was bewildered and incensed. Korean male bully prevails again.

That same day, Isabel and I were getting dressed in the locker room after swimming and showering. Our lockers were right by the door, which is made of frosted glass. I could see a shape on the other side switch off some lights in the hall, then the man walked through the door, turned, and looked at me. I was naked. He stood there. Stunned? Or just looking? I quickly walked around the corner as he turned and left. Isabel said, "Don't be upset, Margaret." She repeated this several times rapidly and in a voice that was phonily nonchalant. Her eagerness to sweep the incident under the rug did a good job of conveying to me that she thought it was deliberate. I didn't know what to think. When we got out to the desk at the entrance to the pool, he wasn't there. I started down the stairwell looking for Percival. Behind me, I could hear Isabel talking to the young man. When we met at her car, she relayed to me that he was very sorry, it was a mistake, he wanted to go home, and thought everyone was out of the locker room. But I wonder. My presence and Percival's—the presence of any Westerner—always gets a lot of notice. Did he really not know we were still there?

I've learned to put the chain on my apartment door in order to prevent my landlord from walking in on me. He succeeded twice—he unlocked my door and came in while I was there. Once I was only half dressed. He smirked like the man at the doctor's office, looked me up and down, and handed me the water bill. I told him to leave, I would pay him later. Now I never forget the chain. He has crashed the door into it several times, and always seems surprised that his way is barred. I asked Mr. Lee if this would be acceptable behavior toward a Korean woman. He nearly choked on his noodles as he assured me it wasn't. I thought he might intervene with the landlord for me but he didn't. I have to fend for myself.

After the event in the locker room, I read in Isabel a jumble of thoughts and reactions: denial, anger, resignation, fear I would recognize it for what it was, and embarrassment for her people. She had just been through the car episode. She's a Korean woman in Korea. Her rights and her power are severely limited.

I'm watching Isabel go through so much now. Her son, Ho-chang, and his girlfriend, Bo-mi, are planning on going to America in about six weeks—first to language school in Georgia, then to Ohio State University.

I suggested the university to him. I spent my junior and senior years there, earning my BFA. Ho-chang has spent several evenings in my apartment while we deciphered the application together. I made some after-midnight phone calls to the school in order to get his questions answered.

Isabel doesn't understand how he can leave her by herself, yet she knows the necessity and inevitability of it. She resents her continuing obligation to support Ho-chang, a healthy man of twenty-six with a master's degree. He's never really worked for money. And he'll be relying on Isabel while he's in school in the U.S. too. Her own plans for language school in Florida this summer fell through because money is too tight.

For that matter, *I* resent Ho-chang for being taken care of for so long—supported, given a nice home and good food, and now going to America with a woman who's as educated and even more intelligent than he is. She'll pull her own weight financially and take care of him as if he were her son.

Isabel's also dealing with aging, losing her attractiveness to men, the prospect of a long and solitary future. Very little nurturing or love, no touching or sex. No wonder she acts squirrelly at times. (Does this sound like me?)

....

I went to a dinner given by the students' mothers for the teachers at my school. It was another elaborate, expensive buffet in a gilded banquet hall—part of the bribery ethic here. I tried to get out of this one, pleading my Tae Guk Kwon class. Other teachers can be excused from dinners. But not the American. Plan B was an early getaway—I told everyone I must leave at 7:15 for my class. Just as I was about to leave, Mrs. Jong made me get up and sing a song in English. She would not take no for an answer. I had already sung the traditional "Arirang" very badly with Mr. Lee (who hates this sort of thing as much as I do). I have not yet memorized all the Korean words. I walked to the front of the room again, accepted the microphone, and stumbled through part of "Bridge over Troubled Water." (Simon and Garfunkel are popular here, and I've taught the song in conversation classes.) Where does being a good guest leave off and being a considerate host begin? I was feeling utterly persecuted. Koreans—in general—love to sing and perform. Do they have to force me to do it too? Mrs. Jong didn't stop there. She tried to coerce me into going to norebang after dinner. What's the matter with her? By the time I emerged on to the rainy street, I was ready to explode. The fact that I couldn't immediately get a cab and was later getting to my class than I intended added to the boiling pressure I was barely managing to contain.

So the next day when Mrs. Song kept me and my after-school conversation class waiting in the hall for fifteen minutes while she talked to her homeroom students, I was pissed. Only three or four girls were still with me by the time we got into the room (several others had quietly melted away). I told off the students who had stuck around (which was not fair) and then I called off class (which didn't make sense). I tried to be sure that Mrs. Song knew she'd ruffled my feathers (also uncalled for).

What put me over the top was when I went to get my pay for the extra conversation classes I teach and discovered they had decided to pay me less based on a clause in my new contract that doesn't take effect until September first. Typically, no one warned me ahead of time.

Emerson got angry. I told them I was done teaching conversation classes. I'm required to teach the regular classes, but the conversation is optional. I'd prefer to cut the regular classes (especially the B and C classes that I have to handle by myself) and only teach conversation—that's what I'm best at and that's what I enjoy—but it's not a choice I have. I'll finish this session of first-grade conversation (only five more classes) and I'll teach one more second-grade session because Mr. Won claims the girls are already scheduled for it. (Is he telling the truth?) Then I'm done. This will be a battle of wills between the principal and me. He told the English teachers to "control Emerson."

Koreans don't have the hang of contracts. Teachers here have never had them. They're offered to foreigners as bait, but employers think they can change them at will, unilaterally. They've done that with my first contract. If I signed on for another year, they were supposed to give me an extra two weeks' vacation. That evaporated. I didn't contest this because, not having a home in the U.S. anymore, I'm not sure how I would distribute myself while there. I hate imposing on people. Charlotte and Percival, however, are defying the authorities and planning a one-month vacation in August.

The non-English teachers who were overtly hostile toward me before are even more so now. But the English teachers have been surprisingly supportive in this confrontation with the principal. I don't know what the others think. I expect this confirms for many of them their cherished image of Americans as lazy, selfish, and moneygrubbing. People have been huddling in small groups in the teachers' room, conducting whispered conversations. I continue to provide entertainment.

Mr. Lee came to my apartment after school to discuss this with me. I ventured to inform him (to a small extent) what life is like for me here. I said I know it's a strain for him to talk to me, and the last thing he wants to do when he's tired is talk to Emerson, but it's also trying for me to converse in English with the English teachers. I explained the process of constant rifling through my brain, rejecting possible words or sentence structures, and searching for ones I think are useable. I never speak freely, I said; I often choose not to speak. And listening is just as challenging—having to penetrate their accent, their wording. I've had two foreign languages to learn. I get an hour or two's relief a week if I get together with the Hamiltons. The rest of the time I'm trying to understand and speak Korean or Konglish. It seemed time to let him in on this. I didn't want to hurt his feelings. He can chalk it up to a lesson in international relations. I told him—as I told Mr. Won—I have to set limits. Twenty-five hours a week of teaching. That's all. I'm interested to see how all this plays out.

....

I just had my first real cry since I came to Korea. Anger and frustration have been ricocheting off each other, breeding each other. I feel thwarted—bullied, twisted, tweaked, bent—by students, teachers, friends, the language.

I'm not a kid teacher. This kind of teaching is the grubbiest work there is. It's often mindless. Only the most brilliant, gifted teachers could survive this system. Or maybe they're the ones who succumb first. Isabel says of my problems with the people at school: "The women are jealous and the men are just stupid." She tells me Koreans have a saying that even dogs, although they eat human excrement, won't eat the excrement of teachers.

I've felt at times this week as if I were breaking down—shaky, physically odd. No identifiable illness, maybe just exhaustion and depression. It's no surprise that it descends on me like a wet, suffocating blanket as I walk to school.

This is my wall. This is where I usually decide to do something else. But change is inconvenient. I want to continue with the Tae Guk Kwon; I like the money of my present job; and I don't like the idea of resituating myself in Korea, especially without the help of the government program. Maybe I'll surrender to inertia.

I feel small, like a child. I have always felt like a child, looking for someone to love and take care of me. I've never developed a protective façade—a hard, smooth shell like so many other people. I've never even really known what I look like on the outside, and inside I'm constantly changing. At times I've thought this was a good thing—it has kept me real. I've admired people who have maintained their awkwardness, their vulnerability. But now I just feel stupid and pathetic. How can I be an adult to these students, many of whom were born more self-confident than I am now?

I've been wondering where my tears were. Nothing came out before. No release, no way to let down.

I dream about my beloved cats. I wrote a letter to their new owners not long after arriving in Korea, but it wasn't answered. Now I'm afraid to find out how they are—one or both may have disappeared or been hit by a car. In my sleep, they are there when I call them—furry and faithful, with loving, comforting eyes. I left them; I had to. So now there's no touching other than when Isabel washes my back at the bathhouse, or a few taps on my shoulder when she's making a point, or the scant comfort I get from the scouring referred to here as a massage.

I was frequently depressed in my teens and twenties. The clouds slowly broke up and cleared off in my late thirties. But now they're back. Hormones and fatigue were always the main components and probably are now. It has been eight months since my last period.

Entry 32
Portland, Summer 1999

    I had some spotting today. Was it my body responding to touch? I've had two massages in one week—the ten-minute one at the health fair and a full-body massage at a massage school. I went to the student clinic where you can get a fifty-minute session for twenty dollars. I have three more scheduled over the next three weeks. I'll also look into a second school. Maybe I can find a therapist interested in trading for T'ai Chi lessons.
    Touch makes my skin sigh and flow into rippling goose bumps. During times when I've gotten regular massages, I could *imagine* hands on my arms or feet or head and reproduce that same feeling of utter peace. I've lost my power to do this. I hope I'll regain it now that massage is in my life again.
    Swimming is another form of massage. The water strokes me. I swim three-quarters of a mile slow and easy. I use flippers for kicking and skim over the water effortlessly. Sometimes, because the Y's pool is covered by a plastic greenhouselike dome, there's a wavering net of sunlight in the soft blue water.
    I tried running a couple weeks ago, overdid it, and came down with a cold. Running is something I can't do now. There is no spring and no resilience in my legs. I've probably been swimming too hard too, even though the speed and distance are much less than what I did prediabetes. It's discouraging to see my athletic ability declining. Will I ever get it back? I've felt very tired these last weeks. The cramping in my legs has gotten worse.
    I had a dream about a week ago that I don't really remember, but I woke up from it with the message that I should eat corn. I looked up corn in my nutrition books, trying to find out what it contains that diabetics need. Maybe it's the Coenzyme Q10, an antioxidant that promotes metabolic reactions, transforming food into energy. Maybe it's the unique combination of nutrients in corn. I bought polenta and popcorn; last night I had corn on the cob. This morning the leg cramping

and the "pinging" of my muscles were significantly reduced. The usual sore throat that I have on waking was barely noticeable.

....

I finally called the editor at the magazine where I submitted my article on studying T'ai Chi in Korea. It's been six weeks. He was on the attack immediately with a series of gruff statements: "Didn't you get my E-mail? I thought I sent you a letter. I'm a very busy man—I'm on-line right now. Why did you wait six weeks?" Without missing a beat he dumped the guilt he was evidently feeling onto me. He was quite skillful—it was obvious he had some experience with this.

I thought I was being patient. I sent the article to him in mid-April. Their nearest deadline for submissions was May fifteenth. I theorized they might wait until then to select articles, so I called two weeks after the deadline. He told me he had decided not to use the piece soon after receiving it—the article was too personal, didn't have enough T'ai Chi in it, and my teacher was really a Wushu teacher. No argument from me on any of these points. (This is the man who had not approved of my second book on T'ai Chi because, my publisher informed me, he had thought it too was overly personal. Yet a couple years later he actively promoted a similar book written by a man.) I was just concerned about getting my photos back—I didn't have copies and I'd left the negatives with Kwan Jang Nim. The publisher didn't seem to know where my article was. The conversation ended with no apology (of course) and no commitment to locate and return the photos.

I cried furiously, and was furious that I cried. He sounded exactly like my book publisher. A stone-wall arrogance that doesn't admit any accountability. This is the way writers are treated. I let go of that second book. (I published the first one myself.) It was too irritating to attempt communication. I couldn't even get an answer to whether it had been reprinted. Why? Later, a new employee let slip that it had been.

I sent a terse E-mail to the magazine publisher. He replied within eight hours, saying the photos would be in the mail the next day. I was relieved.

I knew he might reject the article even after responding positively to my query letter. But it didn't occur to me that he could be so massively rude and inconsiderate. Obviously he had sent no E-mail and no letter. He threw up those statements in a knee-jerk reaction as shields to defend himself—like a little kid.

The incident scooped way down into my depression and hauled the worst of it up to the surface. Any discouragement that still lay buried was exposed. This is life, I thought—or too much of it, anyway. I didn't want to be a part of it. I called a friend in California and poured my unhappiness over her. (The price of being my friend now.) She's intelligent and a realist; she's a writer. She made a few attempts ("Read your own book, *Breathing Underwater*"), but in the end she couldn't contradict me. This was beyond the book, I said. This was someplace else. I blotted out her every attempt to be optimistic—or even tolerant—toward life.

I try not to do this—spread my misery to others. But my outburst was therapeutic. I drew on Sarah's friendship, partly out of blind necessity and partly because I thought she was secure and stable enough to maintain balance against the force of my hopelessness.

It occurs to me that this laying out of my life over the last few years is nothing but spreading misery. I hope there's more than anguish here—for myself and others. I write because I'm compelled to, the same as I always have. It smoothes out the jagged, prickly experience. Maybe the writing is a form of consolation, a way to make this period less overwhelming and more acceptable.

....

I take a nap almost every afternoon. For an hour or two, I "sleep like the dead." That's the way it feels—hands crossed over my heart, gravity pressing me into the mattress. My life force dormant, I listen to long, dragging breaths. There's a distinctive, short rattle noise (swallowing air?) that tells me I'm about to drop off. This is something new. It evokes the phrase "death rattle"—a sound that accompanies so many deathbed scenes in literature. I think of my mother saying she was afraid to go to bed at night for fear she might not wake up in the morning. She had a history of heart disease and was on so many life-draining medicines.

A nap produced this dream: A naked woman was being pushed and prodded through a rugged car wash. She was harried and buffeted, but not seriously hurt. (I took my car through the car wash two days ago.) Cleansing—the work of the tea and the supplements—is a harsh process. I'm forcing myself through, perhaps being overly fastidious about sticking to my exercise, diet, and supplement schedule. In this way the cure connives with my disease. Thus my need for naps.

There was a second dream during the same nap. A woman, assisted by a friend, was sending a probe into the earth—like a plumber using a snake to clean out drains. The flexible probe unwound from a big, turning drum, and went much further than she expected. Periodically she halted the process. But each time she resumed, the probe traveled even deeper. As the omniscient observer, I was able to see underground, to see that it was progressing from one "room" (like the den of a burrowing animal) to another. The probe split off and went several directions at once. Meaning? The process I'm undergoing is profound. I'm finding rooms in me that I didn't know existed. Perhaps I'm creating them. My roots are spreading, expanding my sources of nourishment. It reminds me of the spoon dream—the digging work also provides the sustenance.

What doesn't kill you is supposed to make you stronger. But eventually it *does* kill you.

I think I need to exercise in the evening after dinner and before going to bed. It would help clear out the excess blood sugar, give me a respite from it while I'm sleeping. I acquired a blood glucose monitor that I use mostly in the morning. The readings range from 250 to 350 and climb as the day goes on. Normal is 70 to 180.

I walk slowly, feeling a strange resistance in my thighs. Hills are a challenge. I keep my head down, watching the pebbles of the aggregate disappear beneath me. It gives me a sense of making good progress. My weight seems to be holding at about a hundred to a hundred and two pounds. I don't want to lose any more. My boniness, my skeletalness, scares me.

....

I'm furious with JFK Jr. for recklessly risking and losing the lives of two women. A naïve, arrogant man who didn't know his limitations. He had no right to take others with him.

It came to me during meditation that my anger is not just with John Kennedy, but with myself for running roughshod over my spirit during the last several years: Korea, grad school, city living. I'm violently inconsiderate, ignoring my nature—my limitations. My life as a potter, T'ai Chi teacher, and sometime writer suited me. It *was* me. It's the sort of life I'll have to return to.

I listened to Terry Gross interview A. E. Hotchner on National Public Radio about Hemingway. Hotchner, who was a friend of Hemingway's, thought the author chose to kill himself at the age of sixty-two because he didn't want to live if he couldn't live passionately, producing with the same power and originality as he had in the past. He had burned all his fuel, his creativity, his love of life. To us outsiders it may have seemed he had it great down there in those Florida Keys, a rich and famous author with a wife and kids. Not everyone is built to grow old. Some people are just done sooner.

My mother ran into a catch-22 at the end of her life. Her heart problems had caused her to suffer through several operations and she didn't want any more. When she told her doctor that no heroic measures should be taken to save her life, he replied that she was only saying that because she was relatively healthy—she'd change her tune when her life was really on the line. When he wanted her to submit to surgery again, she balked, telling him it constituted heroic measures. This time he said she was only saying that because she was ill and not able to think clearly. By his reasoning there were no circumstances under which she could have control over her own treatment or death. She died on the operating table. The doctor told me that immediately after repairing a section of an artery, the area just above would tear. Repair, tear, repair, tear. I had a vision of my enraged mother ripping apart her own arteries with her hands so that she could finally die.

....

Today I'll plan a strategy for sending my article out to the four other magazines that responded positively to my query. I want to reduce the time involved, which will mean sending out more than one at once.

I'm about done writing the history of the last fifty years of the Portland Police Bureau. I've spent many hours in the city archives and in the Planning and Research Division of the bureau, reading and taking notes on the annual police reports. Some are full of text and are even rather chatty. Others are just graphs and statistics. I feel I have to go through this exercise. How else can I get an accurate picture (from the bureau's point of view) of what has happened with them over five decades? I can tell from my conversations with current bureau employees that people have a hard time remembering correctly, and in any detail, events that happened even a year ago. Only a couple have maintained records of their sections—the Canine Unit and the Mounted Patrol. The publishing company is definitely getting its money's worth out of me. Who else would do this so thoroughly for so little compensation?

The most enjoyable part of the job has been my interviews with past police chiefs and the current one. They've been more objective and more critical of the bureau than any other sources I've used. Lots of good stories there. But I wonder how many will make it past a bureau-biased editor and turn up in the yearbook.

The people in the department have never been sure what to think of me—an outsider scrutinizing their history and their present. But they're used to me now. I have a small desk in a tiny storage room in Planning and Research. That's where I've read most of the annual reports—the ones not kept in the city archives in north Portland. I know I don't look well; I'm gaunt and pale; I drink a lot of water and snack frequently on nuts and seeds and apples. (*I* would wonder about me.) When I sit still for more than an hour, my head becomes foggy and my body stiff. I want to stay there and not move, just sink deeper while wondering if my brain is functioning adequately. The prospect of lunch at a bakery a couple blocks away rouses me. Fresh whole-grain bread, real butter, and delicious soup.

I leave my car about twelve blocks away from the justice building that houses the bureau in order to avoid paying for parking. My walk back to the car, which is uphill, is slow and steady, each step drawing my concentration. Thus I come and go from the Portland Police Bureau. They're cordial with sidelong glances mixed in. They tolerate me.

I learned a great deal from my time as an intern copyeditor at the engineering firm and gained confidence in my editing skills. I witnessed firsthand how crucial good writing is in international work. The firm was working on a feasibility study for a water treatment plant in a developing country. The part of the document that contained most of the text (as opposed to charts and numbers) was sent out without adequate editing—time and money restrictions prevented the company from allowing its editors to give it the proper attention.

The other two interns and I worked on this section, but they didn't use our input—we were just going through the motions, and I'm sure they thought we couldn't offer any improvement over what had already been done by the editor assigned to the project. The firm's senior editor had been told it was in a fairly finished state, but I thought otherwise. She was surprised at the number of changes I made, and she agreed with them. The other two interns, neither of whom was quite sure what copyediting was, went along with my suggestions.

The translators in the other country couldn't decipher this key section. As a result, the entire project was delayed and a long-planned meeting in Europe between the American firm's representatives and the country's officials had to be postponed. Overseas vacations set up by executives and their families were derailed.

If only people would wake up to how important producing clear English is (especially for international communication) and value the work of writers and editors. If we were paid even at the rate and timeliness of tradespeople like carpenters and plumbers it would be a big step up.

My T'ai Chi classes are going great. I'm back into the swing of teaching again and the students are starting to feel like friends. Besides working for the community college, I've begun teaching for Nike at their headquarters. The class is held outdoors at 6:15 on Tuesday and Thursday mornings. I get up at 5:00 and drive eight miles west to an opulent, parklike campus. We practice on a patio overlooking a large pond lined with willow trees, ornamental plums, and begonias. The air is warm but cool at the same time; the sky glows silvery pink and blue. The water, the fragrances, the V-shaped ripples flowing from the breasts of mother ducks trailed by their offspring are all distractingly beautiful. Sometimes I forget to stop the sequence where I'm supposed to—at the point where my instruction has stopped. It's embarrassing. (T'ai Chi, I tell people, is cultivating an extreme state of alertness.) In the fall I'll add more classes through the community college.

I keep remultiplying and re-adding the numbers (dollars per hour and number of hours), and thinking I must be making an error somewhere. It really does look as if T'ai Chi could be a subsistence living here.

In last night's class at the community college, around 9:00, I taught a ch'i-building exercise. I got home at 10:30 and went to bed at 11. I couldn't sleep. My wrists itched during the night—first the right and then the left. I'll have to tell my students to reserve this exercise for early in the day.

Ch'i. Everyone has it, everyone uses it. We are made of ch'i, we exist in an ocean of ch'i. We draw more into ourselves and learn to direct it with a practice like T'ai Chi. The martial arts train the body and mind to work together. Mental focus and imagination combine all my resources into a wave of concerted movement. Everything flows one way, and then everything flows back. Seamless, continuous expansion and contraction—body, breath, and imagination become all one thing.

But I'm dubious about the spectacular demonstrations of the external power of ch'i. I've heard and read and seen on videotapes accounts of a "magical" ch'i in which a master throws opponents dozens of feet without using muscular strength. I've often thought I'd like to participate in such a demonstration. I suspect the propelling of an individual or a row of people twenty or twenty-five feet is an example of collusion between master and pupils. When I've done Push Hands with masters, they have had to use brute strength to uproot me. One wrenched my shoulder and I gave way in order to avoid a dislocated joint. Another tore the skin on my inner arm. I haven't been able to detect any unusual force—just well-honed technique and greater size and strength.

Humans have a fierce need to believe in a guru and in that person's supernatural power. Do they think acknowledging its existence means they may possess it someday? Do they want to be allied with a powerful being—like the subordinate members of a wolf pack? Do they feel comfortable believing they are intrinsically less powerful and therefore don't have to compete for primacy? Anyway, as I said, I'd like to be one of the people a master tries to throw.

A couple of other students and I were standing with Kwan Jang Nim in his office one day. He lit a candle, then flicked his arm and fingers toward the flame in an effort to put it out. He was attempting a demonstration of his ch'i, and finally succeeded after several tries. But it could have been the air current he generated that did the trick.

I participated in a Push Hands workshop in California taught by an accomplished instructor and attended mostly by T'ai Chi teachers. We did a partner exercise in which two people faced each other with only a few feet between them. One closed his eyes while the other moved the back of her hand close to his torso until she felt she had penetrated his "space." Staying at least several inches away, she circled her hand around his chest and abdominal area, at times reversing the direction. After a few minutes we stopped the exercise and everyone was asked to report what they'd felt. All the participants—the passive and the active members of each pair—reported feeling warmth, or current, or vibration evidencing energy. Until it got around to me, the last person in the circle. I said I hadn't felt anything. The instructor smiled, looked pityingly on me, and said that with practice, I may notice something in the future. We then switched roles and tried the exercise again. Afterward, we listened to feedback. This time more people—especially the more experienced ones—were saying they hadn't detected anything. All it took was one person to give them permission to pay attention to what was really there instead of filling in what they'd like to be there or what they could imagine was there.

Yet I believe in ch'i. I think we are ch'i, and that's why we don't know how to look at it or notice it. I also believe that intense meditative practice enables us, over years, to become conscious of the movement of this white energy and to have more control over it.

Hours of sedentariness let ch'i become sluggish and stagnant. Vigorous exercise at the beginning and end of the day isn't enough. I need physical exercise every hour (or two at the most) to keep blood and ch'i flowing plentifully, nourishing me mentally, emotionally, and physically. Standing, walking, doing light exercise or chores have to be interspersed with anything that requires me to be still. That's why being a potter was so healthful—it was physical work combined with intellect and imagination. T'ai Chi combines those things too. Will I come full circle? Round the curve and turn back into myself?

Entry 33
Wonju, Summer 1997

    A typical Tae Guk Kwon class starts with at least twenty minutes of warm-ups led by a senior student. They include jumping jacks, push-ups, pike-position sit-ups, leg-strengthening exercises, and stretching.
    Kwan Jang Nim was walking among us one evening while we were doing forward splits. Here and there he hooked his foot under an ankle, raised a boy's leg off the ground, and forced him a little lower, a little wider. Each boy groaned in pain when it was his turn. I was thinking to myself that certainly he wouldn't do that to me—I'm an adult woman, a teacher, a guest in his country. But there he was standing beside me and lifting my ankle too. At least he did it with his hand and was gentler about it.
    We take turns counting from one to ten as we hold positions or keep track of the number of times we do something like hopping around in circles while in a deep knee bend. The boys exchanged glances and smiles when I first took my turn barking out the Korean numbers.
    After this phase, Kwan Jang Nim teaches basic skills to the entire class—falls, takedowns, kicks, and strikes. Then we divide up into smaller groups to practice the forms we're concentrating on.
    There's a Korean flag at one end of the room, flanked by Chinese characters. All the students line up in rows at the beginning and end of each class and shout some words I don't understand as a salute to the flag and Korea. I stand respectfully at attention (the same as I do at the beginning of every school day while the teachers pledge their allegiance). Finally we form a circle, make fists with our right hands, and cover them with our left (meaning "we all work together"). Then we bow slightly at the waist, look at each other, and say something else I don't understand. Essentially, we salute each other.

We deserve it. Intense training is a world unto itself. Those who participate in it know something about each other. It changes people, galvanizes them.

Fortunately I've had previous experience with hard training—as a competitive swimmer during my teenage years, I worked out before and after school. In the summer we practiced in outdoor pools with the water temperature as low as fifty-eight degrees. Pushing myself through pain is not new to me. I understand the necessity of doing that kind of work if I want to do well.

Kwan Jang Nim recommends at least fifty repetitions at a time of individual movements. I do some a hundred times a day. It's how I learn to put my whole body into them. I live with aches in my legs, arms, and abdomen. Getting up from my desk after sitting for an hour requires a painful process of restarting muscles. But overall I feel toned and fit, tightly wound and resilient. I have a sense of what I can only describe as an inner *readiness*.

With my teacher modelling in front of me, I was practicing one of the most difficult and complex movements in the sequence—Cover with Hand and Punch with Fist. This is a fast, whipping movement done in a very low horse stance. It's hot and humid nowadays and the fans in the dojang give scant relief. Sweat was pouring off my head, my uniform was sticking to my thighs. (I sweat more than anyone else in the dojang. It's embarrassing.) Suddenly a strong current of cold air swirled around me and penetrated me. This state of refrigerated grace lasted for half a minute while I marveled and took advantage of the evaporation of my fatigue. I poured this new shot of energy into the repetitions. My first cold flash!

Kwan Jang Nim wrote down some things for me about Tae Guk Kwon—principles of the movement. I took it to Mr. Lee and he helped me with the translation. There was one word he didn't understand and undoubtedly it's Chinese. I've read that about fifty percent of Korean words come from Chinese. Mrs. Song says newspapers can be a challenge for Koreans because they use so many Chinese characters. She added that learning their own language is difficult for Korean children partly because the grammar changes about every ten years.

....

I'm having a period. The day before it started, the thought popped into my head that I hadn't had one for about ten months, so I was probably through menopause.

I have a theory on why this is happening now. I think it's the physical contact with Kwan Jang Nim. He was touching me a lot on Monday evening—rearranging my limbs, propping up my leg for the leg lifts. When we went through the whole sequence, it was as if we were dancing together. On the way home from class I felt euphoric. I wanted to go running, charge up the hills at the base. This is astonishing given my usual energy level. Between the stress of living in Korea, the teaching, and Tae Guk Kwon, I don't ever feel an excess the way I did that night.

On Wednesday I almost didn't go to class because I was feeling so sluggish and headachy from the heat. But I'm glad I did. As I was stretching on the damp and malodorous floor mats (a combination of sweat and condensation), I was thinking there was no way he would touch me tonight. My feet and hands smelled noticeably from contact with the mats. So when he stood in front of me and reached out in a handshake-type gesture, I couldn't believe my good fortune. He was going to show me some takedowns. It's such a welcome sensation to be touched by him. And I don't often get to do the touching. The centers of our palms—the *lao gong,* both source and receiver of ch'i—pressed together. I was literally thrilled. It seemed brilliant of him to come up with this idea—an exercise that requires mutual touching. Again I left the class feeling uplifted, ebullient. As he frequently does, he gave me a sports drink ("Pocari Sweat") for the ride home. I had a lemonade from my refrigerator after I got back. Either it was something in the drinks (no caffeine was listed on either container—I checked) or just the stimulation of the touching, but I hardly slept at all. Still, I felt fine the next morning. He enlivens me.

Apparently my body doesn't require much encouragement to gear up for one more chance at procreation.

It occurs to me that this is a very nice way to relate intimately with a man—in a structured, contained environment that necessarily includes some touching. It's no threat to other ongoing relationships; no messy, confusing, perhaps disappointing sex. Pure essence. Maybe the strength of the connection with Kwan Jang Nim has something to do with the ch'i that both of us have cultivated over the years through our practices.

Last Friday something interesting happened on the way to the dojang. I told my teacher that I would be going to America. I'm sure he understood—this is an easy thing to say. I felt him jolt and, as if to cover this, he leaned over toward me and said, "What?" I registered his shock; I "got it" just as clearly (no, more clearly) as if he had spoken it. I quickly added that it was a vacation, I'd be back. He said he understood and tried to appear nonchalant. But I could tell he was feeling self-conscious, afraid he had revealed something he didn't intend to.

Now that I think of it, he probably caught the same sort of jolt from me one evening in the dojang. He introduced a young man to me who had studied Tae Guk Kwon in Beijing and told me he'd be my new teacher. The look on Kwan Jang Nim's face said he expected the surprise and disappointment that registered on mine. Fortunately the man was visiting from Seoul and was only around for a couple weeks. He was very annoying, partly because he was brusque and arrogant and partly because he didn't do things the way Kwan Jang Nim did. I didn't like having to change the form after putting in so much practice. But I would have resented any substitute.

I can be quite sensitive to people's subsurface emotional responses. Maybe this accounts for some of my mistrust of Koreans. I've often thought it's responsible for the general misanthropy I've felt throughout my life. I know too much about what's really going on inside people.

Koreans are psychically strong. If people aren't allowed to express themselves overtly, they learn to transmit and receive in other ways—as a blind person develops alternate senses like touch and hearing. Living in a state of deprivation can make a person very acute. The repressiveness of their culture holds Koreans in a continuous state of deprivation. Likewise, my almost unremitting discomfort here hones these qualities in me.

Dream last night: My teacher sitting back, smiling lazily and saying he'd like me to stay "a little while longer." "A little while!" I said. "I'm staying for a whole nother year!" Thinking: Don't you realize I need to stay that long, I'll be absorbing as much as I can during that time, and don't you want me to stay longer than a little while? Aren't I special to you?

What can be worse than indifference or friendly affection. I want passion in my life.

....

Last week—on July 14, 1997—my school received an official visit from representatives of the Ministry of Education in Seoul. This is Korea's highest educational authority. Weeks of preparation preceded this event. The school was painted inside and out, new brick walkways were laid, new plants and bushes appeared. Students missed classes in order to clean, especially to wash windows. Orchids in flaring celadon vases materialized in the entrance hall, the teachers' room, and the financial affairs office. Teachers and administrators worked late into the night, many nights, preparing documents.

One morning, a couple days before the event, Mrs. Song looked at me and said, "All the teachers are late to come to school these days. They are all very angry."

"Why?"

"Because there are so many lies."

"Who is lying?"

"Everyone," gesturing around the teachers' room. "It's the shame of Korea."

"What are the lies?"

"We are saying we have many after-school classes, but we only have a couple."

"Who made the decision to lie?"

"The education office in Chunchon. If our school does this, they will win an award and get much money."

I was surprised and grateful to be given this information. It's the sort of thing Koreans would normally try to hide from me. She said the teachers won't even tell their husbands and wives about this. I said I wouldn't tell anyone either. Now I wonder if I should have said that. Doesn't it make me part of the deception?

Last year my school won this award. They had several English conversation classes taught by American soldiers hired by Mr. Young. They don't exist this year because the administration didn't want to pay the extra money—teachers who come from outside the school are paid thirty dollars an hour as opposed to fifteen to eighteen dollars for teachers employed full-time by the school. Also, students and teachers were often unhappy with the quality of instruction they got from the untrained soldiers. Mr. Won, who took over Mr. Young's job, didn't want to pay premium wages to inferior teachers. Nevertheless, these classes were essential to winning the award and Chunchon wanted a repeat this year.

I realize now that the principal pressured me to take on so many extra hours because he was expecting me to assume all the English conversation classes that used to be taught by several people.

Anyway, documents were drawn up that listed seven extra classes including three in English conversation allegedly taught by three different soldiers. I don't know if the names belong to real people; maybe they're names of those who taught here before. The documents come complete with attendance records—96.8% to 99.8%. That level of attendance is a joke with my first-grade girls.

Even students were drawn into the lie. Mrs. Song was directed to show my English conversation text to everyone on the fake rosters. This was so they could sound credible if questioned about the classes by our visitors.

A puzzling incident took place that I see now is related to all this. Mr. Lee asked for the attendance record for my first-grade class. I held out to him a page dotted with zeroes indicating absences on particular days. There were more zeroes than empty spaces. He looked me in the eye and repeated that the head of supplemental lessons wanted me to take attendance each day. I was confused. I repeated that I did take attendance each day, and here's the record. After some hesitation, he accepted it. I guess I failed to take the hint that I should create another roster with only a few zeroes.

Mrs. Song told me "all schools lie a little, but this school lies too much." I asked if the officials expected the lies and were looking to ferret them out. She said yes. I decided to venture the opinion that some day Koreans would have to refuse to go along with this. Teachers *had* initially refused, she told me, but the principal had pleaded with them. (I'm not sure if the correct word was "pleaded." Knowing our principal, he demanded and threatened.)

"As you know from reading the paper" (she was referring to the English-language *Korean Herald*), "many officials in Korea are corrupt. My husband says all officials are corrupt. They take bribes."

The morning of the event I noticed the principal talking with Mrs. Jong at the far end of the teachers' room. My suspicions were up. I had been told several times that the officials were particularly interested in observing me teach. Not much later Mrs. Song said to me, "The principal is worried about your answer." I told her I thought that might be the case, and I was unsure what I would say if questioned about the conversation classes. I said I could tell the officials truthfully that I don't *know* the other teachers. She suggested I could say there *seem* to be other classes. I'm sure Mrs. Song was given the assignment of feeling me out on this.

The visit was scheduled from ten o'clock until noon. Students cleaned industriously until twenty minutes past nine, then went to their homerooms for final instructions in how to properly answer questions the officials might ask. Four pages of questions and answers had been distributed to all the teachers, including me. Mr. Lee told me he got up at 5:30 that morning to memorize the answers.

He never saw the visitors. Neither did I, other than to watch them get back into their cars. Apparently the principal decided he couldn't trust me. I taught fourth period that day with Mr. Lee and afterwards he drove us to a restaurant in the country for lunch. He said the only good thing to come of the visit was that we had an extra twenty minutes for lunch that day. I added that the school looked a lot better than it had before. Also, one of my second-grade classes had been unusually cooperative that morning.

Mr. Lee was in obvious turmoil over the lying. "Who will be the victim?" he asked, meaning who will be the whistle-blower? "I am very shy about it. But I am ashamed of Korea."

"Maybe a foreigner should do it because he or she can then leave the country and escape punishment."

"It makes me feel very sad to hear that from you. We are living in the twentieth century. This is not the nineteenth century. When will we progress? We want our children to live in a freer, more truthful world."

I told him about people I know in America who were recently arrested for demonstrating against cutting more old growth on lumber company property. In a democracy, the obligation to protest never ends. I mentioned the editorials I've been reading in the *Korea Herald* that keep admonishing people not to stir up trouble now—when the relationship with North Korea is so unstable and the economy is faltering. So when is the right time? People have to make trouble in order for change to happen. It doesn't have to be just one "victim," I said. People can band together. The teachers' union would be a good place to start.

Two teachers told me this in regard to my dispute with the administration over conversation class pay: "Don't think about it, there's nothing you can do about it." That's the coping method most Koreans have adopted. Learning a different approach won't be easy.

Not everyone on the staff of the *Korea Herald* is in tune with the editors. I found this Armenian proverb in its pages: "He who tells the truth must have one foot in the stirrup." And later this quotation from Margaret Fuller, the nineteenth-century

American journalist: "It is astonishing what force, purity, and wisdom it requires for a human being to keep clear of falsehoods."

Where am I in this? Should I—when in Korea—do as the Koreans do? If I had been questioned by the representatives of the Ministry of Education and told the truth, I would have exposed friends (and enemies) as liars. At the same time, lying isn't in my contract, and no one has the right to meddle with my self-respect or require me to be corrupt. I'm glad I didn't have to drink from that cup.

This is a country of secrets and lies, deceit and hypocrisy. Smiles, cheerfulness, and mild manners mask anger, hatred, and frustration. The stored aggression has all sorts of indirect outlets: pushing, shoving, hitting, reckless driving, and too much drinking.

....

My friend Mr. Shin, the former head teacher who is now working at a school in the country, took me to a Korean folk village on a Saturday afternoon. It was fascinating—a reconstructed preindustrial-age community peopled with mannequins in period dress. The inhabitants are performing mundane tasks, including sitting quite visibly in the outhouse. I was struck by the violence portrayed in so many of the scenes. I guess it should not have been a surprise. The schoolroom tableau depicts a teacher hitting a student with a stick; two farm workers are fighting in a plowed field; two young men, one with a wooden club in each hand, are beating up on a third; and then there's the cockfight. At the hub of the village is a thick stone phallus at least as tall as a man. Women are laying offerings at its base in the hope of bearing sons. (I know two male teachers whose wives recently had their first babies. Both were girls, and both men are disappointed.) It's all way to heavy on the yang side. If North Korea doesn't attack, it will be an anomaly.

....

This week I witnessed the worst incident of corporal punishment so far. I heard the first slap and turned to look. She was already sobbing when the other two slaps whipped her head to one side. They were down at the far end of the teachers' room. My reaction was involuntary. I rose from my seat and said out loud, "Now wait just a minute." The student's chin was on her chest, so the teacher grabbed her nose and wrenched it back up, the better to berate her. Then the slight, elderly man with the pinched face told the girl to kneel and walked out the door. It happened so fast. There was no time to get through the milling teachers and students and over to where they were. What would I have done? Grabbed his hand in midslap? I looked at the others in the room. A few had been paying attention, but everyone immediately turned back to business. They were laughing and talking as if nothing had happened, but a little too deliberately. An act for my benefit, to play it down? My vision was drawn by the very stillness of one teacher seated at her desk. Our eyes locked. Hers were glistening behind a fat layer of water and she looked as stunned as I felt. We spoke silently. A few heartbeats, then Mrs. Jong glanced at me and walked over to the student. She talked softly, seeming to offer some comfort. One of the girl's friends came in, pulled her back onto her feet, and led her out of the room.

....

Mr. Shin asked if I had ever eaten dog meat. I said no. He said he likes it very much and wants me to try it. I said I would not eat it and told him why. Koreans tell me the dogs are beaten for hours before they're slaughtered. There's a belief that the chemicals generated by the dogs in their fright and pain add to the flavor. I asked him if it was correct that the dogs are tortured. He laughed and said yes. Then he again attempted to convince me that I should try dog meat. I declined again, saying that I object to treating animals that way.

When the Olympics were held in Seoul in 1988, the government forced the restaurants that specialize in dog meat to either move out of town or close temporarily. They didn't want to offend foreign dog lovers. Dog meat is a traditional delicacy that embarrasses some Koreans and makes others defensive. I'm hoping this custom will die with the current adult generation.

....

I haven't been able to write about something I saw at least a month ago. I've barely been able to think about it. I feel my center revolt when I "look" at the scene in my mind. It's not sufferable, it's beyond suffering. And it carries the deepest guilt with it. Did I really see it? It will haunt me for the rest of my life.

I was riding to class in my Tae Guk Kwon teacher's van. We were winding down a narrow neighborhood street on our way to collect another student. Parked on the right side of the road was a pickup truck with a tall cage—at least five feet high and three feet wide—in the back. It was packed tightly with ratty-looking fur that was a caramelly brown color. Tufts of hair protruded from the metal mesh; dogs' heads emerged at every level. They were alive but not moving. They couldn't. How did someone get so many dogs into that small space? One wide-eyed head, a sweet and beautiful face, was squeezed out of the top of the cage, above all the others. My heart shrivels, the blood retreats from my hands as I write this. Its eyes landed on me. I saw complete, hopeless, bewildered disbelief in those eyes: Why is this happening? Why don't you help me? My hands flew up to cover my face. And we were past it.

My teacher looked over at me. I knew he would have seen nothing alarming. I put my hands down and looked straight ahead. It's not my country, I told myself.

If I pray for them, if I cry for them, will it help? I can only wish them a quick end.

It's a double sadness. For the poor, dazed, helpless dogs and for the lost humans who can do this. We're not fit to live.

....

In the summer of 1970, after graduating from college, I lived in Denmark. I was a student at the University of

Copenhagen for six weeks, then I worked for a potter on the mainland for another six weeks. I enjoyed being in Denmark. I respected and admired the Danes, and still do. I don't respect or admire this culture.

In a way it's good that Westerners are naïve about Eastern societies. We read or hear the plums of Eastern philosophies, add our own positive spin (as humans do to the exotic) and try to live our lives the way we think they live theirs. We end up distilling from another culture something that's better than the original thing. What we're learning from Asia, most of Asia itself doesn't know.

People in developed and relatively free countries—as groups and as individuals—have the precious opportunity to pick and choose the best elements from both East and West and apply them more broadly and consistently than they have ever been applied before. Believing (even mistakenly) that something has already been implemented in a country other than our own lends us confidence that we can realize it in our own lives too.

Korean culture is set up to make innovation like this difficult. The people in power have an elegantly simple strategy to maintain the status quo. They know that if you keep people busy enough and tired enough, they don't have the wherewithal to consider change. Koreans are in a constant state of anxiety. They can't plan; they can't think. They make bad decisions or no decisions at all. They just keep trudging. Like donkeys. That's the ethic here. How long, how uncomplainingly do you work? Not why are you working, are you effective, or what new thing are you creating or contributing.

A friend who worked in Nepal concluded that the purpose of tradition is to keep things from changing. There's a lot of talk in Korea about wanting to maintain their traditions, preserve them against the onslaught of foreign ways. Which traditions? Can they look at their customs, select the ones that are worth saving, modify others, and chuck the ones that need to go? I think my middle school girls can do this.

....

I had a dream that a young woman was killed in a boating accident. She had sheered off the steering wheel somehow. I embraced her father and a humming vibration passed between us, sternum to sternum. He and I shared the grieving.

A few times recently while lying in bed, my upper lip has convulsed and pulled up over my teeth—like a snarl. It's a brief, one-at-a-time tic. I think of a cornered, frightened dog trying to defend itself.

....

So I'm going home. I'll take care of business, see friends and family, join in some T'ai Chi practices, and link up with a former boyfriend I've been corresponding with. (How will that go?) His gentle, intelligent letters have helped keep me alive.

Will two weeks be enough? I'm afraid I'll be desperate, panicked, the time flying by, then back to this wretched country. But now—just being able to plan for this is making a big difference in my mood. I feel more peaceful. The difficult students seem to be cooperating better. Are they afraid I won't come back? Some of the other native English teachers have done just that, with no warning to the authorities. I can understand. If you followed the contract and gave them notice of your resignation, they would find some way to punish you in the interim.

Entry 34
Portland, Summer 1999

I was scanning the shelves at Portland's Central Library, looking for something to read. I recognized the name Ruth Prawer Jhabvala from stories in *The New Yorker* years ago, so I picked up several of her books. It turned out to be one of those serendipitous encounters. Much of what she writes echoes my Korean experience. Her stories are about foreigners in India, Indian natives (many of whom have spent long periods abroad), and Indians of all castes who have never left their villages or cities. By now I've read everything of hers I can find.

Prawer Jhabvala was born in Germany of Polish parents and was educated in England. She married an Indian architect and they went to India to live and raise their children. I read avidly an introduction she wrote to a group of short stories called *Out of India*. Her candor was stunning. She begins by saying she has lived in India most of her adult life. Her husband and children are Indian, but she is not, and "less so every year." If her family were not there, she would not live in India—it doesn't suit her. She is reluctant to seek out the company of other European women married to Indians, because they all "suffer from the same disease," and "who is to listen to whose complaints?"

There are many things to be said about India, she tells her readers, but the most important thing is that the country is extremely poor and backward. The only excuse for Westerners to be in India, Prawer Jhabvala believes, is to try to be of some help—as doctors or social workers, for instance.

This reminded me of Mr. Young's warning not to think of Korea as a developed country. Korea is much wealthier than India, with more widespread development, but Koreans seem unsure at times whether they want Westerners in their country as peers and colleagues or as Peace Corps workers.

Prawer Jhabvala confused me when she closed her essay by saying that she sometimes visits Europe, but then gets bored there and wants to return to India. This was the only part of the essay that rang false. I notice the bio on more recent dust jackets says that now her children are grown, she and her husband divide their time between London and New York.

....

It seems everyone I know has either taught English in Korea or is related to someone who has. Is it money or wanderlust or both? Especially during my first year there, Americans and Canadians were hard-pressed to find employment in their countries. Sometimes I felt we were preying on the Koreans.

A precocious third-grade student accused us of this when I was a guest in her class. She said Americans only came to Korea because they couldn't get jobs at home—not because they had any appreciation for Korea or its culture. She seemed to be willing to grant me an exception because I had just finished saying the usual things while introducing myself: As a student of Tae Guk Kwon, I'm interested in Asian culture, and as a potter, I admire Korean ceramics as some of the best in the world (the girls applauded that one).

But those aren't the reasons I went to Korea. I went for the money. I stayed for the money (and for the Tae Guk Kwon). I harbor guilty feelings. Not just for myself but for all the people who have flocked to Korea, many of them equipped only with an English-language upbringing. I argue with these feelings by telling myself they hired us after all; we didn't hire ourselves. In their zeal to meet ambitious quotas, the Korean government often overlooked its own employment standards. Many people that I went through orientation with didn't even have bachelor's degrees—including Percival and Charlotte. If some of the native English teachers in Korea are incompetent and arrogant, the Koreans bear responsibility for their selection.

A British man in his sixties so offended Korean English teachers during a two-week-long workshop that they boycotted his final classes. Some of the teachers told me he continually ridiculed them for their clumsiness with English. Of course he didn't speak a word of Korean and when they asked why he didn't try to learn, he told them he wouldn't waste his time on such an obscure and unimportant language. If he were going to spend time studying a language, he said, he would study one that would be useful in the world—like Japanese. Thank god he wasn't an American.

I remember talking to an American teacher in the hallway of a university in Chunchon—it was during a break in classes in that same winter workshop for Korean English teachers. He was deploring the fact that every gathering of Western teachers seemed to degenerate into angry diatribes against Koreans. I had only been in Korea for a few months and I was enjoying my classes at the workshop. The students were lively, friendly, and generous in their appreciation for my carefully planned lessons. He and I were feeling big and mature and above the narrow-minded bitterness of the others.

But as time went on I joined the vituperation—in conversations with other Westerners, and even more so in my inner dialogue. Self-reproach was stirred into this winding-up vortex like subtle seasoning. If I hated the place and its inhabitants so much, what right had I to be there? My fellow complainers and I were not just hating Korea but ourselves too—for having no other place to be.

An Indian woman in Ruth Prawer Jhabvala's short story "The Man with the Dog" says precisely this:

> Sooner or later they always come to this subject, and then their faces change, they look mean and bitter like people who feel they have been cheated by some shopkeeper and it's too late to return the goods. ...How I hate to hear them talk this way, saying India is dirty and everyone is dishonest. ...Once they have started on this subject, it always takes them a long time to stop, and the more they talk the more bitter they become, the expression on their faces becomes more and more unpleasant. I suffer, and yet I begin to see that they too are suffering, all the terrible things they are saying are not only against India but against themselves too—because they are here and have nowhere else to go—and against

the fact which has brought them here, so far from where they belong and everything they hold dear.

A professor here in Portland gave me a handout on the stages of culture shock according to Peter Adler. It's a chart taken from an article he wrote in 1975, and provides an interesting comparison with my reactions. In the first stage, people are curious and delighted with every new thing they see and experience. The phases progress through confusion and withdrawal; anger and rejection; empathy and self-confidence; and culminate in trust, humor, and love. Finally "social, psychological and cultural differences are accepted and enjoyed. The individual is capable of exercising choice and responsibility and able to create meaning for situations." This is a fairy tale ending. What do I do with my critical judgment? My common sense? My compassion? Just stuff it? We're not supposed to criticize other cultures now. But I hate the harshness, the meanness, the rudeness of Korea. I hate the way they treat women and poor people and dogs.

This doesn't mean that I'm unable to see the flaws in my own society. But at least those flaws are more publicly exposed and generate a constant flow of argument and attempts at solutions. The tug and pull of diversity and restiveness and the creativity they spawn are intrinsic to the American milieu.

We have the same problems Korea has, but because there are institutionalized ways to bring about change, they often exist to a lesser degree. And everything is a matter of degree.

It's not a difference of East and West or North and South. It's the difference between freedom and repression. Repression breeds dishonesty and corruption: Power always has the right-of-way; justice doesn't exist; people are brought up in a culture of lies. Asia has at times hidden behind the euphemism of "Asian values" when its policies have been attacked by the West. This is merely the people in control wanting to be left alone so they can stay in control. It's corruption preserving itself.

Some cultures *are* better than others.

I stopped going to see Marilyn after two months (ten visits). At the end, our relationship felt adversarial to me. She was impatient with my questions and barely managed to tolerate my suggestions. She seemed threatened by the knowledge I was acquiring about diabetes through my reading. (When I asked her about the cramping in my legs, she waved at the books on her shelves and said glibly, "If you read a book about diabetes, I'm sure you'll find something about leg cramps there.") I don't want to be insulin dependent like my sister and deceased cousin so I was afraid to ask this question, but I did: "Why do you assume I'm type 2 instead of type 1?" "Because of your age," she replied. "Only children get type 1." It was a relief to hear her say that.

I called the clinic of a college of naturopathic medicine in Portland, talked to the receptionist about my situation, and got a recommendation for a female physician with some experience in diabetes. I think I can trust someone connected with a teaching institution.

I like my new physician, Maureen. She's in her forties somewhere, long and thin, with a casual but patrician way of looking and dressing. The bags under her eyes remind me of my own and my father's and provide a sense of familiarity. She seems intelligent and thoughtful, and assures me she has successfully treated diabetics before. By the second visit she had prepared a two-page treatment plan that includes diet instructions and numerous supplements.

Some of the diet restrictions are based on the new book *Eat Right for Your Type*. I'm skeptical. Is this another fad? Isn't my diet restricted enough already? Further limitations are another source of stress—the root cause of my disease. Maureen says the father of the man who wrote the book spent many years testing various foods with each blood type. Seems to me there's a basic problem here. We almost never eat one food at a time, and foods interact biochemically. Also, he doesn't address the Rh factor. I'm A negative.

It worries me that a series of homeopathic drugs she's prescribing preclude taking basic antioxidants like A, E, and C. Whether a person is ill or well, I think it's important to take vitamins. Ever since I went on the healing program twenty years ago to deal with carcinoma-in-situ, I have taken them daily. Now I'm especially concerned about protecting my eyes. But I'm going along with the program, conscientiously taking my supplements when they're supposed to be taken—some with food, some away from food.

I'm eating as much as I can hold but weigh only 102 with clothes on. Still insatiably hungry and thirsty much of the time. Generally I only test my blood sugar in the mornings. It's still between 250 and 300, sometimes higher. It goes up and down with stress just the way blood pressure does. If I test in the evening, the monitor invariably reads "Hi," meaning over 600.

....

This dream: a basketball spinning on the tip of a finger whose last segment is missing. A week after seeing that image in my sleep, an optometrist who checked my eyes (no damage so far) was responding to my opinion that the diabetes was triggered by stress. He made that spinning gesture with a finger as he talked about people these days trying to keep too many plates going at once. And in the dream, was the missing end of the finger a warning of what happens to diabetics who don't reduce the stress in their lives and whose blood sugar isn't brought under control? The amputation of fingers, toes, legs... My aunt, a type-1 diabetic from childhood, chose to die when she was in her early fifties. She refused to start down that road, beginning with the amputation of an infected toe. That same optometrist advised me to stick with Maureen's treatment program for a while. "Ride that pony" was the way he put it.

....

One of these months I'll be paid my pittance for the police history. The publisher and the bureau have to approve the narrative. I asked for more money—having put in over two hundred hours means I get paid less than five dollars an hour— well under minimum wage. But neither the representative for the police nor the publisher's editor would budge an inch. I'm sure the editor knew ahead of time—much better than I did—the amount of work that would be required. I've been exploited. At one time I was excited about the idea of writing a series of articles on the various divisions of the bureau—the Canine Unit, the Mounted Patrol, the extinct Women's Protective Division, for instance. But now I want nothing to do with them.

I'm sending out resumes for editing jobs, both local and distant. T'ai Chi teaching is going beautifully. It hardly seems possible, but the income from teaching is allowing me to scrape by. I'm making money *my* way.

....

No grad school course this summer, and I'm luxuriating in the reduced pressure. I've been having the usual dreams about driving a car that's out of control because it has no brakes. Now, finally, I'm getting some breaks. I don't have to be doing something "productive" every moment. I can sit. Stare. Write. Read. Sip.

Recent dreams have had softened male images in them, males I love and trust who comfort me. Is my yang side softening, my yin side replenishing itself so that the two can meet as balanced equals? No one force bullying the other.

Maybe society is the disease and diabetes the cure. I remember this sentence appearing inside my head while in my usual state of duress in Korea: "Nothing that a good illness wouldn't cure." Illness forces me to stop, rest, reassess, change.

A new life seems to be materializing, growing up around me. I stepped out of the car the other day and fleetingly "saw" it, felt it—like the petals of a flower surrounding my feet. The forms were translucent green and thick like a succulent, low and not fully formed. Oh. They resembled the bottom leaves of an artichoke, the lotus-like symbol that's been hovering over my life since it appeared in a dream in 1983. It was carved into the back of a wooden throne with an inscription: "This symbol be seen." And I have seen it repeatedly since then, in many different media. This is the first time for it to appear as a waking vision.

My spirits are inexplicably high at the same time that my body is enervated and my head clouded and prone to forgetfulness and omissions. I often feel euphoric—in love with virtually everything around me. A pervasive optimism, a tingling anticipation. I'm serene with regard to money. Why? Nothing has improved in that quarter.

I experienced this once before—this "in love" feeling without being in love with a man. It was the fall of 1990. Fall's my season, but that can't—now or then—fully account for my soaring good will, my sunlit, sparkling blue serenity.

This time, is it the seratonin in my diet (the tablespoon of vinegar I take each morning)? The St. John's wort I prescribed for myself? Did the orum that Marilyn gave me in May finally kick in more than two months later? Is it just being able to finally relax a little?

At least psychically, the wheel is up now.

Entry 35
Wonju, Fall 1997

    The trip back to Korea was the usual eighteen hours of confinement in oxygen-depleted air. I returned just in time for another wave of heat and humidity. As little as a week ahead of time, no one knew when the semester would begin. Now that it's underway, the teachers and students are already drooping. During one of my classes a sleepy (sleeping?) student in the front row sat with her head on her desk, arms folded as a pillow. The friend sitting beside her tickled her under the chin, slowly and gently. I envied that dozing student, and I didn't interrupt them.

    Kwan Jang Nim has been wearing a full sweat suit with the jacket zipped up to his neck. His senior students have been doing the same. He has no air-conditioning in his van, but travels with all the windows rolled up. In this suffocating weather, what could possibly be his reasoning? What is the tactic, the logic behind the tactic? Clearly it's a way of dealing with heat that this Westerner is not familiar with. I've wondered if the rolled-up windows are meant to make people think his van is air-conditioned. Koreans can be so materialistically competitive.

    A few days after I got back, I distributed the small gifts I'd brought from the U.S. to the administrators and some of the teachers at school. I also placed cold drinks on all the desks in the main teacher's room. It's customary in Korea to bring back numerous inexpensive gifts to friends and coworkers after a trip.

    The vice principal noticed I had put a drink on Mr. Han's desk and said to me in English, "Mr. Han is in paradise." Thinking he meant the restaurant—one the teachers like that has an English name spelled in Hangul—I asked if Mr. Han had taken an early lunch. Another teacher who speaks some English was sitting nearby. She looked up at me and said, "Dead." I didn't get it at first, thought I wasn't understanding her English. She repeated, "Dead. Dead." What a jolt! Mr. Han was such a lively, relatively young (early 40s?), respected teacher with a famous sense of humor. "A good man," as the Koreans would say.

He and another teacher at my school, whom I didn't know, were in a car accident. Both were killed. Two people in the other car were critically injured. Mr. Han was speeding—sixty miles per hour in a construction zone with a speed limit of twenty-five. He'll be missed by everyone. He had a number of students professing their love for him every day. His most ardent admirer sat in the chair at his desk for the entire day after the accident. No one tried to move her.

....

The advent of E-mail: Elizabeth's son, Ho-chang, helped me get set up just before I left to go to the U.S. I see the thin stream of electron impulses as a nourishing lifeline, like a tube for intravenous feeding.

....

The two weeks at home were a blur of friends and family laced with jet lag. The experience was a bit frantic, but it replenished me.

My male friend and I camped in a forest close to the ocean. I woke in the middle of the night feeling frightened after a bad dream. I opened my eyes and looked toward a wall of the tent that was opaque (not one of the walls with screens). I could see through this solid wall. In midair under the trees about fifteen feet away was a bright circle of white light, and in the light was a man's squarish, solid face. His black hair was parted in the middle and either it was pulled back or it stopped at about chin level. He looked robust and happy; he was smiling mischievously at me. I could see his hands because they were raised to the side of his face, fingers curled, as if he were holding a small invisible flute. I kept checking that I was awake. I was aware the light shouldn't be there. I knew I shouldn't be able to see through the wall of the tent. While I watched him, I noticed that there was a pulsating, wavelike light inside the tent, not so bright as the one illuminating the man's face. I blinked my eyes, wondering what was wrong with them. The man didn't frighten me, but the strangeness of the occurrence worried me. I wondered how long it would last. I suppose the whole thing took no more than a minute. Then the white circle of light in the trees faded, and the lively face with it. In their place was a deep red glow that died out in a matter of seconds. Finally, to my relief, the light in the tent disappeared.

I went back to sleep and dreamed about a group of deer—both bucks and does—outside the tent. They transformed into people and joined hands in two concentric circles. I was part of one circle; the friend who slept beside me was part of the other. Everyone walked toward the center, contracting the enclosed space. Then we backed up and the space expanded. As we did this repeatedly, we chanted two lines as if from a poem or song—one line as we contracted, the other as we expanded. I thought I would remember the words, but I didn't.

A similar experience happened to me in the last house I lived in before going to Korea. I woke up scared from a nightmare and saw a circle of white light on the ceiling. Characters that looked like runes swirled in a luminous three-dimensional fog. That vision really did frighten me (why this one and not the one in the forest?) I kept trying to verify that I was indeed awake while nervously eliminating possible mundane sources of the light—my neighbor's headlights, a reflection off a mirror? I was grateful when the light vanished after too many long seconds.

Entry 36
Wonju, Fall 1997

Mrs. Song informed me that the school's lying paid off. They won the award for the most supplemental classes and (perhaps this was the true purpose of the charade) the principal has been promoted to the provincial office in Chunchon. He'll finish out his career there. We suddenly have a new principal—a woman, which is a rarity at that level of administration.

....

I didn't realize until after the fact that I missed my chance to be bribed. There was an English speaking contest at school this morning. The English teachers relied on my judgment to choose the winner, and it's a good thing because otherwise they would have come up with a choice that was way off. The girl I ranked a close second was very upset and cried a long time. All the girls worked hard, but I know she was counting on winning. I felt sorry for her. She and another competitor came to my house last Thursday after school. She told me she had a present for me and would give it to me on Saturday—today, the day of the contest. I'm not surprised it didn't show up—it must have been intended as a little insurance, the customary Korean bribe. In addition to being disappointed, the girl may be angry with me for not getting with the program and playing by the rules.

I like the student who won. She's strong and unpretentious. And boy can she memorize—a real asset in a speech contest. It frees her to concentrate on the drama of the folk tale and on the voices of the animals—the rabbit and the tiger. Her confidence in her memory gives her poise. All the girls held it together pretty well.

....

Mrs. Song has been surprisingly disclosive about her personal life. She's married and has a two-year-old son. Her husband, a high school science teacher, lives and works in Seoul. He generally doesn't come to Wonju for the weekends, only for the longer holidays. Mrs. Song used to live with her in-laws, but she moved into her own apartment with her son because she decided "it was better to die than live with my husband's parents." I think she meant it literally. Her father-in-law "cursed her" for it. I'm guessing this translates as yelled and swore at her.

Within a little over a year, Mrs. Song has been pregnant four times. Three ended in miscarriages, and one in abortion. "My womb is not healthy," she says. She got the abortion because she exposed herself to radiation while holding her son for his chest x-rays and didn't learn until afterwards that this could harm a fetus.

Two weeks ago, Mrs. Song looked very ill. She told me she was one-month pregnant and probably experiencing a miscarriage. She had a note from her doctor saying she should take two weeks off from work. She didn't want to approach the vice principal with it because "he doesn't like this sort of thing" (female problems). Instead she went to see the new principal, who was receptive and even suggested taking a whole month off. This would have allowed the school to bring in a substitute teacher—something they can't do if a teacher is absent for any less than a month. The catch is that the officially allotted time for a miscarriage is two weeks, and that's all the doctor could vouch for. I told Mrs. Song that I would gladly help fill in for her during the two weeks and I thought the other English teachers would feel the same way. She wasn't so sure; everyone is overworked and she feared (to be honest, I did too) that they'd resent her for adding to their burden. In the end she made do with the four-day weekend that all of us got for a national holiday.

Mrs. Song's little boy has a congenital heart disease believed to have been brought on by progesterone injections taken to stave off nausea during her pregnancy. He's a sweet-natured and beautiful child with decidedly limited energy. I see him frequently because, in order to spend as much time with him as possible, she brings him to the dinners we teachers have to attend after school. She's quite worried about him. She feels her husband doesn't appreciate the seriousness of their son's disease or the energy required to care for him. Perhaps this partially accounts for the fact that after every school holiday (after each visit to Wonju by her husband) Mrs. Song finds herself pregnant again. Her husband doesn't seem to notice what's evident to me—she isn't ready to be distracted by another child and what would inevitably be a very difficult nine months, if she could hold on to the baby that long.

At her request, I used the Internet to research hospitals that specialize in her son's condition—Tetralogy of Fallow or TOF. I discovered that the Cleveland Heart Clinic has the best reputation, so I contacted them by phone and was told the doctor there needed to see certain test results and surgery reports (the boy has had several operations already) in order to assess his condition. Mrs. Song dreaded discussing the possibility of a second opinion with her doctor in Seoul. But she did. He told her Cleveland is known to be the best heart hospital in the world, but the hospital in Seoul is second best. He refuses to send the records.

I composed a letter to the doctor in Cleveland asking him to write to Mrs. Song's physician and request the necessary information. I thought the Korean doctor would be more likely to honor a request from a peer at a prestigious hospital. Mrs. Song intended to fax it immediately, but was delayed because the school's office was closed that day. In the meantime she showed the letter to Mrs. Yu (the English teacher who resents me so much). Mrs. Yu said our tactic would make the Korean doctor angry and suggested asking him again in person. I'm sure she's right, but either way, the man's feathers will be ruffled, and he'll be irate.

Mrs. Song called me at home in the evening to tell me why she hadn't sent the fax. She was crying. She said she was afraid she'd start crying when she tried to talk with her physician. I suggested her husband do it. She told me she is the one who is "sincere" about their son, not her husband.

That's where the situation stands. I'm tempted to try to persuade her to send the fax, but feel I have to restrain myself. By helping her make waves, I'll likely add to her hardship, with nothing gained for it.

....

I wrote this to friends in the U.S.:

Women have a difficult time here. A Korean English teacher took me to a choral concert last week. She's twenty-nine, has a husband and a year-old baby. On the way to the concert, she said, "Love is good, but sometimes after marriage love disappears." She said she would not marry if she had it to do over—she's too tired and has no time to herself. Almost all Korean women do all the work of maintaining the household. Teachers in middle school work five and a half days a week, a minimum of nine hours a day. This particular teacher's workday extends much longer because she teaches ninth graders who are being prepared to apply to the life-course-determining high schools.

Often people here ask me what I think of Korean men. I say how helpful some of the English teachers have been as colleagues. (I know this isn't what the questioners are getting at.) Then I say I don't think Korean men would like American women because they're too independent and expect a lot from a man. (Dodging the question again.)

....

Mr. Lee just told me about the sensation generated by Donna Ferguson's coming into the teachers' room in shorts last summer while I was in the U.S. Women aren't supposed to reveal skin that way. I don't get it—I see women in shorts and extremely short skirts here all the time. Maybe it's a class difference—a teacher doesn't dress that way. And I think there's some envy there too. Donna's long, slim legs are highly prized by Koreans. The women probably resent an attractive Western female who has an impact on their males. The men probably see her as someone who's not under proper control.

....

I haven't written about my Mt. Ch'iak adventure with Percival (Charlotte wasn't up for a climb to the peak). One Sunday afternoon we got onto the bus that travels the thirty-minute route to the mountain. We were smooshed in with fifty other happy hikers and because Percival and I were some of the last to board, we were standing in the aisle, holding onto ceiling straps right behind the driver. The people behind us were exerting forward pressure. The bus driver kept swinging his forearm, swatting Percival and trying to get him to move back. We *couldn't* move back. Percival was fuming. Finally he hit the driver's arm and said, "Stop bloody hitting me!" The driver was stunned to get an equal and opposite reaction. He grumbled to himself, shook his head, and slowed the bus. I thought he might stop and tell Percival and me to get off, but he didn't. Percival glared and planted himself, waiting for the driver to try it again. He's about had it with Korea. He's in worse shape than I am. As far as I'm concerned, what Percival did was more harshness in a harsh culture, and the wrong way to respond. It was depressing.

Despite the ragged start, I enjoyed being on the mountain again and having something to do, someone to talk to. Percival told me he wanted to visit the U.S. and would even consider living there (!) or in Canada. He says he's not eager to resettle in England—"It's a mean country." I can see Canada, but the idea of Percival settling in the U.S. is mindboggling.

I made dinner last night for Isabel, Percival, and Charlotte. I was glad for the company even though P and C managed as always to get in their barbs toward Americans and Koreans. (No regard for the presence of both.) They showed some restraint concerning Americans until I beat them in a British word game. That was too much for them—they let loose. I can only observe and be amused, and keep my distance.

....

I went to Seoul by myself for a day. I had three missions—to buy books in English at Kyobo Bookstore, to buy some traditional (but updated) Korean clothing, and to have lunch at T.G.I. Friday's. I accomplished all three. The day before going, I made a phone call to Jil Gyung I, the clothing store, and speaking entirely Korean, managed to get directions to the shop. I navigated by bus, subway, and taxi to get from place to place with no missteps. (Ever since I was a kid, I've gotten a kick out of being able to get around in a strange city.) Lunch was good, but not great. It cost over twenty dollars.

....

I've visited various potters and potteries here (including the pottery village of Ichon). The work is nice. All the ingredients are there—beautiful glazes, graceful shapes, refined decorating techniques. But it quickly becomes boring. The few times I've run into work that diverges from the traditional, it looked tentative and scared. The artists don't have enough practice being creative. I have seen a few delightful, playful exceptions.

....

I started noticing allergies when I was in the U.S. and they got much worse when I returned to Wonju. I'm also experiencing more frequent hot flashes, and headaches that appear every week or two and last for a day (if I'm lucky).

I keep thinking about the trucks that were crawling through Wonju's streets last summer, spewing a thick white fog. I believe it was an insecticide aimed at mosquitoes. The smell was pungently petrochemical. I never seemed to get my windows closed fast enough. Did it poison me? Koreans don't spare the chemicals—on food or on the environment. In a related vein: I checked out the ingredients in multiple vitamin tablets. They include nicotine!

Right now I'm mostly sore from the new kicks, jumps, and stretches that I'm doing in the dojang. I go to the army base right after school and on weekends to practice the falls and flying kicks that I'm learning, as well as Tae Guk Kwon. It's a bit raw, windy, and cool, and there's not much light left by the time I'm done with school, but the grass makes a relatively soft landing. Soon I'll have to move into the gymnasium. I wonder what the Korean guard on the hill about a hundred yards away thinks of this flailing, thrashing woman.

I'm having a hard time feeding myself. I can't seem to keep food on hand and what I eat isn't very healthful. By Saturday, I'm extremely hungry. I've started taking the bus across town to a large, well-stocked grocery store. The local ones are more and more unappetizing. They smell of rotting vegetables; they're cluttered and cramped and not very clean. There are mouse droppings on the cornflake boxes in one tiny store. And cornflakes are one of my staples. I need to make more regular trips to the bigger, brighter, cleaner (more Americanlike) store and provide myself with some appealing food.

I'm suffering most, I think, from skin hunger. It's increasingly difficult to relax by listening to music or by conjuring up memories of massage or of being in the presence of soothing people. When I was getting regular massages in the U.S., I could revisit that experience in my mind when I needed to, and bring goosebumps to my skin. That sort of thing is too distant now, too faint to be revivable. The other day a student stroked my hair and lightly brushed my neck with her hand. It was a millisecond. But I used it, reexperienced it again and again. Any time anyone touches me now, I practically go into a trance. Sometimes Isabel touches me, and more and more her intention seems sexual. An example: While we were in the hot tub, she moved in too close and slid her hand along my side and down to my hip. I'm repulsed. I've been giving her a lot of leeway, thinking "cultural differences," but I don't see other women doing any more than linking arms or holding hands. So now I'm uneasy around her, always poised to fend her off, trying to make the limitations clear. Yet I don't have the courage to say anything directly. Confronting someone about something so personal has always been difficult for me. I'm afraid of offending the person and losing the friendship altogether. Is this a new tactic of

Isabel's to connect herself with an American? Maybe she's testing out a theory that my reason for not marrying is that I'm a lesbian.

....

About two weeks ago the head teacher started making some clumsy efforts to communicate with me—in a friendly way for a change. A couple times he told me how nice I looked or how young I looked in a particular color. I thought maybe the change in attitude was the result of my telling Mrs. Song I might leave Korea one semester early. (Like me or not, I'm a bit of prestige for the school.) But I think I know now what he was up to. His son got married last weekend, and he wanted the American to show up at the wedding. Most of the other teachers went. He wields some power—I expect attendance was required. It never occurred to me to go.

....

A disturbing issue with my apartment. My neighbors (there are two apartments up here on the second floor, and a Korean family has just moved in) asked me to open their door for them, saying they had forgotten their key. I insisted my key was different. They insisted it wasn't. I was polite but adamant and not a little confused. Now I realize I was afraid to test the possibility that our keys *are* the same and that not only my landlord can enter my apartment when I'm gone, but they can too, and they know it. In such a security-conscious country, why would locks be set up this way? The landlord must have decided it was convenient for him.

Did I mention that he came to my door and started talking rapidly about utility bills? I couldn't follow him, so I referred him to Mr. Won at school. Mr. Won told me Mr. Go claims I agreed from the beginning to pay him 50,000 won every month for water and electricity. I told him I'd been paying the bills Mr. Go showed me, and the total always came to less than 10,000 won. I wrote down everything I had paid since I moved into the apartment and gave the list to Mr. Won, who talked to Mr. Go again. That was the end of that. Just an attempt by my landlord to extract some extra money from me. He may have figured that with my original guide teacher gone, Mr. Won would take his word over mine. There will be no repercussions to him for his barefaced lie. No sense in my even getting angry about it. This is business as usual here.

....

I've stopped collecting Korea-bashing articles from the *Korea Herald*. I guess my outrage is fading. What's the sense in gathering evidence of the meanness and corruption; what have I been trying to prove? To whom? I'm finally accepting the way things are.

I've always seen this activity of mine as neurotic. I have a view of myself from above (a camera mounted on the ceiling?) while I cut out the articles critical of the government, big business, the school system, and the rigid, belligerent patriarchy (written by Koreans themselves! agreeing with me! vindicating my own disgruntlement!). I write the date of the article on the top, fold it, and slide it into a plastic bag with all the others. How, when, why did I think I would use these things in the future? In what court?

....

On the inside of one of the double doors to my armoire, I've posted a piece of paper, a handmade calendar that charts all the days remaining in my stay in Korea—now at 122. I cross off a day each morning like a prisoner in a cell. When I was showing Isabel my new clothes from Jil Gyung I, I forgot about that paper. She glanced at it, then later—just before she left—asked to see the clothes again. I think she wanted to take another look at the calendar, see if it was what she thought it was. I opened the other door. I'll have to be more careful.

....

I have never had much tolerance for unhappiness. I've always tried to fix things—often by withdrawing from difficult circumstances. Yet I've led a life with long stretches of unhappiness. (For one thing, I don't fit in.) Now I seem to be determined to bear the suffering instead of seeking to change it or avoid it. Is this an improvement? It feels self-destructive. I don't seem to know when is the appropriate time to struggle and when is the appropriate time to endure.

....

I'm reading Olivia Goldsmith's *Bestseller,* and I can't tear myself away from it. It's such a telling, hilarious look at the publishing industry. Books are such lifesavers. I would die of loneliness without them.

Entry 37
Portland, Fall 1999

This is what I'm awake and crying about in the middle of the night: It's been seven weeks since I turned in the police history to the publishers, and I still haven't been paid. It's been nine weeks since I started teaching at Nike, and they haven't paid me yet. The community center where I'm teaching doesn't pay until the end of the eight-week session. I'm supposed to be paid mileage by the community college for classes I teach in a suburb twenty miles away, but the woman who authorizes this sort of thing can't seem to remember to include this in her regular duties. Both *Qi Journal* and *Black Belt Magazine* have accepted my article "Studying T'ai Chi in Korea," but the former doesn't pay anything for articles and the latter only pays a hundred to two hundred dollars—after the piece is published. And who knows when it will actually be published. The woman I've been working with at the Y to set up T'ai Chi classes failed to publicize them at all, and my pay is based on the number of students. Against my long-established policy based on hard experience, I allowed a student to take one of my videotapes of the sequence home without paying for it first. She didn't return to class the following week (the last one in the session) and when I phoned her at home, she told me she had decided she didn't want it after all. Did she copy it? I'll have to pick it up. I was just barely able to pay my rent today.

How do I make money?

....

I had a friend in college who spent her early childhood in Venezuela because her father worked for an American oil company there. When Elsa was fourteen, her family moved back to the U.S. and she found herself in an alien culture. She was so unhappy about the move that she stopped eating. After becoming dangerously thin and landing in the hospital, Elsa gradually started eating again. But she had become bulimic. Elsa and I often sat at the same table for breakfast at the cafeteria. She would start out with a plateful of normal portions—some scrambled eggs, toast, hush puppies. All of us sharing the table were in the habit of trading news while we ate. Elsa would eventually get up for seconds. When she came back, her plate would be piled a little higher than the first time, and Elsa's fork would begin methodically and efficiently mixing ketchup in with her eggs while she talked. At a constant pace that looked machinelike, the fork began to move from food to mouth. I remember the transparent skin of Elsa's long forearms with their well-defined muscles; visible, rounded veins; and no extra on them at all. She'd go back for more. This time the plate would be overflowing, and her scooping and her speech more rapid, as she somehow stayed in the conversation. Her face began to look flushed under her short blonde curls. No one ever commented on the volume of food she ate. Her suitemate complained that she threw up every morning in their shared bathroom. She was one of the stars of her class—very bright, and an accomplished gymnast. But some of her classmates shunned her because of her illness.

Eating disorders. Futile attempts to fill ourselves up or show that we don't need to, we can go without. Diabetes mirrors my fathomless inner hunger and thirst. There's never enough. Everything's always running out. Starvation looms. Feeling retreats to the interior leaving the exterior numb and shut off. Wounds fester and are slow to heal. Is it the pancreas, or is it the heart? (I have not a single childhood memory of my parents hugging me, kissing me, or telling me they love me. If I lay my head on her lap in the evenings, my mother would stroke my head. One time my father brushed the back of his hand along my cheek when he thought I was asleep.) My heart feels as if it's ready to burst and shriveling to nothing at the same time.

I've just read Jean Rhys's *Voyage in the Dark*. "Keep hope alive," she says, "and you can do anything, and that's the way the world goes round, that's the way they keep the world rolling. So much hope for each person. And damned cleverly done too. But what happens if you don't hope any more, if your back's broken? What happens then?"

I do know this: In order to survive, I have to cultivate yin energy in my life (swimming, T'ai Chi, and play, of which there is way too little.) Yin is a force in itself. Yin is not the absence of yang. Yin is not the absence of yang. (I need to say it more than once.) It has to be nurtured and protected in this out-of-balance, dangerously yang world. Yin and yang are neutral forces, only destructive when one overruns the other. We live in a society where yin is always being pushed, crushed, squeezed out by the barrage of yang.

Yin has been less visible to me throughout my life; so I've discounted it. I'm slowly grasping that it works behind the scenes. In studying the history of Portland while writing about the police department, I can't help but feel surprised that Portland still exists. It doesn't seem possible that the people and events selected by (male) historians could produce the city as it is. Clearly more has been happening all along to make such a beautiful, livable community (as cities go). But that hasn't been written about; it hasn't been noticed or given credit for being as influential as it is.

I heard this on the network news: People who spent thirty minutes a day in a hot tub for three weeks brought their blood sugar down thirteen percent. A *New Yorker* article told the story of a young man with a rare and supposedly fatal disease who recovered when he changed his work to what he felt passionate about instead of "following the money." A *Prevention* article says a daily glass of wine is good for diabetics—alcohol decreases the cells' resistance to insulin. It's all just stress reduction.

....

I told Maureen that I was unhappy with her treatment program. My blood sugar levels have not come down. Early on, she said it was important to deal with this problem quickly because of the destructive side effects of high blood sugar over time. When I asked her how much longer it would take to reach normal levels, she said three months—that would mean late November, five months after starting with her. I objected again to the homeopathic drugs (Unda is the brand name) because they preclude taking the antioxidant vitamins I think I need to protect my circulation and my eyes. Plus they haven't had any noticeable effect. When I pressed her, she was unable to explain how they worked and referred me to another naturopath at the college. After several tries, I still haven't actually talked with him. I also told Maureen it worried me that she's not prescribing any of the supplements I keep coming across in my reading—gymnema sylvestre, fenugreek, ginkgo, chromium picolinate, alpha lipoic acid, and others, They all have long, successful track records with diabetics.

A month after my complaining, Maureen has changed my regimen—no more Undas (so I'm taking vitamins again); and I'm using a tincture that includes gymnema sylvestre, ginkgo, fenugreek, and bilberry.

I'm feeling better. Haven't weighed myself in quite a while, nor have I checked my blood sugar. I like that. I'm tired of checking my blood sugar every morning. It's another source of stress—a "test" that I have to pass—and never do.

Entry 38
Portland, Fall 1999

Spent the day at Cannon Beach. It's an easy hour and a half drive—I'll have to go more often. I parked downtown and strolled the beach south to Haystack Rock, twenty minutes through the touchless touch of sun-inspired fog lifting from the sand. The rock is a tourist attraction, but on a weekday in the fall, hardly anyone is there. I'm fascinated by that big outcropping in the surf. It's part bare, part green, and part covered with birds. Big chunks have toppled into the water—you can see the divots and the missing pieces of the puzzle below. Those rocks of varied sizes are in dialogue with the waves; they prod and enliven each other. It's the active interaction, the quickening, that attracts me.

I planted myself across from the rock and did T'ai Chi, then lay down on my bedspread and dozed. Later I walked through town, looking at clothes and earrings, pretending I could afford them. The food in the restaurants—at least the ones I know of at this point—isn't as healthy as I hoped. But it's pretty difficult to satisfy all my requirements and restrictions. I had packed plenty of food—my security and my lifeline.

....

I have a cat who visits me. She's sleek black and white, very solid. No collar, but seems well fed and cared for. She comes in through my dining room window in the late evening or middle of the night, investigates the apartment, tries to open all the doors. I sometimes think she only comes in in order to prove that she can. She doesn't act hungry or beg for food.

I was suspicious of her at first (and she of me), but we've warmed to each other and I do feed her. We were sitting beside each other on the couch one evening when she reached out her paw, looped it around my arm, and pulled herself close so she could lay her head on my thigh. So human.

Last night she came in around 9:00 when I was already in bed. She yowled to see if I were home and I came out to the living room to welcome her, then went back to bed. She followed me and lay down by my head for some minutes before getting up and leaving. I appreciated her closeness. God knows how many people she's sleeping with.

Keeping a cat is grounds for eviction in this building. I keep her food and water bowls out of sight of the windows. How can property owners refuse tenants the right to have pets? Living without animals is a real deprivation.

I was getting out of my car—I'd parked in the alley behind my apartment—when I saw the cat dash across the road and disappear between two buildings. I noticed a neighbor sitting in the sun on her steps, and I asked if she knew who owned the cat. "Oh, that's the visiting cat," she said. "Everyone knows her."

I call her Scappoose—after the town north of Portland—just because I like the sound of the name. Maybe it should be Scappuss. I wonder where she is now.

....

Directly across from my apartment, separated by only about eight feet, is another apartment in another building. A young man lives there by himself. He's frequently visited by a male friend who has a laugh like a hyena—in a human it sounds forced, unbalanced, and crazed. And it easily penetrates my old single-pane windows. The two men get in around 1:30 or 2:00 at night (after the bars close) and wind up from there, blasting heavy metal and preternaturally loud voices to the outside world all the way till morning. Sometimes they scream at each other (or rather hyena-man screams at his friend) and every other word is "fuck" or "fuckin'." Judging from their conversation, I think they're a gay couple. They must be on drugs, because I can't imagine sustaining that level of hysteria for that long unassisted. One morning, as I left the apartment around 7:00 to do T'ai Chi (I couldn't wait to get out after a sleepless night), I heard one of the men shout out the window, "It's fuckin' light out there!"

The same neighbor has an alarm clock that sounds like the backup signal on a garbage truck. It lets loose at about 9 A.M. and continues for hours—while I'm studying or writing. The snooze alarm apparently gets punched now and then, allowing an intermittent fifteen minutes of blessed silence. Some days they must leave the apartment during the snooze phase, with the alarm still activated. Maybe they're partially deaf from too many rock concerts.

I've talked to the manager of my building (who's sympathetic but helpless), the manager of the other building (who's rude and unhelpful), and finally the police. A visit from the police quiets them for that night, but I suffer too long before calling, and the last time they said they only have jurisdiction over "amplified sound." If the guys aren't playing music, the cops don't want to be called.

I talked with some of the other tenants in the building about this problem. They're furious too. A male who lives above me has shouted in a booming, angry voice, "Keep it quiet over there!" and that worked a couple times. One man (who was quick to add that he doesn't own a gun) said he fantasized about shooting them. Yet I'm the only person who has complained to any authority that might be able to remedy the situation. Why?

I heard a discussion on the radio the other day about noise in the city. The expert on the subject said that we're naturally reluctant to confront people who disturb us because we instinctively recognize that only aggressive, belligerent people do this sort of thing; their behavior is a form of violence; and what happens if we draw their anger? I'm sure that by now the young men across from me know I've been complaining. It has crossed my mind they might try to retaliate. They're scary.

Sleep has been elusive enough. Being barred by these guys from what little sound sleep I can get is pure torture. They've brought me to tears several times. I slammed a window so hard that I cracked the glass. I need to get out of the city.

....

I was relieved to be admitted to an overcrowded memoirs writing course at PSU. It's providing a good writers' group for me—my first. The alternative was a newswriting course that wouldn't have been relevant to what I'm doing. I sat in on the first meeting of the news class in case I didn't get into the other. When the class was over, I stood by, waiting to talk to the teacher while a young female undergrad asked him if the news stories she would be generating as a full-time employee of the student newspaper could fulfill class assignments. The man hemmed a bit, then said, "No, that didn't work in the past…" and drifted off. Then he added, "And besides, you're getting paid for that writing." He sounded as if he were grasping for rationalizations for a decision he had never thought through. I ask you, what kind of an answer is that? In what way is it relevant that she's getting paid for the articles? She'll be writing for the paper precisely the kinds of reports he'll be requiring for class. Why invent additional, redundant hoops for her to jump through? Isn't it enough that she's in school and supporting herself simultaneously? Doesn't he have any conception of what her life is like? Why do humans *want* to make life more difficult for each other? If nothing else, a good teacher has to like people and have compassion for them.

....

Tantalizing wisps of memory envelop me now and then. They're fleeting, yet come complete with sight, sound, fragrance, and state of mind. They come unbidden—I find myself in familiar, lovely settings that are wholly different from my actual surroundings, and in the company of cherished friends. More than memories, these are brief recurrences and must be my inner self's attempt to come to the rescue. The feelings they bring—of being at peace and at home—are comforting. And frustrating, because this state of grace is out of reach. But these ephemeral gifts provide hope.

....

I snagged a couple proofreading jobs with Portland publishers. I like being able to work at home—in my pajamas, at ten o'clock at night if I want to. Catching errors is an intellectual game. I'm being very thorough, and have brought the work in on time and under budget. One publisher actually paid on delivery!

One of the books was about all the summit attempts made thus far on Denali (Mt. McKinley). It contained some interesting comments on Korean mountain climbers. The Koreans were largely responsible for a rash of rescues and deaths on Denali in the early 1990s. A U.S. park ranger, after ten days in Seoul as a guest of the Korean Alpine Federation, discovered that Korean climbers feel it's absolutely necessary to reach the top, regardless of the circumstances.

"Koreans are driven by a set of pressures that are, for lack of a better word, foreign to us," the ranger reported. "They have a lot more invested in their trips to Denali than [Americans] do." The book's author explains that Koreans, as a rule, receive only five vacation days a year. If they want to participate in a Denali expedition, they have to either quit their jobs or convince their company to sponsor them. Corporate sponsorship adds its own pressures—failure to reach the summit is considered shameful and would likely mean the withdrawal of support. Success on a big-name peak like Denali, on the other hand, can bring fame and riches in a country where climbing is a national passion.

The Koreans themselves were embarrassed by the accidents on the mountain. They agreed changes had to be made.

....

I've decided to make this first session of T'ai Chi classes at the Y my last. It's too difficult to fit my teaching into their rigid schedule of six- or seven-week sessions. I need more time to get across the material. T'ai Chi just doesn't work well as a drop-in class. But the fitness director at Nike wants me to continue teaching indefinitely. That was good to hear. The community college classes are well attended and fun, and I'm beginning some substitute teaching at an athletic club within walking distance of my apartment. It *is* tough getting home from a

Monday night class at 10:30 and having to get up at 5 the next morning to teach at Nike. I almost wish I could sleep overnight at the Nike campus on my way back into town from the class in Hillsboro. On Thursdays, I teach the early Nike class and then teach in town until 8:30 P.M. By the end of that class, I'm so tired that I can barely walk straight.

....

Here's my plan: (1) finish my degree by spring 2001, (2) gradually establish myself as a freelance copyeditor and writer (3) get out of the city and go back to Humboldt County, California. I want to be able to see the sky through my window, and have a flower garden. Having something to look forward to energizes me.

....

This from Jane Austen's *Emma:*
Harriet Smith: "But still, you will be an old maid—and that's so dreadful!"
Emma: "Never mind, Harriet, I shall not be a poor old maid; and it is poverty only which makes celibacy contemptible to a generous public! A single woman with a very narrow income must be a ridiculous, disagreeable old maid, the proper sport of boys and girls; but a single woman of good fortune is always respectable, and may be as sensible and pleasant as anybody else! And the distinction is not quite so much against the candour and common-sense of the world as appears at first; for a very narrow income has a tendency to contract the mind, and sour the temper. Those who can barely live, and who live perforce in a very small and generally very inferior society, may well be illiberal and cross. This does not apply, however, to Miss Bates. ... Poverty certainly has not contracted her mind.

Can I be a Miss Bates? I *want* to live gracefully, but I'm so often frightened, worried, threatened, irritable.

Entry 39
Wonju, Winter 1997-1998

I woke at 2:40 last night and wrote down this remarkable dream: A male friend and I were going somewhere in a taxi when he informed me that he was not only pregnant but thought he was about to have the baby. I was baffled and concerned at the same time. He wasn't acting as if he were experiencing really painful contractions, so I asked about that, and joked about the cliché of having a baby in the back seat of a taxi. It was only slowly dawning on me that this was happening, and it was happening fast. The understanding between us was that it was my baby, and I dimly remember thinking it was natural he would be the one to have it, because he's more open to that sort of thing—has had children before.

The setting shifted to a large, empty room in a building. My friend sat on the floor with his back against a square pillar, his legs straight out in front of him. The room reminded me of the dojang, and also of the basement of the Episcopal church I went to as a kid—overlaying T'ai Chi and my religion (T'ai Chi *is* my religion?). I knelt on the floor in front of him, trying to ascertain what to do. There was a third person there—a male, I think. I said to him, "You have to help, too!" But he wasn't responding.

My friend said, "The baby is coming *now!*" So I hurriedly pulled off his jeans. The baby came out in one smooth push. (Out of nowhere in a way—this was not an anatomically correct dream, and there was no mess.) He—I think it was a boy—slid onto the floor and lay in front of me on his back. He was very big and developed, more than a newborn. Beaming with joy, he was bloomingly robust, entirely alert, and seemed elated to have arrived in the world, not upset or shocked like all the slapped-on-the-rear babies.

Trying to make myself useful, I took a towel and started to massage the baby's leg. But this made him cry, so I stopped, and he went back to being his cheerful self. He needed nothing.

In the past, my dreams of being pregnant or having babies always came when I was about to give birth to a creative project—my books for instance. And there was the dream of having my cat. This dream seems to presage an easy birth—the less assistance, the less "massaging," the better.

Why did I dream that my friend had the baby instead of me? Maybe because I feel so shut down and shut off now. He had to act as my surrogate, representing my more hopeful, happy, nurturing self.

It was a wonderful dream. I can't express how vibrant and strong and beautiful the baby was.

....

The Korean economy is collapsing. The won per dollar exchange rate is close to 2000. It was about 850 when I arrived. The recent prosperity was in many ways false—it had rotten underpinnings like the modern bridge in Seoul that fell recently and the department store that crumbled a few years ago. Too many shortcuts were taken in the building of those structures. They were victims—along with the people on them or in them who died—of the corruption that riddles big business and its adjunct, the government.

And now the IMF has been called in. Koreans are angry, ashamed, and resentful. Most politicians and businessmen are busily pointing the finger at ordinary Korean citizens, blaming *them*—for being too extravagant, for taking too many trips abroad and spending their dollars outside of the country. True to form, the Korean people—at least partially—are buying this and readily shouldering the responsibility. They're mounting campaigns to live more frugally, stop buying Western products, contribute their dollars to the government, and turn in their gold jewelry so it can be converted to dollars. Students gather in public places to burn foreign-made pencils and pencil cases. The real problem is that the *chaebol* (business conglomerates), with the help of the World Bank, got too grandiose and expanded way beyond their true capacities. Now the loans are due—in dollars—and bankruptcies and layoffs are mounting.

Despite the public rhetoric, not all the Korean people are taken in. Many are privately disgusted with big business and government—they know who has brought this scourge down upon them.

But I think Korea will come out of this much stronger. Big business will have to get its act together in order to survive here and in the world market. Corruption is not only unjust, it's also inefficient and costly.

Antiforeigner sentiment is growing, especially toward the Japanese and Americans. Koreans equate them with the IMF. Their fear that the developed countries will use this opportunity to gain greater access to their economy is probably well founded.

Someone knew this was coming. The first year, we foreign English teachers were paid in dollars. Our second year's contract changed it to won. The American liaison between the education office and the native teachers says there has been some talk about giving us a raise, but I can't imagine it will come close to compensating for the devalued won.

The head teacher has been glowering at me with renewed anger. I made a point of telling Mrs. Song that I'm being paid in won this year, not dollars—so I'm hurt by this catastrophe too. I knew she would relay the information to all the faculty and staff.

I feel sorry for Charlotte and Percival. They've been keeping their money in one of the local banks instead of wiring it home, and since September that money has been in won. Something about avoiding taxes back in England.

If I don't have the incentive of saving a significant amount of money, I can hardly rationalize staying where I'm so unhappy. Even the Tae Guk Kwon training, a life raft I've been desperately clutching, is too flimsy. I know I'm hoping we don't get a raise—I want a good reason to leave.

Ordinarily I would have transferred money to the U.S. today—a bimonthly task that always gives me a sense of accomplishment. But I'll put it off until (with luck) the exchange rate improves. This makes me nervous. Especially now, I want my money safely out of here. It's true I'm part of the dollar drain; I'm one of the foreigners changing won into dollars and sending them out of the country.

Entry 40
Wonju, Winter 1997-1998

I asked my conversation students to draw a twenty-four-hour clock, big enough to fill a sheet of notebook paper. Then I asked them to write sentences at appropriate places on the dial, telling what they did yesterday. It's an exercise in past tense. The clock of one of my best students showed that she got four hours' sleep and didn't eat an actual meal all day. I stood over her shoulder, looked at the drawing, and then looked at her.

"Really?"

"Really."

The next day she came to school with a red, swollen nose and bleary eyes—a bad cold.

I have a break from teaching while the girls take their finals—twelve tests in three days. There are written tests in art, music, and home ec. All subjects are attacked as academic subjects. I monitor some of the tests and I can see how nervous the students are. But they're well-trained test takers, underlining each row of print as they read, making sure they don't miss a single word of the directions, the questions, or the answers. It's nearly all multiple choice with a few one-word written responses. Machines can tally most of the results.

Shin Young-sook is a third-grade English teacher who coaches students for their high school entrance exams and helps them decide which school to apply to. Different schools specialize in different subjects, and there's a strict hierarchy from the most to the least prestigious. The high school a student attends determines the course of the rest of her life. Shin Young-sook told me that from their high school placement on, many students are destined to live unhappy lives. I was incredulous—it seemed so unrealistically final. "Their whole lives will be unhappy?" "Yes," she said. Korean society only bestows respect on "scholars" or a least college-educated people with jobs in big corporations.

....

I sent five letters home—all essentially the same, all to friends who are (or were) public school teachers. I sketched a picture of the school scene here and told them I wanted to know some things: How do you keep order in the classroom? What's the disciplinary process for repeat offenders, from the most minor punishment to the most severe? How do administrators and other teachers support you? How and when are parents drawn in?

One couple took copies of my letter to their respective elementary and high schools. The other teachers, my friends reported, were "dumbfounded": "The concept of striking a child for discipline is so foreign to us. To beat a child as you described is inconceivable."

I'm grateful for the lengthy, thoughtful responses, although I feel so rattled and besieged that I can hardly even take in the suggestions—varied, creative, and effective as they are. That world seems hopelessly far away.

A high school teacher writes that Governor Wilson in California is pointing to the high Japanese test scores as reason for extending the American school year. How ironic that the U.S. wants to copy Asian methods of education just when the Asians are wising up, turning away from their old system, and trying to emulate the West! School reform is a hot topic here. They're reducing the number of allowable after-school classes so kids can go home earlier and (this is critical) legalizing the teachers' union as of next July. Korean schools *do* prepare students for standardized multiple-choice tests, but they don't prepare students to think. Too much knowledge is changing too fast to waste time memorizing it. Students need practice being inventive and resourceful.

As for extending the American school year, every teacher I know at home is wholly committed to their students and performs way beyond their job description. I can't imagine asking them to do more. And reducing them to "teaching to the test" would be everyone's loss. The best teachers would be thwarted; they'd leave the profession. And for the students, school would be pure drudgery.

I once said to a group of Korean English teachers that learning is fun. I was met with blank stares. Fun wasn't part of their educational experience, and they don't expect it to be so for this generation either. Mr. Won looked at me and said, "Students don't want to learn. That's why we must hit them."

The same high school teacher who told me about Governor Wilson said he doesn't have discipline problems because his subjects—geology and biology—are inherently interesting to teenagers, and his school stresses a hands-on approach that keeps students actively involved. My mother taught fourth and fifth grade for seventeen years, and she always said you can't really control children, you can only keep them curious and busy.

....

The Korean approach: Never pause to think, never look ahead, never yield. Just put your head down and bull your way forward. And if something doesn't work, deny it.

The cornerstones of a repressive society:

Keep people frantically busy and tired. This way they have no time or energy to assess or evaluate their abusive or inequitable situation, let alone mount a protest or complaint.

Promote nationalism. Focus on the general (or specific) outside world as a threat. This diverts attention away from internal abuses and corruption.

Make sure everyone is married with children and bound up in family. These people are less likely to take risks because of their heavy responsibilities.

Confucianism—unquestioning respect for and obedience to superiors—is perfect cement for a repressive society. The status quo, the current hierarchy, must be maintained.

I look at Korea, and my advice to Koreans is: emigrate.

....

I was in the snack bar at the army base and noticed two young soldiers, a white male and a black female, sitting in a booth. They were listening to a tune on the jukebox and the woman was singing along, moving with the music, grooving. I was struck with her vibance, the healthy life force within her. And with the contrast between her and me. I feel like a stick of dead wood—rigid, brittle, graceless, lifeless.

More and more I stay in my apartment, windows closed. I don't like to go out into the neighborhood. It's dingy and depressing. Instead of shopping for groceries, I improvise with what I have. Made pancakes this morning with water instead of milk. They were fine.

Entry 41
Wonju, Winter 1997-1998

Standing at the front of his high school classroom, Percival paused in the middle of the lesson to remove his glasses and clean them with his handkerchief. At that moment, Charlotte and I burst through the door at the back of the room. With bandanas tied around the lower halves of our faces, we brandished our guns, sprayed the delighted, flinching boys with water, and shouted at Percival to put his hands up and turn around. Then Charlotte demanded his wallet. Having obeyed our commands, he was facing away from us as he took the wallet out of his back pocket and laid it on the desk. She rushed forward, grabbed it, and we ran out the door, dampening as many students as we could on the way.

It was a demonstration English lesson given by Percival. Because he had his glasses off and was turned away from Charlotte and me most of the time, he had to rely on his students to describe the bandits to him—gender, height, weight, hair color, clothing, and so on. The perimeter of the room was lined with observers—administrators and teachers from Wonju schools. The lesson was a big success, largely because of that stunt (although a smart aleck told Percival that one of the bandits was his wife, and surely he must know what *she* looks like). At the lunch afterward, Percival's principal toasted him as the best English teacher in Wonju. He feigned modesty.

I remember when I gave him the idea for that lesson. It was interesting to watch his reaction to hearing from an American an idea that he knew would be the high point of any class. It wasn't invented by me—I had seen it done at the school for teaching English in San Francisco. His first response was that my suggestion had come too late—the lesson plan had to be submitted the next day. Then, hardly skipping a beat, he said he thought he remembered the idea from his training in Britain. ("Thank you for reminding me.") Charlotte nodded vaguely in agreement. Percival did express his gratitude again, after the lesson was over, this time without any pretense of having known of it previously. But he basked in the admiration of all the others who assumed it was his idea.

I was seated beside Percival at the lunch after the demonstration. He told me he planned to use my lesson on English words adopted by the Korean language at a workshop for teachers where I would also be an instructor. I told him he couldn't do that—it was my original lesson and I intended to use it; we couldn't teach the same lesson to the same students. He blustered and I could see he expected me to object and was ready with his defense: "The idea is in the *Five-Minute Game Book"* (a book of suggestions for people teaching English to non-native speakers). "With a list of 200 Korean words?" I asked. He claimed to have added a few to my list. But then he backed down. We both know he's not capable of constructing a lesson like this because he doesn't even know the Korean alphabet. I gave the list to him months ago and I'm glad he's been able to use it, but he can't use it at the same workshop where I'm teaching. A minute later, Charlotte told me she had thought of including the lesson too, but decided I would probably be teaching it, and therefore she shouldn't. I thanked her. Percival was listening.

I suppose he'll use the lesson on emotions that I gave him too—he told me he shrunk the cartoon heads that illustrate the emotions and added a line on which students could write in the Korean word, in addition to the line that's already there for the English word. The drawings aren't mine, but it took me a long time to arrive at the correct translations. I consulted several teachers, and they didn't always agree with each other. Again, this is a lesson that someone without an understanding of the Korean language couldn't develop. The drawings and miming aren't enough to get across the precise intent.

Where are Percival's ideas? Charlotte has at least shared some of her resource books with me.

....

Health update: I got conjunctivitis again, this time from the swimming pool. (My precious swimming! One of the few pleasures I have here.) Again, the eye doctor wasn't interested in knowing how I got it. Simultaneously I came down with the flu—full-body aches and fatigue. Between that, the eye infection, and another round of antibiotics, I've been in bad shape. I haven't skipped any school, though—I don't want to make life harder than it already is for the other teachers.

About ten days ago I received the herbs and food supplements that I requested from my doctor in the U.S. They're making a difference. My energy level is rising, I look better, my dreams have improved. The hot flashes—I was having as many as a dozen a day—are almost entirely gone. I didn't even notice the usual flush of heat when I woke this morning.

....

During my last Korean lesson with Isabel, I wrote a sentence and she made a correction. I expressed surprise at the change she made, and told her why I thought I'd chosen the proper verb. (It's right out of Lesson One of my Korean conversation book—one of the ways to say "it is.") She launched into an elaborate explanation of why her way was correct. It was pretty impressive—pure fabrication off the top of her head, spoken to someone who she apparently thought was more ignorant than I actually am. I pulled out the beginner's book, opened it to the first chapter, and pointed out the verb. She made a U-turn.

What's going on? I'm baffled. What other malarkey is she feeding me? Or is it just that the Korean language is slippery and resists being pinned down to a (Western) academic grid?

Isabel is fading out of my life. She's busy with her master's degree and teaching English conversation to Koreans and has other worries as well. Her son, Ho-chang, is asking for more money, and the shift in the exchange rate means it's literally doubly hard to support him in the U.S. He and his girlfriend, Bo-mi, finished language school in Georgia and were accepted as undergraduates at Ohio State. Isabel seems to take it for granted that Ho-chang will be going to school there—despite the fact that thousands of Korean students are flocking home from their studies abroad.

I was surprised by a flurry of activity on my behalf—Isabel made a special trip to the bus station to pin down the departure times for Dragon Valley, a ski resort a few hours from here. (I'm planning to meet two American friends who are teaching English in Singapore for a few days' skiing over Christmas.) She also brought me some tangerines. I instantly connected the favors with a request she made two days later over the phone: "Do you have any dollars I can borrow?" I was relieved to be able to tell her that I have almost no dollars here. How could she pay me back? Who knows when the exchange rate will improve, or if it will ever return to the precollapse level. Helping to support a healthy twenty-seven-year-old man with a master's degree from Seoul University as he embarks on his freshman year in college is not a compelling cause. In any case, I'm sure his father will continue to help him.

Isabel had a crushing headache and severe nausea after we went swimming a few months ago. She left the pool only minutes after we'd gotten in, saying she wasn't feeling well. When I got back to the locker room after my swim, I found her dressed and lying with her head on the cool tiles. We had to stop the car on the way home so she could get out and throw up at the side of the road. (Ho-chang was with us that time, and fortunately he was driving.) Later she told me her left arm was really bothering her. When I wondered aloud if she had had a slight stroke, she claimed she'd fallen on her arm. She seems to be recovering slowly from that original event at the pool. I think knowing Ho-chang was about to leave for the U.S. on a five-year visa was too much for her.

All the doctor told her was that she should be careful to warm up slowly when she swims. He sounds naïve. Or is that really what he said? It took her a long time even to go see a doctor. I think she felt she couldn't allow herself to be sick just then.

....

I was excited to find a new person to help me study Korean, but actually getting together with her is proving to be a problem. Three weeks ago I gave her 100,000 won for five lessons (more than I get paid for teaching conversation classes at school). We've had one so far, but she—Beth—seems to feel no obligation to plan another.

She's a native Korean who married an American soldier that she met here twenty years ago. He was stationed at Camp Seward and she was working in a small grocery store located just outside the base's entrance. Although neither spoke much more than "hello" and "thank you" in each other's language, they fell in love, married, and settled in California. They have a seventeen-year-old son.

Beth's husband, Russell, signed on for the same English teaching program that I did—it's given them a chance to return to Korea for a couple years (maybe more?) so that Beth can be around her aging parents. Their son, Clay—over six feet tall, handsome, thoroughly bilingual, and an American—is a big hit with the girls here. His phone doesn't stop ringing. For some reason his father still doesn't speak any of his wife's language, but Beth is the most fluent English speaker I've run into among native Koreans. Her English is much better than Min-hi's even, probably because she was forced to speak it at home. Min-hi lived within a Korean-speaking community in New Jersey and shared a home with her mother. I noticed Beth is reading *Angela's Ashes.*

Beth said she would come to one of my classes at the dojang—I wanted her to ask my teacher some questions and translate his answers. We fixed on an evening, but she never showed up. I told Kwan Jang Nim she was coming, so it was embarrassing as well as disappointing. I was hoping Beth would help me make faster progress in my language study, but that looks doubtful now.

....

I took Mr. Shin and his wife to dinner at the army base. I wanted to repay them for the two dinners at their house and for

Mr. Shin's continued friendship even after he was transferred to the school in the country. They relished the dinner, seemed thrilled to be at an American army base, especially to be admitted to "the club"—the restaurant and bar. The place isn't opulent, but there are white linen tablecloths and subdued lighting. It was their first really Western meal. I had to explain salad and dressing and A1 sauce. They were awed by the size of their T-bone steaks. (The A1 bottle on the table triggered childhood memories for me, and the glistening steaks looked inedible.)

I made an effort to keep the conversation in Korean or make sure Mr. Shin translated for his wife when I had to resort to English. I didn't want her to feel excluded. My Korean is raggedy and limited, but I thought I was doing pretty well. It was one of the rare times that I've felt comfortable and relaxed around Koreans. Then Mr. Shin said, "You are in Korea almost two years and you speak little Korean. We think it is the same for Koreans when they go to America." I guess it was gracious for him to acknowledge that learning each other's language is difficult for both of us, but I was stung.

....

I'm newly obsessed with learning how to wield the staff from Kwan Jang Nim. The thing is about as big around as a stout broomstick and cut to exactly my height. Maybe I'm fascinated because it's a chance to use my hands again after more than a year of doing no pottery. It's a good thing I can practice in the gym at the base on the days that I don't go to the dojang—my apartment won't accommodate a whirling five-foot four-inch stick. I know because I tried it. Miraculously, I didn't break anything. The other miracle is that thus far I've avoided knocking myself unconscious. In my hands, the staff doesn't qualify as a weapon yet. But I'm definitely a majorette with an attitude.

....

Last Sunday evening I trained in the gym at the base and then went to the library to look for more books. It was 7:45 when a man walked in. I recognized him as the chaplain—we had met before, but we reintroduced ourselves. He told me he'll be going home in a couple months. He's reluctantly leaving the army because there's no vacant slot on the ladder he's been climbing. The number of positions decreases as rank increases. I'm guessing he's in his late forties. He's not looking forward to starting another career, and talked unenthusiastically about his possibilities. None of them will pay as well as his current work.

The important thing is that from the time he turned toward me, at ten feet away, I felt a silky wave of serenity break over me. I shivered in the way I do when I'm getting a massage. The unhurried pace of his speech, the softness of his voice, his large brown eyes and full lips. My whole body tingled, melted.

It was time for the library to close and he said he was just out walking around, would I mind if he accompanied me to the gate? As we walked in the cool, dark air, I held my mouth open slightly—as if I could absorb more that way. I soaked it up through my skin. A painful, knotted muscle in my shoulder sighed and let go. When we got there, he asked if he could walk me the rest of the way to my home. Of course I said yes. I wanted what was happening to last forever.

We talked about living in Korea. I toned down my opinions, worried that my rankling would quash the feeling. But it didn't.

When I got into my apartment, I didn't turn on my TV for company as I normally would. I was sufficient. I went to bed, still feeling the effects of the chaplain's presence and slept well, as I knew I would.

Other people have had this sort of effect on me, but never so marked (perhaps it's a measure of my current neediness). Some of those people I've liked, some I've disliked. All of them had a dreamy slowness about them—their speech, their movements, the casual way in which they conducted their lives. Perhaps, on some subliminal level, they're my complement—an antidote to my directedness, my ambition, my fight-or-flight, adrenaline-packed existence. They soothe me and I love being around them. I'll gladly put up with boring or irritating conversations in exchange for the chance to bathe in their atmosphere.

The chaplain is no soul mate; he's not at all attractive to me sexually; he's married and devoted to his family. The differences in our backgrounds, lives, and personalities would make even a friendship difficult. But I'll try to be around him when I can. He invited me to a church dinner at the base. I doubt he'll have the same effect on me with the commotion of so many others around.

What does he feel around me? He wanted to talk with me, stay with me as long as possible. Does he get the same effect?

....

I woke at five o'clock this morning and got up to go to the bathroom. Curious to see what the U.S. armed forces were broadcasting at that hour, I turned on the TV. Wildflowers—orange, red, yellow, and blue—rippled across a mountain meadow, accompanied by the caressing sounds of harp and piano. I sunk down on the floor and let it in. After a few minutes, I was treated to a video of Norman and Nancy Blake and friends, sitting in a circle, playing their arrangement of "God Rest Ye Merry Gentlemen." Seeing those relaxed musicians smiling across their instruments at each other (guitar, cello, mandolin, fiddle), playing so well, dressed so unpretentiously in the clothes of my tribe, was soul soothing. The scene exuded what I like best about the U.S.—people doing what they do for the sheer love of it, and the perfect excellence arrived at by that unselfconscious route.

Entry 42
Portland, Winter 2000-2001

Y2K came and went not with a bang but a whimper. A friend from Arcata spent the weekend here, and we watched on TV as the new millennium swept across the planet—so anticlimactically, as it turned out. I had filled two big new white lidded buckets with water and stockpiled a small store of canned goods. My portable radio was fortified with fresh batteries and the cookstove I have for camping stood by. I appreciated not spending New Year's Eve alone, but I don't make a good companion. My energy is limited. When I'm tired and hungry I get cranky, and I'm tired and hungry most of the time.

....

How about that lemon balm! It's in a tea that Maureen prescribed, along with oat straw, bilberry, and spearmint. I'm sure that's what's helping me sleep. I feel a little sedated during the day, too, which concerns me. But being calmer is helping me write; I don't get so bollixed up. I'm grateful for the sleep—I have sufficient energy for teaching and my legs aren't trembling at the end of the sequence.

I'm still overeating, but not as much as I was. I actually had one day last week when I wasn't hungry or thirsty. The hair has started growing on my legs again (hairless legs are a symptom of diabetes). Food is definitely my primary sensual pleasure. I only wish I could feel satiated.

For the last several weeks I've been practicing Liangong, a set of thirty-six therapeutic exercises that came out of China in 1975. It's based on ancient healing practices as well as modern sports medicine. It uses breathing, stretching movements, and self-applied acupressure to work with ch'i. I'm more and more impressed with how it seems to strengthen me and raise my energy level.

My students like it too. I've been squeezing it into my intermediate classes as a complement to T'ai Chi. I'm just about done composing the handouts—six double-sided pages with three exercises on each side. I've made drawings to accompany the directions. It's been a slow process; I keep checking everything against the videotapes by Wen Mei Yu, a really outstanding Chinese teacher who's been living in this country for the last fifteen years. I also have my notes from her classes at training camps put on by the Pacific Association of Women Martial Artists. My thinking must be blurry because the more I edit, the more errors I find. I'll be glad when this project is over.

....

Some days ago I called Joanna, a friend in Humboldt County. I can talk to her on a deeply personal level, and the conversation was comforting. She exudes a certain peace, although I know her life has not been easy. Today I received a colorful note card from her with nourishing words inside. The cover drawing shows an exuberant red fish leaping above curly stylized waves; the inscription reads "Boundless Joy Arising."

What a nice sentiment to offer! I've always admired—and wanted to emulate—the people who go to the trouble and expense of picking out special cards and keeping up a regular correspondence. Some obviously mark all their friends' birthdays on their new calendars at the beginning of each year. I limit myself to family birthdays and a couple of others.

The hand-written word means so much to me, and so much more than E-mail. E-mail was a necessity while I was in Korea, but here it's another way to separate me from friends—it's used too often instead of the intimate phone call or letter. My usual excuse for not giving friends the gift of a card is that I'm too rushed, too distracted, and too poor. But isn't it just a matter of priorities? I'm reexamining mine and aspiring to Joanna's unhurried grace.

....

Min-hi writes this from New Jersey: "I was almost dying this summer for the pain of the chest as the result of the failure of the last conventional chemo treatment. …Then the hospital proposed me to join a clinical research program which is an utter experimental one. I had no choice but to accept it." The new medication alleviated her pain but worsened her fatigue. "Margy, I'm closer to God ever and feel him listen to me. Through these turbulences I retrospect the past with regret or joy and hope and dreams for the life ahead. Life is so precious." She wanted me to tell her about my "vibrant life." Everything is relative.

I've written back, wondering if I'll hear from her again.

....

I bought finger paints at a toy store in Cannon Beach. I've been filling ripped-out pages of my sketchbook with primary colors applied without thought, without preconception. The materials are cheap and expendable. This is not art for keeps, it's art for experience. Sitting at my antique maple table with golden asters in the slim black vase I made years ago, I dip my fingers into paints that are cool, jellylike, and slippery. I place red beside yellow beside purple beside green. The trails of my fingertips waver like plowed rows following the land's contours. I spread the pages around on the floor to dry, a process that takes more than a day because the paint is gobbed on—I want saturated color. Some of the paintings work better than others as compositions. Some charm me; some are indictments, evidence of my inferior talent as an artist. I try to be charitable toward all of them.

....

A local publisher finally paid me for an invoice handed in seven weeks ago. Their stated policy is to pay every two to three weeks. I got the old "check is in the mail" runaround from the executive editor. He said accounts payable informed him they'd mailed the check two weeks before, and if I didn't receive it within a few days, he'd have a new check sent. After another week and several sincere- and concerned-sounding E-mails from the editor, a friend suggested I call accounts payable directly. I took the advice. It turned out they had never seen my invoice. The woman I talked to seemed surprised that I hadn't been paid and assured me they always pay "within terms." She sounded annoyed with the editor and clearly wasn't interested in covering for him. She said she'd write a check that day and send it to me. I said I'd be by that afternoon to pick it up. The editor told her he would call me about this, but of course he hasn't. I caught him in a very undignified series of lies. At least I got a good reference letter out of him before our relationship came to an end.

A dream: I'm standing among a group of people, working myself into a fury. "You're taking advantage of me!" I scream. It's about money. People use me until they have to pay me, then they disappear. A woman reminds me that I have to work within the community: Don't get too angry, too hysterical.

Entry 43
Portland, Winter 2000-2001

I was so estranged from myself by the time I got back from Korea that I had become my own alien environment. Then, choosing an exterior to match my interior, I decided to live in a city. Cacophony inside and out—a perverse harmony.

Now it feels as if I'm floating, drifting on the periphery of the day-to-day of my life. I can't tell—am I resting and healing, or am I just sick?

....

Vision while meditating: I hover upright, several feet above the ground in the park where I practice T'ai Chi. A TV is suspended between my feet and the green grass. I interpret it this way: television comes between me and healing. I've been watching the news (which means being assaulted by the commercials even more than by the reports and pictures), sometimes *Seinfeld.* No more TV.

....

Why do I feel so strong in the water and so weak on land? I take baths, sit in the hot tub at the Y, and swim. I'm thirsty this evening, too thirsty. I'll keep drinking until I'm not; until whatever is in me is all cleared out, cleaned out, rinsed out, washed out. My Chinese herbs are brewing. Then sleep. Saturday morning T'ai Chi class tomorrow. I look forward to it.

....

Every day I ingest these things: a tincture of gymnema sylvestre, ginkgo, fenugreek, and bilberry (one-half teaspoon, twice a day); a tablespoon of vinegar mixed with a quarter teaspoon of honey in eight ounces of water (fifteen minutes before each meal); a multiple vitamin that's heavy on the antioxidants (twice a day); two teaspoons of a mixture of borage, flax, sunflower, sesame, and pumpkin oils; a tablespoon of brewer's yeast; and at least one serving of soy protein powder. The regimen is formulated to provide nutrients diabetics tend to be deficient in, protect vision and circulation, and help me hold onto or even gain weight. The vinegar is supposed to aid digestion; Maureen isn't sure why it's combined with honey.

People around me covet jobs that offer health insurance. It wouldn't do me much good. None of the "medicines" I take would be covered (and they do add up). The cost of a comprehensive policy would be more than I spend by seeing Maureen once a month. Besides, the people I know who have health insurance complain about the restrictions of managed care, and not being able to see the physicians they want to see, used to see.

Before I left for Korea, I had "disaster" insurance—a $2,000 deductible and coverage for falling off a cliff, that sort of thing. I've always been able to handle everyday medical expenses. In Korea I was automatically covered by their national health insurance (when will the U.S. catch up with the other developed and developing countries in this area?). After living outside of the country for six months, my American health insurance was cancelled, as per their usual procedure. I didn't buy new insurance when I returned.

Tomorrow a massage—something else an insurance policy wouldn't cover. It's been over a month since the last one.

....

I'm enjoying my writing class—it's turning out to be very useful as a writing group. Carol Franks and Tony Wolk designed the course with the assumption that the students are sincere and interested. How refreshing! It's the opposite of the adversarial approach taken by most teachers. Before we break up into smaller groups, Carol and Tony read excerpts of their favorite writing to us. We get to listen, savor, and talk about why it works.

The writing department is posting job openings via E-mail. Some are internships with no pay, just the possibility of being eventually hired by the company. I mentioned this to a friend of mine who has been working in computers for a long time. He raised his eyebrows. The computer companies, he informed me, always pay interns working in technological fields. He sounded scornful of writers—that they would be offered such an arrangement, and that they would accept it.

The paying jobs that are being posted are often down around minimum wage. One particularly insulting one popped up on my screen the other day. It requires two years of college, computer skills, and the ability to write and edit—all for $6.50 an hour. I told a professor I thought they should refuse to relay this sort of thing to students—in effect, the department is collaborating with the exploitation of writers, encouraging businesses to devalue our skills. He was short with me, told me lots of writers are willing to work for nothing in order to get a foot in the door or get published. Too bad he's right.

Entry 44
Wonju, Winter 1997-1998

    Skiing in mild, sunny weather! Speaking English at full speed using compound sentences! Swimming, sauna, and hot tub! Exotic food catered from Singapore!

    Just returned from Dragon Valley Ski Resort yesterday afternoon. Two American women friends who are teaching English in Singapore met me there for a few days over Christmas. I requested they bring herb teas and real peanut butter without the sugar and additives. Suzanne went crazy and brought at least five different teas, two jars of peanut butter, cheeses, baguettes, hummus, pate, avocados, salsa, and chips. I feasted—and continue to enjoy the leftovers here at home.

    We discussed my moving to Singapore to finish out the year. The living and teaching situations would be vastly better. I could teach adults; the money would be comparable. But those few days of fun make it seem possible to last through the final semester in Korea. I think the economy will improve. I'll lose some money, but still come out okay. And I don't want to leave my training now. I suspect the Koreans would try to impose some penalties on me—even if I give them the proper notice. They can't be relied on to stick to the contract. I hate knowing they have this unfair leverage. Money really is the root of all evil.

Entry 45
Wonju, Winter 1997-1998

I was two weeks in Kangnung, teaching at a workshop for elementary school teachers. The change of scene, the adult students, and the other native English teachers who were there provided welcome diversion from my usual Wonju life.

One of the native teachers was Brad Kelly, a thirty-year-old American who infuriated me with his arrogance and shallowness when I met him a year and a half ago at the program orientation. This is the guy who was chosen to speak for all two hundred fifty of us native teachers at the end of the week. I squirmed with shame and embarrassment while he stood on the stage and told us he had not prepared anything to say ahead of time—even though the Koreans had asked him to. He proceeded—arrogant and oblivious—to do a perfect rendition of the Ugly American. I'm sure the Australians, New Zealanders, Canadians, and Brits were reveling in this validation of their prejudice. But the Koreans didn't know the difference (or maybe some of them did, and they liked having their animosity confirmed too). They chose him because he's male, American, and looks good in a suit.

I dislike Brad less now. He speaks Korean more glibly than I, although he murders the pronunciation and grammar even worse than I do. What bugs me is that Koreans seem to understand him better at times. I wonder if they're pretending to understand him because he's male, whereas they wouldn't bother to do the same for me because of my lower status as a female.

Being in the company of a group of people here reminds me of how men—here and in the U.S.—dominate conversations with their loud voices and their knee-jerk one-upmanship. A person who speaks slowly and softly isn't listened to. Even when a woman manages to get something in, it's frequently ignored or interrupted. If a man repeats her comment, however, he'll draw a response. Korean culture encourages this unevenness.

Mr. Won called me while I was in Kangnung. He told me Inspector Ho from the provincial education office had asked me to come to Chunchon to help in the interviewing process for Korean English teachers. Another female native teacher was also chosen. I was surprised that he picked women for the job. I reported this news (and the fact that I'd be paid extra for the work) to Charlotte, Percival, and Brad as we walked on slushy sidewalks to the training center where the workshop was being held. Brad and Percival acted as if no one had said anything. After a moment of silence, they started talking about something else. This kind of information is the sort of thing that native teachers *live* to talk about—who's selected to do what special job for whom. And most importantly, how much someone will get paid. Only Charlotte pursued the subject with me and the men gradually joined in. They couldn't swallow the fact that I'd been invited instead of either of them. By ignoring me at first, they were trying to pretend it hadn't happened. What children! They come from male-dominated societies and they've been getting fat on the attention given them by this even more lopsided culture.

....

Anyway, I'm writing this while being held prisoner in the Swisstel, a hotel in Chunchon. I and Lucy (the other native English teacher) as well as all the Koreans involved in the interviewing process are confined here for three days. We're composing questions for the prospective Korean English teachers. On the third day we'll be sprung to do the interviews at a local school. We're literally not allowed to leave the hotel. All our meals are brought in. The phone was removed from my room; my notes on questions to ask the candidates have been collected from me and destroyed; no one is supposed to know which hotel we're staying in or what we're doing here. (I'm sure there isn't a teacher in the entire province who doesn't know who we are, where we are, and why we're here.) The measures seem extreme, but Koreans assume everyone will try to advance themselves in any way possible—honest or dishonest. A person in my position could make some money out of this. If only I knew some of the applicants!

This is another odd experience in Korea, but any break in my routine is appreciated. I like my room with a view—I look out over bare-branched alders, an apple orchard, and snow flurries fleeing the wind in all directions. It's a Western style room with a bed, and it's clean and new and the bathroom has a bathtub. Long, hot baths every morning and evening.

Entry 46
Wonju, Winter 1997-1998

Back in Wonju and teaching daily conversation classes until the semester resumes. Twelve girls come to my apartment every morning. After class today we went ice skating on the frozen river only a few blocks from here. Every winter the American army sets up big tents beside the ice so people can get out of the wind, buy hot chocolate, and sit down on benches to put on or take off their skates. Soldiers sweep the snow off the frozen surface and maintain a smooth rink. Korean vendors spread tarps on the hard yellow dirt and display skates for rent. Mine didn't fit very well and didn't offer much support. I found myself skating mostly on my ankles as I alternately chased and ran away from girls in our game of "it."

....

Our plans are set. My male friend will fly from San Francisco and meet me in Bangkok for a week's vacation in the end of February—I have some time between the end of this school year and the beginning of the next on March 2. We'll go to the tourist destination of Phuket and then on to the smaller island of Koh Phi Phi for snorkeling. I desperately need to vacate Korea.

Entry 47
Portland, Winter 2000-2001

I'm listening now. The Celtic harps and pipes slow my runaway heart. The music is a gift from a T'ai Chi student, someone who gives me hugs too. Several of the people in my classes have shown great kindness to me. Where does it come from? I'm always surprised by kindness. I wonder if they see or sense my illness and if the affection is a sign of concern. In any case, I'm grateful.

This week I'm scheduled for a haircut and a perm—an attempt to fluff up my life, lighten my countenance. It would be the first perm in decades. Will I go through with it? Yes.

One of the advantages of living in Portland is the many thrift stores—three within walking distance. There are lots of wealthy people here and they freely discard expensive clothes in excellent condition. Once through the wash, and it's mine. I think seven dollars is the most I've paid for anything, and that's extravagant by my gauge. I'm buying clothes that I like and enjoy wearing. I can afford to experiment and shopping is not the painstaking, demoralizing process it's been in the past. This way I don't feel obligated to wear something until it disintegrates. And I can be my own sloppy self, getting ink on my clothes when I write, and olive oil on them when I cook. I buy some, I redonate some—the clothes cycle through my life and reflect my varied moods.

The Nike class has been rescheduled for lunchtime. No more 5:00 alarms; I can sleep. I have great lunches at the cafeteria where the food is healthy, appetizing, and cheap. I read the newspaper and luxuriate in the flavors, the chewing.

I slept last night—was only up once to pee. Tigger padded into my dreams. I petted her and hugged her. Piglet came too. She kept putting her cool orange nose up against mine. Happy, loving feelings. When I woke, I spent ten minutes "palming." I lay there with my palms covering my eyes, shutting out all the light because black is the most restful color for eyes. I breathed deeply into my abdomen, rolled my eyes up as I inhaled, held them there briefly as I stopped my breath; then dropped my eyes down as I exhaled. It's an exercise to improve eyesight that I also like to use as meditation. My heart was pounding, so I calmed it by seeing it nestled in green grass, then floating and spreading out into a sunlit blue sky. I also told it to relax (a powerful word, I've discovered) and it listened to me.

....

I spent a few days in Arcata during the break between terms. My friends treat me lovingly and I love them back. The redwoods, the ocean, the marsh were all there for me to draw on. I got an acupuncture treatment and as usual, it helped—it enlivened me. Staying in the guest house of some friends allowed me to take my long afternoon naps. It was hard to stay awake while driving the four hundred miles, even though I divided the trip into two days. I couldn't possibly make it in one day, as I used to.

I'm determined to move back to Arcata.

....

I almost don't like to write this, because I so resent being poor—but sometimes I feel rich. What more could I want? I just had three good nights' sleep in a row. I cook delicious, wholesome food—salmon, great salads, sugarless scones and cookies. No TV and lots of good music like the Celtic tapes, David Darling's *Eight String Religion* and Dean Evenson and Li Xiangting's *Tao of Healing*. Saw a good movie yesterday (*42 Up*), went swimming, and practiced T'ai Chi in my own private rose garden (or so it seems that early in the morning). I have time to write, a good writer's group, and lovely T'ai Chi classes with delightful, respectful students. I have a Shiatsu session scheduled at a massage school next week. I'm feeling less tired. There are yellow freesias and burnt-orange asters on my table.

Entry 48
Wonju, Spring 1998

    I feel so well fed—by the soothing, stimulating words and touch of my friend; by the lush colors, shapes, and food of Thailand. Warm blue-green water invited me under. Propelled by long fins through coral canyons, I pursued fish whose crazy color combinations and patterns required extra seconds for my brain and eyes to comprehend. I was scared off by sea slugs that look like short, fat snakes, and I'm afraid I harassed sea anemones by putting my finger into their centers just to watch their aqua fringe flutter and close. Who could have invented such things! What an imagination! When no one else was around, I took off my suit and swam nude. It seemed necessary.

    We were walking along a sidewalk in Phuket when a man passed us leading a baby elephant that was just about my height. I didn't notice it until it was already beside me. The elephant's fluid footsteps made no noise at all. I felt privileged to be so close to that placid, flowing grace.

    I've hung bright sarongs on my apartment wall—orange turtles, red fish, and blue elephants. I look at them and scavenge crumbs of Thailand.

....

    Now I'm back to the brown and gray of Korea, but luckily spring has come early here. People at school seem to be in a good mood. Korea's financial crunch is forcing the vice principal to cut back on the number of supplemental lessons, and kids will be spending less time in academies in the evenings. There are benefits to bankruptcy.

    I'm a much better teacher than I was last year at this time—I have lots of tricks up my sleeve, and I'm more confident. When the teacher is relaxed, the students relax too. There's lots of humor and energy in the classes; I have the best relationship I've ever had with the girls.

Four months—sixteen weeks—to go.

....

I got Henry, the chaplain at the base, to mail a couple boxes home for me. He says the army doesn't charge soldiers for getting things across the ocean—they don't want to penalize them for being overseas. I sent a box of winter clothes to a friend who will put them into my storage unit and a box of gifts to my family in Portland.

Henry has been kind and is someone to talk to. We get together now and then for tea. I empathize and sympathize with the hard transition into civilian life that he's facing. He's also concerned about one of his two daughters—she's twelve and has a history of depression. Judging from the look on his face yesterday when I was in his office, he gets the same soothing effect from me that I get from him.

....

Min-hi called at seven o'clock this morning (Saturday). She just got back to Korea after going home to New Jersey for the break. She extended her stay while the doctors tracked the return of her breast cancer. It's reached both lungs, following the usual path from breast to lymph nodes to lungs to brain. The hormone treatment didn't work. So now it's back to chemotherapy and she's dreading the nausea and weakness and going bald. This could go on for a long time, even if the treatment's unsuccessful. At one point in the conversation she said, "I have plenty of time to die."

I'll visit her in two weeks. She's moving out of her apartment to live with her sister until she leaves for the U.S. at the end of April. Min-hi wanted to finish her contract, but she can't. What a weight she's carrying every day! Sorrow.

Entry 49
Wonju, Spring 1998

Instead of coming to school on Monday morning, a first-grade student jumped from her eleventh-floor apartment. Jumping from high rises is the Korean weapon of choice when it comes to suicide. When I was told about it—in a whisper by Mrs. Song—I felt the downward pull on my heart. How could one so young make that choice? How could she have such courage? How bad can life be at that age? (These are the questions of a person who has forgotten the morass of adolescence.)

Since then, I look at the faces in the river of students passing me in the halls and streaming out of the school gate at five o'clock. I wonder, "Which one of these girls killed herself?" It could have been any of them. She was a small particle in the flood of students I see every week. I didn't recognize her name. Would I even remember her if I saw a photograph?

I asked which homeroom she was in. Before I completed the question, I realized I had a hunch about that. She was in the homeroom of a lumpy, dowdy woman who, when she first arrived at our school last year, existed in a nearly catatonic state—her feet barely cleared the ground when she walked; her body and glance hardly varied from a narrow straight ahead. I was told she was on medication. Her class is the most unruly of all the first grades, and the room is littered and in disarray. Devoid of personality, no sustenance or life force could be gained from that teacher; she could only contribute to a student's sense of isolation and hopelessness. I doubt that she could detect a problem in one of her charges or have the wherewithal to address it if she did.

Recently she's been acting more alert. I've come to realize that she's a person of goodwill, and I like her. She was the only teacher who reacted with any emotion to the suicide (maybe she understands depression) and it endeared her to me. She must have felt some guilt, some remorse at not being able to catch this girl.

I'm told the student wrote a letter and showed it to her classmates. It said she was "very unhappy, had no friends, and would die." No one took it seriously.

Mrs. Song was not eager to discuss this incident with me, but I gleaned the following information from her: The faculty decided not to talk about the suicide with the girls unless an individual asked. Mrs. Song is not aware of anyone who has asked. The parents wanted the funeral procession to come by the school. A group of teachers objected, claiming it would upset the students. When the mother was told of the school's decision, she "fell down" (meaning, perhaps, that she fainted). The family members requested a meeting with the teachers and administrators. At this meeting the family pleaded that it could have been an accidental death. A compromise was reached—one car could come to the school and it would be met by a delegation of teachers and administrators. On that day, the third period class was started ten minutes early, just to ensure that all the students would be occupied when the car arrived. That was Wednesday. In the Thursday morning teacher's meeting, one of the oldest faculty members—a man who keeps telling me that he writes about Buddhism and is searching for the ultimate reality—spoke for a long time. He got vociferous in a light-hearted way. At one point, all the teachers laughed. I couldn't follow him, but I was told later that his subject was the argument between the girl's family and the teachers.

I asked one of the English teachers if suicide is a shameful thing in Korea. She said it's considered bad form to die before your parents (I presume because you can't fulfill the compact of taking care of them in their old age), and it's especially inconsiderate to take your own life.

That poor girl couldn't even garner anyone's attention by dying. What do you have to do? Her sinking hardly caused a ripple in the sea of students.

I'm left with the kind of feelings I have after watching a teacher furiously beat a kid. Who are these people, my colleagues? What lurks underneath the modern, educated, civilized-looking surface? And what about me? I'm part of this education factory. I'm participating in the mass production of carbon-copy people. I reward the ones who do well in the few sanctioned academic subjects, knowing there are plenty of creative, eccentric kids for whom recognition will only come in the form of punishment.

I saw a particularly lively, flamboyant student in the teachers' room the other day. I was about to compliment her hairstyle—short and a little spiky on top. It looked good on her. Then I realized that was why she was there. Later I watched her patting down her wet hair, trying to flatten it. She has been hit before for not wearing the proper blouse or socks with her uniform. She and so many others will be knocked into shape over the next years. Some of them will survive to be innovators and artists. But many will sink. Who is sinking now?

Charlotte mentioned the suicide to a teacher at her school. The teacher said she had heard about it, and added that the faculty there had just been warned not to hit students because suicides often leave notes, and if they mention such treatment, it reflects badly on the school. I wonder what all was in this last note?

Not long before the girl jumped, I was shaken by a particularly vicious example of hitting. The male art teacher struck the girl on the backs of the legs with his stick—hard—two or three times. Then he shoved and kicked her. I'd never seen a student kicked before. Through all this she was sobbing and trying to turn away. In disbelief, I said to an English teacher who was standing beside me, "He *kicked* her!" She walked down to the end of the room where it was happening and whispered to him that Emerson was watching. He took the student out of the room. I sat down and waited for my heart to recover.

Another depressing incident: I was teaching with Mr. Lee in the eighth section of first grade (an extremely bright and energetic group, the best of the lot) when he discovered that many of the students hadn't done their homework assignment—previewing a couple of pages in the text. He ordered each errant girl to stand and hold out a palm while he walked up and down the aisles, thwacking them with his hard plastic stick. It wasn't just a tap. He wanted to hurt them. I watched the squinched-up look of concentration on his face, renewed with each strike. The girls were obviously in pain—they were blowing on their hands and shaking them for some minutes afterwards—yet they took it in stride.

I sat still and watched this oppressive scene, mortified. Mr. Lee noticed my reaction, and later in the hour when the students were working on their own, he asked me how I was feeling. I said I felt depressed. He seemed dismayed and said he was sorry, but he was smiling, even grinning while he spoke. (He and I had discussed some weeks earlier the Korean custom of smiling while they express concern, and the likelihood that a Westerner would take it the wrong way.) He said he probably shouldn't be smiling. I said probably not. By then I was struggling to hold back my tears. I've seen too much of this brutality.

Why did he do it? He's managed to restrain himself in the past when I'm in the room. I think he's afraid his classes are not as controllable while I'm there because the students believe he won't hit them in my presence. Maybe this was his way of asserting his primacy—to himself, the kids, and me. I've always been impressed with how remarkably attentive and responsive that particular class is—what does he require?

I suspect him of hating women. He speaks rudely, disrespectfully of his new wife—calls her fat, tells the girls her nickname is *dung dung*, which means something like "fatty."

When one of the English teachers went to England for a month, I taught Mr. Lee's classes by myself while he filled in for the other teacher. I think this bothered him—another shred of control over his classes lost. He doesn't like the idea that I can successfully teach using only English. It puts more pressure on him to stop using Korean, something the government is urging teachers to do.

Hitting students became officially illegal in Korea with the beginning of this new school year. Will the policy change make even a dent in the stone wall of tradition?

....

Americans do a good job of contributing to the high level of testosterone that fills the air of this military town. Men's football, basketball, and baseball as well as other manly sports like studio wrestling pack the AFKN TV programming (American Forces Korea Network). I had the best laugh I had in weeks when I saw a football player who had just made a touchdown celebrate by head-butting a cement wall. You could just see the stars and birdies circling his head as he stumbled backward. He injured his neck and won't be playing for a while. In the same game (these were ESPN highlights) a kicker injured his pelvis and hopped around while clutching his crotch. It's not nice to laugh at another's pain.

At dinner at the army base restaurant, I see the usual examples of young male soldiers who look excruciatingly uncomfortable in their bodies. And if you happen to talk to them or overhear their conversation, they seem to be equally uncomfortable with their minds. One notable guy was dressed all in black—like a cowboy, complete with hat. He must have been doing Garth Brooks. Behind all the stiffness and rigidity is fear—fear of doing something incorrectly—and knowing they can't trust themselves to think independently. Many are control freaks, some of whom are probably working hard to control their need to control.

They're mostly very young and going through ordinary adolescent awkwardness. It can't be easy for them to be plucked from their home states for the first time in their lives and set down in a very foreign country.

I saw *GI Jane* with Percival and Charlotte last night. Horrifying, oppressive violence. Then I came home to the news show *20/20* on TV. They covered the story of a fourteen-year-old boy who raped and killed an eleven-year-old neighbor boy. The fourteen year old had been involved in a homosexual relationship for a year with a pedophile he'd met on the Internet. No wonder I had difficulty getting to sleep.

I awoke talking aloud—trying to explain to my mother and father why I had spent so much of my life intensely devoted to work that didn't bring me money. We were seated in the living room of our family home. I'm not lazy (I pleaded my case): witness my two years in Korea.

But I could never make a career of this work. Suicide would be preferable. The dream provided no answers, only a statement of where I am now and how I got here: trying to please my dead parents (who remain a stubborn part of me) by making money.

Violence comes in two forms—outward and inward, physical and emotional. They're inseparable, really, and equally destructive. I'm doing violence to myself by living and teaching in Korea.

Yet I believe in choosing life, in choosing the life of the soul—giving it what it requires to not just survive but flourish. The sticking point is, can you make a living if you choose life?

Percival's right hand is in a cast. He broke it across the back when he slammed his fist down on a desk, an inch from a student's head, in order to wake him up. It's time for Percival to go home. Me too.

....

Samulnori. A great Korean tradition. A quartet of drummers sitting cross-legged in a circle. The girls whale away, heads bobbing, drumsticks flying, eyes intent. Sound joins forces with color—the vivid gold, red, or blue of pantaloons; shirts crisscrossed over their chests, and headbands tied in back. Anyone within earshot is whisked into the soaring exuberance. Not Korean boys or men but Korean girls! I watch them practice on the dirt playground and I have hope for these kids. They can go at it, they can throw themselves into their tall and narrow or wide and short beribboned drums. The other girls in the school cheer. I know that this too is a disciplined art that demands years of training, but the performance escapes discipline and training and bursts into pure inspiration and emotion. The human spirit finds a way.

Entry 50
Portland, Spring 2000

First this dream: A sickly, demented woman—her skin opaque gray-green, her limp black hair drooping over her face in matted clumps—is naked and sitting astride her lover. He lies motionless on the ground, the life almost entirely gone from him. In appearance, they're a matched pair. The woman exhorts him to keep going. He's unable to respond.

Two who should be feeding each other are instead devouring each other. It's a fight to the death, and it's nearly over. My yin, my yang.

During a nap, I dreamt of sailing—something I did as a child and when I lived in Illinois. I was conscious of trying to show off my ability, but I was "in irons"—no matter how I turned the sails, the boat made no headway in any direction. Bewildered and embarrassed, I couldn't read the wind.

A series of dreams like the one of sailing have played out my flawed performance, battered self-confidence, and confusion. But some have been reassuring too, arguing with my misgivings and showing me a way out of this dark maze: Be flexible. Change. In one, I use a supple tree branch to swing myself upward to a new ledge, a new level. And in another, I'm dancing with a group of people who are showing me how to bend my back in ways I never have before.

Then there's last night's dream. I was sitting on a grassy slope watching a turtle. Its shell was an unpleasant mottled yellow-green with a ragged brown edge. I was a little afraid of it, and didn't want it near me. I said to a woman friend beside me that it was the ugliest turtle I'd ever seen. Joyce, who knew more about turtles than I did, protested. I modified my comment by saying okay, it's one of the uglier turtles I've ever seen. Joyce pointed out that its color was already improving. She let the turtle crawl up her arm and from there to the top of her head. Then it leapt into the air and flew into the branches of a tree where it began feeding. Several times it managed short flights from one tree to another. I noticed it had a long, thin tail. Joyce said at least it wasn't the kind of turtle that bites and it didn't have a sucker attachment coming out of its neck like some turtles do. I admired her for the love and charitable compassion that she offered the turtle. It responded to Joyce's warmth and grew steadily more beautiful.

Ever since Korea, I've felt an affinity for turtles. In Asia the turtle is a symbol of longevity; in this dream I think it's a symbol for my whole life, my self. If I can love myself, I can blossom (and live long?). And the turtle is slow, yet it wins the race. I have always needed to slow down, to live my life the way I do T'ai Chi. Maybe the elongated tail is there for the same reason as a monkey's or a squirrel's—it provides balance. The part about not biting, not having a sucker attachment—does it mean that at least I'm not deliberately harming others? Or, more likely, is it that I need not be afraid of myself.

....

Ninety-four pounds this morning. I'm losing weight again. As of today I will begin to gain weight. I'll go back to the soy protein powder, and take it twice a day. I'll take more of the tincture (gymnema sylvestre is a sugar metabolizer) and more of the multivitamins. I've tried running at the track at the Y a few times in the last two weeks—I was hoping I could get some of the spring back into my legs—but I'll have to stop that. Swimming will be limited to twice a week, only about twenty-five minutes at a time, and no real exertion.

My ankles are swelling. Why?

City living is not conducive to healing—the noise, cement, and pollution. A day trip to the ocean is good for a week.

I'm disengaging from popular culture. No TV, and I'm not much interested in the newspaper either. My one magazine, *The New Yorker,* is bound up in the patriarchy—too male, too harsh. It's becoming tough for me to find books that I really want to read. There are few movie possibilities. I spend more time doing nothing.

Friends of mine—a married couple—say no one should work more than four hours a day. In their fifties, they've managed to achieve that goal, at least for the most part. I'd like to get there too. I'm doing okay with money. Paying tuition is the hard part, and the proofreading jobs have been helping with that, but they crowd my time. I have Stanford University's proofreading and copyediting tests on hand. I'll do them soon.

I'm keeping my dining room table cleared off and fresh flowers in the vase.

Entry 51
Portland, Spring 2000

    Today I'm stopping. It's my first real stopping in a place that feels like home in several years. It's Memorial Day and the neighborhood is peaceful.

    A T'ai Chi friend—Sarah—came for dinner last night. She brought banana bread and the pink roses that are on my table. I slept from 9 P.M. to 6:30 this morning with a reading interlude somewhere in the middle (Maeve Binchy now). After getting up, I went to the park and did a barefoot, floating practice. Then breakfast and back to bed. I slept an hour and a half or more before getting up to wash dishes and make a pasta salad for a family dinner tonight. Lunch was a reprise of last night's dinner—potato leek soup, olive bread, fresh greens from Sarah's garden, cold chicken, and banana bread. I did some ironing—it seemed like a nice, mindless thing to do. My legs continue to cramp off and on, especially at night. And the swelling in my ankles comes and goes. I'll cover them with long pants today instead of wearing shorts.

....

    My own T'ai Chi practice is so different from the T'ai Chi I do in class. When I'm teaching I have to make everything crisp and distinct so the students can see. By myself, the outer movements are soft and muted—the real current is inside, swirling to and from my center. I take off my shoes and grip the cool wet grass with my toes; the soles of my feet open, and green light streams upward to fill every cell. I'm engulfed in a spiraling wave. I *am* a wave. All around me the blades of grass arrange themselves into spirals, circles, and pinwheels—a phenomenon that's accompanied my practice for at least ten years. The elements of the ground I'm standing on—it could be the mismatched grain in narrow wooden floorboards, pebbles in aggregate, cinders in a driveway, mottled linoleum, or grass—all take on patterns that I couldn't see before sinking into T'ai Chi. We reflect each other. Although I've never seen this sort of thing in the sky, the designs remind me of van Gogh's "Starry Night." Maybe I, a woman, resonate more with the earth; and he, a man, with heaven.

On the way to the park I climb cement stairs bordered by emerald-colored boxwood. I place my palms on the miniature wet leaves and receive their sparkling vibrance.

Sometimes I take my breakfast to the park—tea, toast, hard-boiled eggs—just so I can linger after my practice. The scattered picnic tables are empty except for the squirrels that pester me for food.

I know it's artificially fertilized, and who knows what they spray on it to keep down the dandelions, but the grass here is a heart-piercing color, and so lush. I stare at it and imagine myself lying with my head downhill, arms outstretched, so that a river of sunlit green flows into me, entering through the bottoms of my feet and pouring out through the tips of my fingers and the crown of my head. On its way, it cleanses, caresses, heals, and nourishes every particle. When I'm sitting on my bed meditating, this is one of the places I see myself.

....

I tried going to a meditation center a few times, looking for a place to sit for extended periods in the presence of others. It's in an old house, and the walls are white and the ceilings high. The space is immaculately clean and elegantly simple. The altar holds flowers, lazily smoking incense, and a few colorful artifacts. Three or four others showed up on the Sunday mornings when I was there. I relished the silence and the company, but the space is often not available for meditation on weekends because it's used for workshops. Another obstacle is that I just can't get behind gurus, and theirs is no exception. Now and then, excerpts are read from his books; he states the obvious in rambling, vague, and unartful words. The chanting done by the disciples sounds robotic—very annoying. I hoped going to the meditation center might become a regular part of my week, but I can see now that it won't.

....

    A member of my writer's group brought in a parable written by Olive Schreiner called "A Dream of Wild Bees": A woman sits sewing at a window on a hot afternoon. Her ninth child lies within her. As she drowses, bees circling her head seem to elongate into human forms and speak to her, offering to touch her womb and bestow certain gifts on the child. One offers health, another wealth, another fame, another love, and another talent. A final one offers none of these things. As a matter of fact, what this careworn-looking bee/phantom wants to give the baby pretty much precludes all the other rewards. Yet the mother grants only this being permission to touch her child. Its gift is that the new soul will see the ideal as real. Always conscious of and striving toward a vivid, irresistible light, the child will likely leave behind health, wealth, companionship, and recognition on its way. It's a noble life—to follow your own path, and be willing to pay the price. It has to be its own inspiration and its own reward. Olive Schreiner knew how a person could decide again and again to live without ordinary human comforts, eventually sacrificing her or his mortal life to pursue something that gives that life meaning. And what does this dream say about mother love? How wise and brave and unselfish it was for the mother to willingly launch her child out into the full mystery!

....

    "I think I have a twin sister. She made a womb in my heart." I heard these words as I woke in the middle of the night.
    Both sides of me are down to nothing—yang is used up; yin was a long time ago. It's either rebuild from nothing or die. My other self (thank god for reinforcements!) has evidently created a new womb for me in the place where love resides: I become my own mother. Can I be as loving and strong as the mother in "A Dream of Wild Bees"?

Entry 52
Portland, Spring 2000

I'm under the trees, camping at Ft. Stevens State Park for three days. Most of the surrounding campsites are full and there are wails and shouts from kids during the daytime. Still, it's a blessing to be here. My tent has screens on both sides, so I can see bushes and firs and even stars when I'm in my sleeping bag at night. A still lake rimmed with evergreens and the borderless, rolling ocean are nearby.

First thing this morning, I walked across a wide beach to the water and waded in—all the way in, over my head. I knew it was what I was supposed to do, had to do, despite the steely coldness of the saltwater and the inability of the sun's weak rays to compensate. I'm obeying a command when I do this. Is it the ocean's, or is it my body's? I'm returning. Not ashes to ashes and dust to dust, but water to water. Either I'm on the way out, or I'm being reborn.

I woke at midnight and cried a long, overdue cry. In a dream, both a man and a woman tell me I have to learn how to breathe properly. The man touches my face gently with the back of his hand (an allusion to Dad) and says I'm pretty, but I just have to learn how to breathe properly. I turn furiously on both of them, grab the woman by the lapels, and say I have something to tell her: "When you tell me how to breathe, you're telling me how to *be.* You can't tell me how to be. Get it?" She says yes, she gets it. The look on her face tells me that this is a hard one for her to accept.

Then the vision: Two women made of white light sit beside each other. They're larger-than life and imposing like Michelangelo's sibyls. Their glowing robes are luminous clouds, the folds outlined in even brighter light. All is soft and flowing. As I look at them, I'm the woman on the right. I tell my companion that I have something for her. In slow motion, a radiant egg rolls down my right arm, somersaulting on its long axis. It floats upward from my palm and drifts over toward her.

The egg continues high into the air and to her right. She almost lets it get away before reaching up and pulling it in toward her center. She sighs with agreement and delight. She gets it.

This idea again of two lives, two me's, a new second existence. And no one can tell me how to be, not even myself. Especially not myself—the person who absorbs all the injunctions of family and society, who is always on the outside, self-conscious and critiquing. I have to learn how to be who I am from moment to moment.

The night yielded another dream—of a plump, rosy-cheeked, tow-headed, blue-eyed baby. The child was bursting with health and joy, continuously laughing and smiling. He or she was surrounded by a group of people, all adults. But the baby was the leader, the director, and had a surprising vocabulary.

I woke with Madonna's song "Like a Virgin" in my head. I'm not a fan, but the phrase was apropos. This often happens—I wake with the melody of a popular song on my mind, a song I haven't heard recently. Sometimes it's hard for me to dredge up the words, but the lyrics always reveal something about my current state—something I'm resisting acknowledging.

....

Only Randy and I showed up for our last writer's group meeting. Instead of reading our work, we just talked. It turns out he's as disillusioned with life as I am. As I walked back to my car, I realized I felt more relaxed than I had for a long time. My legs were working better and walking was easier; some of the resistance in my thighs had disappeared. It shows what talk therapy can do

I need to express my sadness to a person, not just on paper. I'll make an appointment with someone that Maureen recommended. She does "process work," a therapy that relies heavily on dreams and uses a Jungian approach. More than taking any medicine, more than getting massage, I have to talk to someone.

Entry 53
Wonju, Spring 1998

If it hadn't already existed, Koreans would have invented April Fool's Day. The girls outdid themselves this year and I walked into it oblivious of the date. For starters, the darlings switched the room numbers on the doors. I was probably the only teacher genuinely confused and embarrassed by this because I visit twenty-one different classrooms every week and still have to look at the school map before taking off for class. They reversed all the furniture in the rooms, putting the teacher's desk at the opposite end; wore their blazers backward; and were generally rowdy. Desperate for revenge, I waved a bunch of papers in the air and told them they were all getting pop quizzes. That silenced them for a few seconds. I didn't discover until the following day that some of the first graders had attended second-grade classes and vice versa. That trick sailed over my head and must have provided plenty of amusement, as well as proof positive that all Asians look alike to Westerners.

....

The new school year is running surprisingly smoothly. There seems to be a new attitude toward Emerson. Maybe it's because they know I'm leaving in July—the middle of the semester—and they've planned the schedule as if I'm not here at all, so there won't be a gap to fill when I'm gone. Mr. Won actually *asked* me how many supplemental lessons I wanted to teach. It took me a while to understand what he was saying. I took advantage of the opportunity to cut down on my hours. Also, I've consistently had Korean teachers present in the B classes. The girls and I are having fun. It helps that I'm more confident and know more Korean—we can indulge our sense of humor.

Not everyone is enjoying this time. I saw three girls slapped in the face recently. One got a nosebleed.

I've been moved to a different desk in the teacher's room. Lee Yon-shil, newly assigned from third grade to first grade, requested to sit beside me. I miss Mrs. Song, but my new neighbor is a blessing. Her English is unusually competent and she *talks* to me. I'm always so grateful for any conversation. She's a sturdily built, vigorous woman in her early thirties and a dedicated teacher who's ready to try new methods. We come up with some lively, exhilarating classes together.

Lee Yon-shil encouraged me to bring my Korean language textbooks to school so I can occupy myself gainfully during some of the long hours between classes. It relieves my boredom and she's there to answer questions. I'm learning much faster—too bad I couldn't have started this earlier.

Kim Sung-gi is a new English teacher at our school who's close to retirement and, I've come to realize, quite burned out. I suppose he's around sixty, a nice-looking mild sort of man always on the lookout for diversions from the drudgery of teaching. He told me he has twenty contact hours a week, and that's too much. He doesn't like to come to the classes we're supposed to be coteaching, but he comes when I ask him to. It's a joke between us, really. He pretends to forget about the class; I stop by his desk on my way out of the teacher's room and remind him. We both laugh. I only require him to attend the B classes, sparing him a couple of hours. We like each other and I enjoy teaching with him, although I can see he has no patience left for the students, is rough with them (probably much more so when I'm not there), and they respond with open resentment. I think the girls count his age against him. His English is pretty good.

There's another woman I'm working with for the first time—Shin Young-sook. She's about my age, relatively fluent, and a superior teacher. I'm learning a lot from her, even though she tells me she hates teaching because she doesn't enjoy controlling kids.

This is her last year. After more than two decades, she'll start collecting a pension. Then one more year of studying to be a Presbyterian missionary and she'll go abroad to spread the word. Part of that word, I've discovered, is that you can't be a Christian without believing in creationism. She didn't like hearing that there are plenty of devout American Christians who would disagree with her.

She's a widow with two sons, aged thirteen and fourteen. The boys will travel with her. Her elderly mother with the bent back and poor health, who cares for the boys while Shin Young-sook is teaching and studying and going to church, will have to move in with one of her other children. I respect Mrs. Shin's intelligence and marvel at her energy. I appreciate her presence, her willingness to sit beside me at school dinners, and accompany me on school outings. She kindly praises my efforts at school and my attempts to learn Korean, and I lap up this encouragement.

She's becoming a better and better friend and has come to my apartment several times—invited herself, but that's okay. I don't feel comfortable letting her out of my sight when she visits because she does the usual Korean snooping. She looked into the box where I keep all my supplements and asked about them. She looked into an envelope with the words "Kwan Jang Nim" on it—it contained the money for my monthly fee at the dojang. Twice I've caught her looking around in my bedroom. Once I came out of the bathroom (I tried to be as quick as possible) and found her standing in the doorway to the bedroom. I thought she was safely occupied looking at some newly developed photos in the living room. Both doors of my armoire were open, revealing my check-off-the-remaining-days calendar and a list of the things I want, need in life to be happy—having friends, human touch, time to read and write and meditate, that sort of thing. This is all very private to me, not to mention the fact that I don't want Koreans to know I'm counting every day.

She asked if I have a Korean boyfriend. I acted surprised at the question (I *was* surprised at the directness) and told her of course I didn't. I always have the sense that these personal sorts of questions are being put to me by the entire surrounding Korean community. Certainly my answers are instantaneously broadcast. Well, maybe this will clear up one matter of speculation. I think Mr. Young is the only real candidate they could have in mind, and he has been entirely out of my life—and mostly out of my thoughts—for months now.

While we stood on the sidelines of the playground and watched the girls compete in sit-ups, chin-ups, and team games on Sports Day, she grilled me on why I'm single. I gave her my stock response—I've always been very involved in my work, and I didn't want children. She pressed it, saying some people marry and decide not to have children. Finally she said, "So you have never experienced married life?" I said no. It always bothers me to lie about this. It wasn't until the next day that I realized by "married life" she probably meant sex. She wants to know (along with everyone else) if I'm a virgin. Not a proper question in any country. But I think the main reason it bothered me was because it's repulsive to think about being forty-nine years old and a virgin. I hate having people here trying to trap my life and history inside their narrow, rigid culture. It scares me, as if I could be infected by such prolonged close contact. Part of me wants to tell them about my wildest sexual adventures (not wild by American standards) and make up a few too, just to let them know a woman can live a whole life, her own life, without society's interference in such personal decisions. Not that American society didn't influence some of my decisions to *have* sex.

....

Three and a half months to go and I'm already preparing to leave. I look at all my possessions in terms of what will be thrown out, sold, given away, or mailed home. I've always enjoyed the winnowing process.

In the last week or so I've been developing a more positive attitude toward my future. Before this, I didn't even want to think about it—there didn't seem to be any appealing ways to make a living on my horizon. But now ideas are bubbling up. Why not see it as if I'm embarking on a second adulthood? Fifty sounds like a nice round starting point. In a way, I'm just graduating—from my former life. I've accumulated certain hard-earned skills and credentials. Now what do I do? Another degree? Smarter ways to use my current education and abilities? Whatever the plans, they're going to include some money and some comfort and security for myself.

A master's in teaching English would be a good way to use my experience in the field and make myself eligible for more professional pay. I'd have to become more computer literate (always a good thing in this high-tech world, right?) and add to my knowledge of the language. Both of these things would increase my chances of getting jobs as a freelance copyeditor. Teaching T'ai Chi is another possible source of income. Eventually I'd want a ceramics studio in my home—with no pressure to generate money from it. Writing would always be happening. I'm thinking Portland for school. Who knows.

I'll be "composing a life" as Mary Catherine Bateson called it—doing several different things with no one thing crowding out the others.

I've been gradually transferring money to the U.S. despite the high exchange rate. (It's slowly coming down.) If the current rate holds I'll still manage to save about $13,000 this year. That will mean a total of $30,000 for the two years. Not bad. It helps me feel this time in Korea has been worthwhile if I can at least fulfill my goal of making some money.

....

I've tentatively signed up for a two-week tour of China after leaving Korea. I figure I should visit that country while I'm in the hemisphere. A stroll along the Great Wall sounds nice. Charlotte and Percival brought up the idea, and I asked if I could tag along. It's not that I'm eager to prolong my contact with them, but I don't want to travel in China by myself. After China I'll visit my friends in Singapore for a week, then to the U.S. The Koreans tell me summer is not a good time to travel in China because it's too hot and the public restrooms smell bad. This from people whose school toilets can be detected from fifty feet away.

....

The school week goes fast, but that doesn't satisfy me. Only leaving Korea will satisfy me. I fantasize sitting down to slow meals—good food and good conversation with friends—in my own country.

I'm so hungry. Don't know if it's psychological or physical. I overeat sometimes, looking to fill myself up, looking for any sensual gratification.

And then there's the endless mind chatter: I seem to be always either explaining something in my head to some phantom critical companion, or counting. I count everything (just as I always have): number of teapots thrown, number of laps swum, number of seconds that I stretch or hold a pose. My inner mouth runs on. I tell it to stop. It waits a little while until I'm looking the other way, then it starts again. It feels like a hammer—like a hammer coming down. I try to slow my heartbeat, soothe myself, but that ability is fugitive to me here.

I check off the days. I wait to leave. But I haven't forgotten that I also waited to leave the U.S. In the meantime, in the midst of all this chafing restlessness, my life is happening. I do learn things, but I resent the harshness of the lessons.

The other night I imagined (not for the first time) that I could feel Tigger stepping softly on the comforter, padding from the bottom of the bed up toward my head. I opened my eyes and fully expected to see her. Then I remembered where I was.

Entry 54
Wonju, Spring 1998

  The Koreans are so rough on their kids that it seems puzzling or maybe hypocritical that they'd devote a national holiday to them—Children's Day. At least it's a day off school. One of the many events planned throughout the city last Tuesday was a martial arts demonstration in Wonju's big indoor gymnasium. Along with others in my dojang, I participated. First on the agenda were Korean soldiers doing their very lethal-looking stuff—destroying boards and cement blocks, yet having less effect when whaling on each other's torsos. Mighty impressive. Then came the Wushu. There are three Wushu dojangs in Wonju and they all performed. My teacher is the captain (*Kwan Jang Nim*) of all three, although he only teaches in one. His former students are the head instructors at the other two. The boys in my dojang dazzled me with their exhibitions of forms, sword, and staff. The complex routines they demonstrated were apparently practiced in the late evenings after I'd gone home.

  I was expecting to do the long form Tae Guk Kwon by myself. But when I showed up at the gym—two hours early as I was told—Kwan Jang Nim handed me a white satin uniform to match his and informed me we would do the sequence together. Not only that, we would do it to music and speed it up, pausing for dramatic effect at strategic places. Driving and powerful, the tape sounded like a modern rendition of traditional Chinese music. With a boom box on the grass beside us, we practiced a couple times before going into the gym for the start of the program.

  I'm not sure why he did it this way. Maybe he was afraid I couldn't handle it on my own. He might have detected my stage fright kicking in, something that has always gripped me when I've had to "perform" T'ai Chi in front of an audience. Maybe he wanted Tae Guk Kwon to be better represented—we were the only ones demonstrating it.

But what a blast! It was a dance, a form of artistic expression. I didn't know my teacher had it in him. I managed to keep up and got through it without falling on my head. By the end I was euphoric.

This relationship with Kwan Jang Nim. Two ill-matched people on almost every plane. But the best that's in us connects when we do the sequence together. Between the two of us, the energy swells like a big wave and we get to ride it. We see each other under duress—I'm training and sweating hard, and he's teaching too many classes and trying to keep up with a bunch of high school kids. Often we're tired, irritated, or sick. And we still like each other. I like that. Better than sex. Which is inappropriate.

....

I'm pretty much "one of the guys" now at the dojang. Except when it comes to getting swatted with the wooden stick for being too rambunctious. Kwan Jang Nim sends me into the other room when he does that. There's a new little girl, about ten or eleven years old, who has come to two classes so far. The last time, she looked long and piercingly at me more than once. I thought she was going to speak, but she didn't. Later she plunked herself down on the windowsill beside me as I did some stretching exercises. I asked her name—it's Su-young. She told me I do well and I thanked her. She sticks close when she can. I wonder if she'll last there, especially after I'm gone. The boys are rough with her. We're the only females.

How long does it take to learn a T'ai Chi sequence? I'm repeating some movements a hundred times a day and I feel I'm just beginning to glimpse the interior of the form. Stretching is still a challenge, but not excruciating the way it was. I'm surprised that I've been able to achieve this degree of flexibility because I'm not naturally limber. It continues to amaze me how trainable bodies are.

Beth finally showed up—unannounced—at the dojang. She arrived twenty minutes before the end of class and sat down on a bench to watch the proceedings. Afterward she talked briefly with Kwan Jang Nim about my progress and rode home in the van with us. She relayed to me what he thought I should work on, but it was all stuff I already understood. I was gratified to find out that he thinks I learn quickly. I've worried that he may see me as incredibly slow and clumsy.

Beth asked about Kwan Jang Nim's new baby—his second child, both of them boys. She wondered if he wanted a girl this time. He said no and bragged about how large both babies were—about four kilograms.

She also talked to Kwan Jang Nim about the practicalities of making a living teaching Wushu. I learned that he has had to move the dojang several times—rents are high in Wonju. The current one is spacious and located beside his apartment complex. I hope he continues to succeed. It's a rugged business and sometimes I wonder how he can keep up such a punishing teaching schedule. For months he's had a chronic cough.

Beth explained to him that I'll be leaving in July—my contract is up, she said, and the financial situation in Korea doesn't encourage a foreigner to stay on. He has asked me several times since that evening, "Why are you going to America?" I always steer my answer toward the contract's ending, but he doesn't seem to understand the word "contract." Even in Korean it's probably unfamiliar to him because it's still a foreign concept here. I'll be sorry to leave him.

It just occurred to me to write an article on him for an American martial arts magazine. I wonder if there's an appropriate outlet for such an article—I wouldn't be writing from the usual macho point of view. I'll need photos, but I was planning on taking some of all the people at the dojang anyway.

....

After a Friday class two weeks ago, Kwan Jang Nim handed me a copy of a chapter from a book written in English about maintaining high-quality medical records. He asked me if I could translate it for his wife. Happy to have a chance to do him a favor, I said sure, it's easy. I assumed his wife worked in the records department of a hospital. I tried to explain to him in

Korean that first I'd rewrite it in easy English, then I'd work with a teacher at school to translate it into Korean. Later I decided Beth would be a better choice because she's more fluent than any of the teachers.

The next day, Saturday, I spent three hours reading, comprehending, and condensing the eight-page article into translatable English. The author's wording wasn't too bad, but it wasn't great either, and there was plenty of jargon. I knew that trying to go directly from the original to the Korean would waste too much time and probably result in gibberish—I wouldn't be able to make the meaning of the sentences clear to Beth. I chose the vocabulary and sentence structure carefully, avoiding as many of the pitfalls between the two languages as possible. I typed my version into the computer, leaving space between the lines for the Korean, and printed two copies. That night I got together with Beth and we worked on the translation.

At first I despaired that she could do it. She wanted to look up every other word in her electronic dictionary. I thought the sentences would be fairly easy for her. Again I was struck with the difficulty of bridging the two languages. But gradually we picked up speed and had completed all but two sentences by the time I left, after two and a half hours. Beth finished up and rewrote it neatly on the second copy the next day.

I took a basket of fruit to her the evening we did the work. When I met her downtown the next day to pick up the article, I gave her two wool sweaters I'd bought in Korea. One I had only worn once.

I was happy with what we'd accomplished. I've decided this is the best way to translate the two languages—with a native English speaker and a native Korean speaker. It would be better if I knew more Korean. But as long as the two can communicate effectively with each other, they can keep checking on the accuracy of the translation. I suppose having two people work together is impractical, probably cost prohibitive, but it's ideal. Otherwise, all sorts of misinformation could get invented and passed on. Good editing is needed too—the original writing has to be clear and pared down before even starting the translating.

I returned the material to Kwan Jang Nim the following Monday. What service, I thought! Back in two days. And a translation that was accurate. And it was free.

On Wednesday evening, when he picked me up to go to class, his wife and three-year-old son were in the car—a first. When I try to remember how she looked, I see huge red red lips and the rest of the makeup mask—the Korean standard of feminine beauty. I think she was pretty, but I worry that I wouldn't recognize her if I saw her again.

When Kwan Jang Nim stopped the van to wait for another student to emerge from his apartment, he turned to me and, holding the original version of the article in his hand, asked if I could do a line-by-line translation. His wife has no English, but she spoke the word "summary" in English and made it clear she didn't want that. I wasn't comfortable with the word because it didn't describe what I'd done, but speaking in Korean I said it was only a summary in the sense that I had made the language less complex. I stressed that—nevertheless—the Korean was true to the original. I said Beth and I could not do a line-by-line translation.

Crestfallen. That's a good word here. My crest had fallen. I was hurt that she was dissatisfied, but I tried to slough it off. I told myself that I should have expected this. They have no way of distinguishing a good translation from a bad one, no way of appreciating the time and work and expertise involved. Still, it seemed rude. They were looking a gift horse in the mouth.

In class that night Kwan Jang Nim worked with me for a while, and as he often does, changed his instruction on some movements. This is a gripe I have with him—the variation in the instruction after I've worked hard to incorporate certain elements. He never admits to any conflict, only jumps on the old way as my mistake. (My Chinese teacher did this too and in the Asian culture, students are not supposed to point out inconsistencies. They just have to roll with it and think—or pretend to think— they had it wrong.) It was a bad night to be perpetrating this on me again.

I talked with Beth's husband, Russell, that night on the phone and with Beth the next evening. Russell thought the situation was deplorable and that they had indeed been rude. Beth called Kwan Jang Nim and explained why we had done the translation the way we had. This was all I was hoping she would do but she went on to tell him I felt he didn't appreciate our work, that I had done him a favor because I like him, and it had required serious effort. All true, but it seemed unnecessarily and embarrassingly detailed. He wanted her to impress on me that he did appreciate the work. He said he was afraid my feelings were hurt, but couldn't express that because of the language barrier. He was evasive about who the translation was for—evidently it wasn't for his wife after all. I feel even more taken advantage of. But I appreciate his concern for my feelings.

The constant discomfort of living in Korea! I'm so frequently chafing, feeling out of place. I wasn't looking forward to seeing Kwan Jang Nim, but I knew I wouldn't forgo a class. The next day was Teacher's Day, so I dutifully wrapped a gift for him—a double wooden picture frame—and gave it to him when he picked me up. He handed me a collapsible T'ai Chi sword. I'm pleased with the gift, even though he hasn't taught me any sword work. I've learned some in training camps in the past and can always pick it up again in the U.S. That evening he spent a lot of time with me. So I got some compensation.

....

Teacher's Day is quite an extravaganza. The presents pile up on and around all the teachers' desks—everything from flowers to jewelry to small appliances. It's partly a popularity contest and the size of the pile is a graphic rating system for all to see. But mostly it's just the entrenched custom of bribery. The wealthier the parents, the more impressive the gifts. Extra largesse is bestowed on teachers that control crucial subjects, especially if a grade is in question. I don't determine grades, but still I got bouquets, cards, and various souvenirs of traditional Korea. The math teacher whose desk faces mine seemed both pleased and embarrassed by the gifts stacked to shoulder height on either side of her—who doesn't like being on the receiving end of Christmas? But she knows this is an indulgence whose days are numbered. I remember the endearing but economically valueless kid-bought trinkets my mother used to bring home from school.

....

Inspector Ho called me from the education office in Chunchon one evening last week. He offered me a job teaching at Kangwon University. I thanked him but said no, I'm a little homesick (an English word I know Koreans are familiar with because they ask me about it all the time). It's a reason I can give for wanting to leave Korea without creating any hard feelings. I didn't even think to ask about the pay. "Are you kidding?" I fantasized saying. "I'll be out of here like a shot the day my contract is up." But I left it at homesick. It was nice to get the offer—it shows some level of appreciation.

....

June 4, 1998. Election Day and a miracle has occurred. Kim Dae-jeong is South Korea's new president. It's the first truly democratic election since this country ostensibly became a democracy after World War II. The military-industrial complex may be on its way out. Kim has been compared to Nelson Mandela, and rightly so. He has survived jail and assassination attempts at the hands of the powers that were. He'll still have to deal with the entrenched bureaucracy and their cronies in big business, but real change is finally stirring. I'm surprised a majority of Koreans voted for him. Even thirty-three-year-old Mr. Lee, as disgruntled as he is with today's Korea, couldn't bring himself to vote for this reformer. Change is just too unfamiliar and too scary for many people. Labor and education are top priorities for the new administration. Korea has a chance now.

....

I've grown to truly love the girls at school. I walk down the wide stairs after a class and feel love pouring out of my heart, exuding from my skin, and cascading like a waterfall. It's a physical feeling, almost painful. Every last one of them is dear to me, even the insolent ones, the dull ones, the disruptive ones.

Entry 55
Portland, Summer 2000

    I walk slowly down the steep hill that my apartment building leans against, concentrating on using my legs to stop me from tumbling forward. By now, not having to think about something like this seems part of an unreachable past. I can only surmise that most people are thinking about other things besides whether their legs will hold up from one step to the next. I empathize with the fragile-looking seniors who pause here and there on their trudge upward to their condominiums and apartments.

    I come to the welcome flat of Northwest Twenty-third Avenue and have only a few blocks to go—Everett, Flanders, Glisan (they're alphabetical) and turn right. I catch my reflection in the windows of restaurants and stores, turn my head to watch myself go by. My legs are so narrow, yet my stomach protrudes behind a blouse that's hanging out and billowy, chosen to hide my misshapenness. But I detect it easily. I wonder if the people I pass are looking at my strange form, or if they're looking at me looking at myself. Anyway, effort that it is, the destination is well worth it—another of my weekly appointments with Hannah, my therapist.

    Hannah's a student in process work, and an intern at the clinic. I linked up with her because she's cheaper than anyone else there. It would cost seventy to ninety dollars per hour for me to see a certified therapist. The clinic only charges twenty dollars for my time with Hannah. I'm not sure that she gets any of that. But she's good! She listens and she gets what I'm saying. She has helpful, kind, supportive things to say. I have to be careful not to offer up my dreams as a way of entertaining her, making her admire me, and therefore (in my worldview) like me. I cry a lot. That's really why I go to see her. I need someone to cry to.

    I told Hannah about the critics that hover over me and make their disparaging comments on how I wash the dishes or park the car or spend money or swim or poach eggs. It was the first time—the only time—I've mentioned it to anyone. After all these years. All this time I've spent absorbing their blows, defending myself, arguing with them. The faces change—they're friends, relatives, acquaintances, enemies—but the tone of the chatter is unremittingly the same. They've been my company. Hannah said she has these too—usually it's her father. Does everyone live like this? When I first exposed them, I wondered what I would do if they weren't there. What would fill the vacuum?

As soon as I told on them—brought in a witness—they became surprisingly meek. The curtain was drawn aside and the wizard exposed. How strange! How simple it was to knock them off their base! They still pop up, but they're fainter and I can cut them off—cut myself off. The key to disarming them was to know them as myself. Looking at them and telling them to go away is one of my practices. What takes their place? Sometimes just quiet, sometimes loneliness. They won't be entirely gone until I have enough love and compassion in me to fill that space.

Hannah has given me two good pieces of advice. One is to examine my dreams more rigorously, see every character, every element as a part of myself. This is not news to me, but she has made me be more disciplined. It's so tempting to see people in dreams as those people in waking life—it often takes the onus off me, gives me someone to blame, and diverts me from looking critically at myself. It's a childish, unsophisticated way to interpret dreams. The other piece of advice is to invest more of my spiritual self into my teaching in order to make it more intriguing and less boring. With all the classes I have now (twelve hours per week), repeating the same instructions around the same movements—often word for word—gets old. I've taken her advice and it works. T'ai Chi is so much more than the motions. And students are as hungry for the inner purpose as I am.

....

I went to a Fourth of July potluck at the home of one of the members of my writing group. I intended to take a pasta salad, but was broke and couldn't buy all the ingredients, so I just added to the beans I already had and made a chili. I took it in the covered saucepan that I used for cooking. Operating out of a hyperglycemic fog of fatigue and fuzzy thinking, I was dimly aware that it made a lackluster presentation, but it was the best I could come up with. When I set it down on the table at the party, my pan of chili looked noticeably depressed compared to the bright, colorful elegance of all the surrounding dishes. They had a joie de vivre that mine lacked. It's just as well that my chili didn't appeal to people—I brought most of it home.

I was already full when I went, having eaten two containers of yogurt with fruit and some fructose-sweetened butter cookies. Nonetheless, I tried most of what was there, including salmon, shrimp, polenta, and grilled vegetables. I also sampled the flan, strawberry shortcake, white cake with chocolate icing, and brownies (I've been craving chocolate lately). By the time I was ready to leave, I was uncomfortably stuffed and swilling water.

On the way home, I drove to the rose garden where I sat on a bench and absorbed. Walking was too difficult with such a crammed stomach. I went home and napped until it was almost time for bed.

Red meat is my other recent craving, so hamburgers are a new addition to my menu. Sometimes it seems to be the only thing that "holds" me for very long. I've also started taking alpha lipoic acid supplements. It's mostly found in red meat and it's the one thing I haven't been taking that's mentioned over and over again in the literature on diabetes.

....

I'm making my way through school—over halfway there. Three more courses and eight hours of thesis to go. And I'll have to pass a Spanish proficiency test.

A Vermont publishing company sent me a book to edit. It's by a Buddhist teacher on self-applied acupressure. The trouble is, it was written in Chinese and translated into English by a native Chinese. The book really needs more than editing, it needs to be rewritten in order to make it publishable. That's essentially what I'm doing. I'm learning from it—some of the acupressure techniques are helping me cope with the cramps in my legs and feet.

I also accepted a proofreading job from Stanford University Press (I passed their test!) The idea is that I'll eventually work up to doing editing for them. This book is on Jungian psychology—also interesting.

Both books have to be completed by the end of the month. Why did I take on all this work? How will I get it done? When will I rest? Again, I'm doing it for the money.

....

I dreamt of walking on a sidewalk in a Korean neighborhood (but it looked more like America). I was leaning into the wind, barely able to move forward, when I was blown over. Some of my students were across the street and I didn't want them to see me on the ground. Wanting to show them I could handle it, I scrambled back up and struggled on. This was another dream of being embarrassed by my weakness. Maybe I should admit that I'm down and stay there. Maybe some of this would blow over.

Am I off course? Is this a stupid question? What's the right course? How can I heal? I look for release. These are the releasing things in my life: eating, swimming, being under the trees, finger painting, writing, meditating, practicing T'ai Chi, listening to music, talking to Hannah. Even peeing is a release—so much water washing through me. These are the confining things in my life: school, editing, proofreading, and too much teaching. If I give up the confining things and follow the releasing things, I give up making a living. Do I just go back to following my bliss? Somehow, sometime, there has to be joy in my life again.

....

Last weekend, after my Saturday T'ai Chi class, I drove out to the beach. The state parks were full, so I set up my tent at a small private campground south of Seaside. I was in an open field with lots of other campers. Not being under trees was a disappointment, but it was quiet and the air was fresh and laced with the sweet smell of cut grass. I could hear the ocean.

Again I felt compelled to submerge myself under the cold, salty waves. First thing in the morning I padded across a very wide beach to the receded surf. As I peeled off my sweatshirt and set it down on my towel, I noticed two fishermen standing in the foam about a hundred yards away. I was afraid I'd frighten them—this sticklike ninety-pound weakling walking into the water. I frighten *myself.* Were they wondering if they'd have to come rescue me? I waded in past my waist and dove through a swell. Just as I used to do in the Atlantic Ocean when I was a kid, I swam to the lift of a wave, turned around, and rode it in toward shore. After a few minutes of body surfing, it was a long cold trek against a stiff wind back to my car. I warmed up under the shower at the campground. The rest of the day was spent in the sun on the beach—blue sky, blue ocean. I was very tired by the end of the afternoon and longing for shade. On the way home I discovered Saddle Mountain State Park, seven miles off the highway up a rocky road. What a find—secluded walk-in campsites in the forest. I'll have to try it next time.

The camping weekends are great—they get me out of the city. But they're also draining and not good for weight gain.

Entry 56
Wonju, Summer 1998

    Last week the girls took their finals in the mornings and had the afternoons off. It gave the teachers a chance to go on a picnic. The drive through unspoiled countryside was charming—forests, mountains, thick green fields, and monsoon waters pouring over wide, flat rocks in the rivers. I was so grateful that I had come along. Shin Young-sook was beside me to speak English; I couldn't have asked for more. But my respite was soon spoiled. We were eating our lunch beside a stream after visiting a temple. One of the male teachers who had had too much soju started throwing silly, repetitive comments at me. He asked about San Francisco—said he wanted to visit me there, he'd been reading about it on the Internet. We divided into groups of three or four and played a Korean game to see which team could pile up small rocks the highest before their teetering tower collapsed. All through this he explained over and over to me what the goal was. The other teachers were as exasperated with him as I was. On the way home, we stopped at a restaurant for dinner. He drank some more and the heckling got worse. He shouted at me from another table that it was rude to wear my sunglasses on my head. Shin Young-sook explained this was true in the country but not in the city. I took them off. (Charlotte further educated me over the phone that evening that smoking and sunglasses signal a loose woman to Koreans.) Later during the dinner I asked Mrs. Shin to translate something else he was slurring at me. She wasn't sure who I meant at first and asked, "The rude one?" I said yes, the rude one. I did understand him when he said he wished he could converse with me, but can't because I don't speak enough Korean. The head teacher sitting near me applauded this. Mrs. Shin told my harasser he should slow his speech and be willing to repeat things. He giggled and said he couldn't. At this point Mrs. Jong across from me launched the all-too familiar theme of why aren't I married and did I have any plans to marry. I answered with a curt no. By now I was fuming and barely containing the tears. If anyone said one more offensive thing, I was determined to walk out. My discomfort was obvious to all of them and I had the impression they were amused and entertained by it. They started on the usual flattery—I look younger than I am, my complexion is so clear. I responded with the bare minimum. As we climbed into the cars after dinner, the rude one came up to me and bobbed up and down repeatedly, saying good-bye in English each time. He was afraid he had offended me, he said. The principal waved her hand dismissively and told him not to worry about it.

The next morning I was standing beside Mrs. Shin in the teachers' room and the rude one came up and asked her to explain to me that he was sorry for his behavior, he had drunk too much soju. I told him it was okay. At least he apologized.

What a nightmare that was! The Koreans seem to be getting squirrelier and squirrelier as my departure gets closer. I feel a deep, pervasive, almost universal hostility. Some of it may come from envy that I'm leaving the country and they're not. I think it's very difficult for Koreans to accommodate or be kind to a foreigner, especially a Westerner and a United States citizen. The pattern I've mostly experienced is that they flatter you, befriend you, see what they can get from you, and then drop you when those possibilities are exhausted or they see you can't benefit them materially. Right now I see them (in general) as cold, materialistic, calculating people full of contempt and derision for—who?—everyone really, not just foreigners. They treat each other with the same lack of respect.

....

Like the dope that I am, I agreed to teach some extra conversation lessons during the last six weeks of the semester. How bad could it be? It was bad. There was no conversation book, so I had to create another new lesson every day. They put me into a tiny library with too many students, all sitting in carrels so I couldn't see them and they couldn't see me. No blackboard, and I could barely squeeze through the aisles to get to the students. After three days I told them I wouldn't teach there anymore. Mrs. Shin stepped in and traded rooms with me. She gives the students two pages from an English grammar workbook to complete each day—that's her way of coping.

....

Papers from the Wonju Education Office appeared on all the teachers' desks last week. It's a list of over a hundred words that may be used in directives coming from the higher-ups. It's feared the teachers won't understand these words, so they're accompanied by their definitions in everyday Korean. Probably many of them derive from Chinese characters. It makes me wonder again how well Koreans communicate with each other.

....

Gradually I've been taking the English teachers, two or three at a time, to dinner at the club on the army base. It's my parting gift to them. They all order steaks and try baked potatoes and rolls (with real butter) for the first time. I've not invited Mrs. Yu—she's been so disapproving and unhelpful all along, and she moved to a different teachers' room, so I never see her. But I wonder if I'll regret this later—see it as smallness on my part once I'm out of here and my feathers have had a chance to smooth down.

....

Things haven't been going well in the dojang. Kwan Jang Nim is doing a good job of eroding my self-confidence. I never know what will be wrong with the way I do something. It changes every week. In some cases he taught me one way then months later changed it, and after I struggled to unlearn and relearn, he changed it back to the original way. Maybe he's getting different input himself from other teachers, but he doesn't bother to explain. He belabors criticisms way past the point where I understand, and his exaggerated mimicry of my mistakes isn't funny anymore. I know I'm lucky to have found him—he's so skilled and of all the people here he's been one of the kindest and most sensitive. I think he understands the internal source of the movement; his teaching has brought me around to the same principles that I emphasized to my own classes even though the sequences are quite different. But I'll be very happy to leave the dojang. I'm looking forward to getting back to a softer, gentler T'ai Chi than what I'm struggling with here.

It's too hot to be training this hard anyway. One night I opened all the windows in the dojang so we could get a cross draft. The most senior student arrived a few minutes later and closed them all. Then he turned on two fans. He was wearing a full, zipped-up sweat suit. I just don't get the Korean strategy for dealing with this oppressive weather. Mrs. Song asked if I've been heating my apartment at night. She says all Koreans do during the rainy season—I guess to dry things out. But the heat barely lets me sleep as it is. I have a fan blowing directly on me all night.

After a frustrating evening in which I discovered the battery in my camera needed to be replaced, I finally took pictures of Kwan Jang Nim and the students. I'm glad to have this record. Kwan Jang Nim wore a special summer uniform—brown satin and sleeveless. Some of the other students dressed in their best too, and made sure every shot was carefully posed. My only candid pictures are of the youngest kids horsing around before class. I'm not in any of the shots—I don't enjoy having my picture taken—but I do have two that Kwan Jang Nim gave me from the Children's Day demonstration. All of us had gathered by his van afterward. I'm standing beside him; the boys are hanging on each other and looking eagerly into the camera. The hand of a young man who has at times helped teach is on my shoulder—the only discordant element. No Korean man would presume to show that kind of familiarity with a Korean woman. I look at that photograph and I can feel that hand. But I do like having a photo of Kwan Jang Nim and me.

I wonder what life is like for a thirty-five-year-old martial artist. He'll continue to gain rank because of his teaching and judging at tournaments. But he seems physically tired. His cough still hasn't gone away (it's been months) and recently he's much less active during class. Perhaps some of the earlier aerial acrobatics were for my benefit.

My feelings toward Kwan Jang Nim have been so changeable—hero worship, attraction, annoyance, hurt, frustration. Most consistently I've felt uncomfortable, awkward, out of place, constrained, confused, and embarrassed—the story of my Korean experience.

....

Things are going badly with regard to final arrangements between the native teachers and the powers that be in the provincial education office. I'm worried they won't honor the contract and give us our last month's salary, severance pay, and the cost of our flight home before we leave the country. I have no hope of ever getting the money if I leave here without it. As it is they rigged the dates of our second contract to be just short of a year so they wouldn't have to give us severance pay for that year. None of the faxes Percival and the Canadians in Chunchon and I have sent over the last two months have elicited even an acknowledgment that they were received. Brad keeps telling us Koreans consider it impolite to discuss contracts. Of course they do! This is strategy—not etiquette. They don't want to be held to the provisions of the contract. And talking to someone about such things would mean acknowledging that he or she is worthy of talking with instead of at. This is what's euphemistically referred to as "lack of transparency." The word "honesty" can be more accurately substituted for "transparency." I'm especially apprehensive because of the swelling anti-American and anti-Westerner sentiment. The economic crisis continues to spawn both justified anger and scapegoating.

Twelve of us—Canadians, Brits, a Korean family of three, and myself—have made reservations for a China trip based on a July 27th departure date. But now it seems they're changing what they said earlier about when our contracts are truly complete. Koreans don't plan ahead, but travel arrangements have to be made well in advance, especially when you're travelling in the busy season. The "papers" they keep saying will be coming soon to finalize the dates and the financial settlement have not appeared.

I have this fear that I'll somehow be forced to stay in Korea, won't ever escape. Irrational, I know, but very real.

....

I've often wanted to explain to Korean acquaintances who don't understand why I'm so agitated about my battles with the school authorities that "it's the principle." It may also be the money or the too heavy demands made on me. But principle enters into it too. That's a foreign concept to most Koreans. Fighting authority is a foreign concept. Objecting or drawing attention to yourself by criticizing the status quo and its supporters only draws punishment. Consequently the vast majority of Koreans have internalized docility and passivity. The solution to any problem is always for the person who is objecting to stop objecting, buckle under, and get with the program.

In what way is the mystery of how well do Koreans actually communicate with each other connected to this behavior? Communication among people brings movement and change—they follow naturally and inevitably. I can see why good communication wouldn't be fostered in a culture where all attempts to change are considered threatening and subversive.

Common sense is the enemy of tradition.

....

More rankling: I understand why Koreans don't wear outdoor shoes in the house. The streets are littered with vomit, spit, human urine, and sometimes even excrement. I watched a mother hold her two-year-old over the curb of a busy street while he defecated. Saturday morning there were three big piles of vomit on the stairs to my apartment. People are constantly spitting on the sidewalks. Many of my students think nothing of spitting on the stairs inside the school. There are so few receptacles for garbage. It's strewn everywhere.

....

     I went to Seoul with Charlotte and Percival. We met the Canadian couple from Chunchon and the five of us trooped from travel agency to travel agency, slowly finalizing arrangements, paying for and picking up tickets. Even though in all but one case the reservations had long been made and the agents knew we were coming in, not one of them had tickets ready for us. It was a long, drawn out, typically Korean process.

     At our last stop, Percival surprised everyone by insisting on paying for Charlotte and his China trip with a credit card. He hadn't checked this out ahead of time, but they fairly readily went along with it. Then he refused to pay the four-percent fee. He lied to them, saying he didn't have enough money in Korea to pay cash—he *had* to pay by card and in his goofball reasoning this meant he shouldn't have to pay any more than the cash amount. Charlotte first tried to get him to pay cash and then to at least consent to the fee. He waved her off and told her she was embarrassing him! The rest of us thought the fee was reasonable because he's paying with funds that aren't even in Korea. And this is basically a cash society. After about thirty minutes of angry huffing and puffing, he finally wore them down. By that time the rest of us had retreated outside, too ashamed to stay and witness any more of the spectacle. Charlotte said she would have it out with him when they got home. Victorious, Percival joined us and we started down the stairs to the subway. I told him I was just glad he wasn't an American. A rash comment that pissed him off even more.

....

     I think Percival is close to snapping. He's having shouting matches with teachers over our final arrangements and is in constant conflict with his colleagues over the wholesale beating of students. He tells me the boys are made to roll up their pant legs and then struck on the bare calves with a whip. Apparently Percival had enough of this during his school days in England and knows it only embitters kids. He asked to be transferred to a less violent teachers' room. The vice principal didn't move him, but he directed Percival's office mates to do their hitting elsewhere. They acquiesced for only a couple weeks. Now they're back at it. None of the teachers who share his room even say hello to him.

It's strange—he seemed to be the happiest, best adjusted of all of us for a long time. He was basking in the status of being a male Brit teaching in the "best" high school in town. Now the antiforeigner fury is unleashed in his school and rearing its ugly head toward Percival. Ironically, his placement in the "best" school meant he was actually in the worst. Because of the way people are selected for advancement in this country, the most respected institutions harbor the most rigid, blindly obedient, reactionary, chauvinistic, narrow minded, punitive, dishonest, arrogant, and uncreative people. I feel sorry for him, but I've also thought that turnabout was fair play—he's perpetrated his own share of arrogance and prejudice. It's a sort of poetic justice.

....

Lee Yon-shil took me to an art museum in Wonju. As we sat in its courtyard—walls draped with ivy, a fountain spraying graceful patterns into the air—she asked, "Don't you wish you could stay in Korea?" The question struck me as disingenuous—could she really wonder about that? "No," I said, "I'm a little homesick and I'm anxious to go back. Two years is a long time to live in a foreign country." My leaving seems to be causing some anxiety in the Koreans around me. For the most part they don't like me, but they're worried about what I think of their country, what I might have to say about it. And most of them wish they could go with me.

....

I suppose it's not surprising that in the midst of all this I'm back to feeling shaky about my future. I thought these two years would crystallize my direction—that by now I'd have an inspiration or at least a plan. I'm not sure I've gotten anywhere beyond where I was when I arrived. Am I the kind of person who gets a master's in teaching English as a second language and becomes a full-time teacher? My heart isn't in it. I think of telling Miss Waugh, my high school debate coach, that I didn't want to join the debate team in college. She was indignant. I was good at it, she argued, it was a step toward success in life, and therefore I should do it. Theoretically I could have, but my temperament wouldn't allow it. I wanted to be a writer, immerse myself in literature. Then I fell in love with clay and started a twenty-four-year-long love affair. Then I became obsessed with T'ai Chi. I would follow my heart now if it would just speak up. Maybe I've smothered it in practicalities. Maybe it doesn't bother to speak to me because it knows I won't listen unless what it has to say includes money.

Entry 57
Wonju, Summer 1998

I'm free! Done with teaching and suddenly fifty pounds lighter. I worked on Saturday because we had the school English speaking contest and a closing ceremony before the summer vacation. The best part of the day was when the principal invited me into her office, gave me a small present, and told me not to worry about my salary, severance pay, and reimbursement for my plane ticket home—it will be in my bank account before I leave. Why did she wait this long to tell me? Either she hadn't made the decision until now, even though I brought this up with the school and with the provincial office two months ago, or she—and they—were adhering to the Korean custom of not letting employees know anything until the last minute. It's a good way to assert rank and keep underlings in their place. Anyway, it's such a relief—antiforeigner sentiment keeps growing and I'm sure many Koreans would feel justified if they didn't pay us at all, let alone meet the provisions of the contract.

Yesterday—Monday—was quite a finale. In a teachers' meeting, I was presented with a cash gift of about $230 from the non-English teachers and a fancy plaque with two dragons wrapped around an inscription that thanked me for my teaching. A nice memento. The English teachers had already given me an updated version of traditional Korean clothing—a jacket and skirt in a beautiful lavender that I picked out myself. I was wearing it. I gave a short, carefully rehearsed speech to the teachers, each sentence first in Korean and then in English. Later I gave another speech in the same way to the students over a video broadcast to all the rooms. My hands and voice shook—it was hard to control my emotions, although I'm not even sure what those emotions were. Mostly I'm utterly depleted from recent frustrations and from the whole two years. And I've contracted a killer cold with a disgusting, chronic cough.

A week ago I started saying good-bye to my students in each classroom. It was difficult. After the first day, I wasn't sure

I could make it through the next four. I love these girls. Kids are wonderful and amazing, aren't they? I know some of them are not kind or honest or compassionate, and some will grow up to be despicable adults, but there's a purity and energy and newness. Potential. They have hope and great expectations. Even though the culture and school system will quash some of it, they have typhoon-force creativity.

I finally slept well last night. This morning I tore down my handmade calendar that started with the day I returned to Korea last August—all the days are crossed off. I burned it in a ceramic cup.

One week to go before we get on the ferry to China, and I have very little left to pack. Shin Young-sook has been given the job of inspecting the apartment to discover if I've taken furniture that belongs to the government. Despite what this says about the school's opinion of me, I welcome it. I don't trust the landlord not to grab something as soon as I walk out the door to get a taxi—and blame the missing goods on me.

I've packed my computer to mail home via the U.S. Army post office. It was scary to unplug it and put it into its box. It's been my lifeline to friends and I suppose to myself too. It's my diary, and I've always been fond of my diaries. Who would have thought that I'd be anthropomorphizing a machine, calling it "my little gray buddy" as I have in recent E-mail.

Sometimes I think it was an accomplishment to make it through these two years. Other times I think it was pure folly. Why did I do it? There's always the money, and I did learn a lot. But what a cost! One compensation: I met with one of the English teachers who no longer works at my school. She gave me a set of brightly painted ceramic dolls—two childlike women in traditional clothes, one ironing silk by beating it with clubs, one stirring something in a kettle; and a tearful little boy from old Korea walking with his sleeping mat on his head as punishment for wetting the bed. She included this sweet note written in English: "I was sorry when I heard that you are to leave here soon. Although we couldn't often meet, I'm so happy when I think about the days with you at our school. So I am very sad now, and I'll miss you. I hope you'll be happy wherever you are and God bless you. You are the first person who change my thoughts (prejudice) about Americans."

I'm looking forward to traveling some in the U.S. and visiting friends after I get back. I was recently asked to write something for dear, long-time friends celebrating their fiftieth wedding anniversary. The words of many loving people will be collected for them in an album. It was a pleasure to reminisce about these rare, luminous people who entertained me many evenings with detailed stories of their life adventures. They introduced me to John Dewey and Edith Piaf and have been models and mentors for me for more than two decades. Gentle people of integrity who have always lived simply and according to their conscience, there's no pretense, no artifice in Charles and Alice. I hope to go to Colorado to see them. In my final E-mail to another couple, I placed my order for a dinner of pesto made from the fragrant basil in their garden, olive bread, and wine that they produce—expertly—in their garage. I'll be glad to get back to these people and others who compose my own comforting, nourishing culture.

Mrs. Song tells me the city's education office has decided there won't be supplemental lessons for first- and second-grade middle schoolers this summer. She'll have her first real vacation in a long time—no teaching and no surgery scheduled for her son. "I am happy," she said.

She explained why schools have had so many ineffectual classes before and after school and during summer vacations— it's because the principal and vice principal get a cut of the fees, even though they don't teach. Mrs. Song also told me that an older male science teacher who still maintains the custom of keeping a record of the gifts he receives from each student has been pressuring her homeroom girls to be more forthcoming. They complained to her and she reported it to the vice principal. The teacher was told to stop. He was furious with Mrs. Song and her class—the government is launching a new policy of forcing "incompetent" teachers to retire, and he's afraid this kind of attention will mean he'll have to go. Mrs. Song also explained to me why fourteen second graders spent so much time in the teachers' room last week. They were extorting money from first graders and some second graders. They had just raised their price from 3,000 won to 5,000 won. A few of them may be expelled, probably to be reinstated later. One other item from my informant: The homeroom teachers have to write about each of their students at the end of the year. Their comments are recorded in a big logbook. One of the categories is "community service"—girls are supposed to do so many hours of it each year. She said that column is filled in with almost pure fiction.

After relating all this, Mrs. Song looked at me and surprised me with the question, "Will you write a book?"

Will I?

Entry 58
Portland, Summer 2000

Maureen inserted the needle into my scrawny up-turned arm, and I broke into tears. "I need my legs," I sobbed. "I'm losing the use of my legs." It was the fifth intravenous infusion of vitamins and minerals in five weeks. Each time I've had to sit very still for about two hours while the saline solution dripped into my vein. Maureen told me the IVs would give me energy and help me gain weight.

Partly to explain the tears and partly to express my extremity, I told her about a phone call from a friend who has been type-1 diabetic and dependent on insulin since she was a girl. "You're dying! You're dying!" She shouted at me. "Your body is eating itself. First it eats the fat and then it eats the muscle." I knew she was drunk at the time and I hung up on her. But I had been watching precisely this happen to myself for a year and a half. Maureen took her eyes off the bag of yellowish liquid suspended from the IV support. She handed me a tissue and sat down and listened, but had nothing new or encouraging to say.

After the first couple IVs, I thought I noticed increased energy and my weight was up four pounds. I hoped the B vitamins might be the missing ingredient—maybe they'd save me. But standing on the scale in Maureen's office, I wondered to myself if the new pounds were only water weight (by then the swelling included my entire legs as well as my ankles and feet) and I almost said this to her. Not wanting to spoil the mood of progress and optimism, I swallowed my words. This possibility didn't seem to occur to Maureen.

A few weeks ago, although Maureen hadn't asked me to, I took off my socks to show her my fat feet and ankles. She diagnosed warm weather and prescribed cell salts. I had to remind her to weigh me during that visit. I considered taking all my clothes off to show her how wasted I am. It puzzles me that she doesn't seem to grasp the seriousness of my situation.

The day after I cried in her office, Maureen called me at home and asked a brief series of questions. Based on the answers, she prescribed a homeopathic drug—the kind you only take once. I was reluctant to take it. When I went to a homeopath in Chicago during my healing program for carcinoma-in-situ twenty years ago, I was interviewed for two and a half hours before the doctor chose my remedy. Maureen's practicing outside her area. And as she reminded me, a properly prescribed homeopathic remedy can lead to the resurfacing of symptoms as it works. How can she consider piling additional strain on my body? Yet I did take it. My only excuse is that I haven't been thinking clearly. Now I'm drinking mint tea (mint is an antidote to homeopathic drugs) in the hopes of thwarting the remedy and heading off any new ailments.

My weight has dropped back down to ninety-three pounds and who knows how much of that is the swelling in my legs and feet. Maureen is hedging on her claim that the IVs would help me gain weight. Now she's saying she only told me they "could lead to weight gain."

Each treatment costs eighty-five dollars. Maureen is as oblivious to the burden of the expense as she is to my skeletal appearance. I sit there watching the drops of disappointingly ineffective nutrition slide down the tube and into my arm and have the simultaneous sensation of money leaking out of me. Maureen's expenses have gone up lately—she has moved into her own office, away from the auspices of the college. It occurs to me that this is a good way to "tap" patients for money, and I do feel like the sap is being drained out of me. One afternoon I shared the room with another of Maureen's patients. It was ghastly—the two of us tethered to our flimsy, dubious lifelines. He was on his sixtieth week of treatments. I don't think so.

The results of some new blood tests came back from the lab—Maureen wanted to check for hepatitis and asked *me* if I wanted an insulin test. I leapt at the chance. There's no hepatitis, but the insulin output is down at the bottom of the scale. Maureen says she's not sure how to interpret the reading. I asked if she can prescribe insulin. She thought for a moment, then said, "Some forms." She says she'll make it a priority to find another naturopath that she can refer me to—someone who specializes in diabetes. Because she's going on vacation and the week afterward is booked, it will be more than three weeks before I see her again. I'm not sure I can survive till then. How long does she intend to let this go on?

I didn't tell her that I've been trying for several weeks to get an appointment with an M.D. recommended by friends. He's a diabetologist and apparently open to combining conventional and alternative medicine. I'll have to put aside my past experiences with conventional doctors.

....

I'm one of several people sitting at a gleaming wooden table in a room. A male friend sits beside me. Oregon's governor, John Kitzhaber, is about to sign an execution order. If he does, a man will be executed today. I'm certain the governor won't be able to bring himself to do it. The official forms are in a folder in the center of the table. I cover the folder with one of my own blank pieces of notebook paper, thinking this will halt the process. I begin to cry. With a flourish, the governor pulls out a very bright white, gilded, and ornately signed certificate that stays the execution. I release the breath I've been holding. But I'm thinking: This isn't the best way to do things—at the last minute. It's hard on all of us.

Kitzhaber is an M.D.

Entry 59
Portland, Summer 2000

"We can fix this."

Just what I longed to hear. Dr. Matthews' light blue eyes looked intently into mine as he spoke the words. He's clean-cut and crisp looking, middle aged with gray-white hair. He had already spent some minutes looking over my records and test results of the last year and a half before coming into the exam room. He dropped my file onto a counter and sat down on a stool. I was seated on a chair beside the examination table, my bare feet resting neatly on a folded white towel. Earlier, the young woman who led me into the room had told me to remove my shoes and socks. I was conscious of looking ill and puny. I could feel the lines in my face—the skin sagged and seemed to pull my eyes downward. In contrast, the skin was stretched tight around my stumplike legs and feet.

He diagnosed me immediately as a type-1, insulin-dependent diabetic. I asked why he knew that. He said because I hadn't responded quickly to the usual therapies for type-2 diabetes, and my insulin level was so low that it was barely measurable. It's not common for adults to develop type-1 diabetes, but it happens.

I weighed ninety-three pounds on his scale and he estimated I'm carrying at least five pounds of water weight. The swollen feet and legs are from malnutrition—a protein deficiency. My protruding stomach is what happens when you've eaten all your muscle and there's nothing there to hold in your intestines and liver. Very Third World.

I felt grateful and relieved; I felt desperate and beaten.

I was also suspicious—the doctor rides in on his white horse and scoops the flailing woman out of the rushing current just before she's dragged over the pounding falls. "We can fix this!" I guess it's ludicrous for me to criticize, but it sounded melodramatic and smacked of the god complex. Besides, type-1 diabetics don't get fixed, they get treated. So when he said that, I sighed and winced at the same time.

I was shaky and shell-shocked in addition to my usual bleariness. Should I be glad or grieving? Help had finally arrived, but I was permanently broken. I'd never be cured; I'd never fully emerge from this.

I told him some of my history with natural healing—how it had worked for me in the past and that it was not easy for me to be sitting in this room, in this hospital, looking for help from an M.D.

I will be ever thankful to Dr. Matthews for telling me it was natural to resist accepting that I had an incurable disease— denial is always the first stage, he said. I so needed that kindness, sitting there wondering why I had allowed such devastation to overrun my body. It could have been avoided.

He started me on insulin that day. I was lucky—the nurse educator was available so I went straight from my consultation with Dr. Matthews to another small room where I met Carolyn. She showed me how to draw insulin and how to give myself an injection. Normally a shot would be given in the abdomen or waist where there's some fat to put it into and from where the insulin is most easily absorbed. But there was only skin and my abdominal wall. I pinched some flesh on my thigh and stuck the needle in there. I was slow to take in all Carolyn's instructions and she seemed impatient. Give me a break, I was thinking—I just learned that I have a serious illness that will require me to take several injections a day for the rest of my life.

I drove home slowly, carefully, knowing that a bomb had just exploded inside me and my faculties might not be functioning properly.

I guess my biological clock was set to stop at about fifty. Without the stress of these last years, would this have happened? Might it have been put off? With an easier life—more security, less pressure—might my death from other causes have come much later and before this genetic predisposition kicked in? I think probably yes. But at least in part, I created my stressful life. Could I have chosen a different life? Did I have other choices that would have been do-able by the person that I am? It's easy to think so. But that doesn't take into account my essence and the myriad ways in which my immutable core doesn't fit with the surrounding world. The fact is, I do have limitations.

Anyway, now I have this existentialist question staring me in the face. My body decided enough was enough. It quit. But because it's possible to manufacture insulin outside the body, I can do an end run and go on living. Does my subconscious want to? My conscious? Is insulin just an artificial way to keep a person who's incompatible with life propped up and in the game? Should I honor my body's decision? I'd better have some good excuses for making it go on. I can't keep putting it through the kind of stuff I've been going though over the last several years. So that means there *must* be other choices, other paths that the person I am can take, and I have to find them. And some of what I think of as my "immutable core" may have to mutate.

I'm back to seeing my life as two side-by-side hoops. I'm more definitively on the second hoop than I ever suspected I would be. There's no returning to the first now. No going home. When I embarked on this transition four years ago, I had no idea how complete the metamorphosis would be or how it would manifest in my body.

Entry 60
Arcata, Spring 2001

I'm in Arcata for a few days before starting my last (phew!) quarter of grad school. This morning I got into my car and drove a few miles north to Moonstone Beach where I joined friends for their usual Sunday morning T'ai Chi practice. They're all former students of mine and it was a chance to flow through the sequence with an experienced group, all of whom savor the ritual as much as I do.

Waves and smiles as people got out of their cars in the parking lot, hugs and the usual how-have-you-been's when we got close. Singly or in twos, twelve of us accumulated on the sand. I stood and listened to the expected comments about the transformation in my appearance. (I've been hearing a lot of this lately.) When they last saw me, I'd been taking insulin for only about a month, so I was still disturbingly thin and they let me know it. Since then I've gained twenty-five pounds and now I look as if someone reinflated me with a bicycle pump. My strength is returning and I knew this practice would be very different from the last one at this beach six months ago.

We stood in a circle to do ten minutes of warm-ups, then arranged ourselves on dark, packed sand that had been smoothed and finely corrugated by the tide. Behind us the mouth of the Little River sloshed against a light surf and butted its way into the final body of water. In front of us and to the right, sculptural rocks in mottled gray and black jutted thirty feet upward. Further off, past a long stretch of beach, successive bluffs reached into the surf like claws, their dark purples fading and softening one by one, until the last was indistinguishable from the atmosphere. To our left, the blue, blue water with its oscillating white fringe. We chose a large rock that sits in the waves across from the bluffs to mark our north direction, our front. Camel Rock it's called, because of its two humps.

The air was liquid, imbued with the ocean's breath. Microscopic prisms softly blurred everything the sunlight caressed. There was the fecund smell of the beach—the presence of so much life that always some of it is in decay. Floating gulls lazily crisscrossed the sky, emitting casual, half-hearted screams, and lowering their heads to look down at us, curious to discover if we might be the source of food. A hundred yards away, several dogs were in heaven, their spirits unleashed in pure space. We heard their distance-muted yelps as they tore between owner and waves, chased neon-green tennis balls, and occasionally paused for a ginger sniff at dogs they'd never met before. The closest one dug wildly into the sand. Either she was on to something, or it was just another way to work off excess energy. The background for all this was the sound of the ocean's steady, relaxed pulse—diastolic and systolic, expanding and contracting, advancing and retreating. This is the pattern for all movement in T'ai Chi.

We lifted our palms to begin. In the middle of each palm is a point called the *lao gong*. The Chinese believe that it's through this invisible aperture that we take in ch'i from anywhere—from the air, the rocks, the trees, from other people. I think of revival meetings where members of the congregation raise their hands in a receiving, welcoming gesture.

I bent my knees deeply, held myself low, and burrowed in with my feet. Two years ago, the first sign of the onset of diabetes was trembling in my legs when I did T'ai Chi. But this morning my legs were solid. Now I can think about something else besides whether one leg is capable of supporting me while the other sweeps the air in a slow-motion kick.

The sequence kept us continually turning to face first one direction, then another—the bluffs with their wind-bent cypress, the river, the rocks, the shore. Each time the shore came into view, I could see a large woman walking toward us, following the ocean's edge. She was trailing behind and shepherding a tow-headed, impish girl of four or five. The girl squealed ecstatically as she played tag with the waves. Each time I re-turned toward her, she had shed another piece of clothing. I marveled at her hardiness—she was oblivious to the cool March air and the temperature of the water that had to be well below sixty degrees.

Finally the prancing, splashing sprite was entirely naked. Her joy filled me up and spilled over in a smile.

I'm grateful to that little girl. Her playfulness was a life-affirming contrast to my own desperate connection to the ocean, my instinct-driven immersions. I wasn't longing to disrobe and submerge myself this morning. I was content to look at the water or at most take off my shoes and socks and wade up to my ankles, maybe dip my fingers in and touch them to my lips. It seemed way too cold for getting naked and jumping in as I did last summer under harsher conditions. Besides, the little girl did it for me, and did it better.

You're supposed to avoid distractions and focus on what you're doing while practicing T'ai Chi. But you're also cultivating an extreme state of alertness. While I'm doing the sequence, all my senses and perceptions are intensified. I absorbed the vitality of the girl the same as I absorbed the healing force of the ocean, the sky, the rocks, and the peacefulness and goodwill of my friends.

Epilogue
Arcata, Summer 2005

It's been five years since I started taking insulin. As the doses were slowly increased, blood sugar levels dropped. It took several months to adjust to operating with something close to normal amounts of insulin in my body. In the first weeks I woke up shaking, hardly able to hold a pen.

My introduction to insulin shock—meaning I'd taken too much insulin for the food I'd eaten—began while walking back to my apartment after teaching a morning class at a nearby athletic club. My legs started feeling weak and wobbly as I trudged up a steep hill. When I got home, my blood sugar tested at seventy-two—an all-time low for me, although still within the normal range for nondiabetics. I needed to eat and began making a sandwich. But within seconds my entire body was oozing sweat. Rivulets collected on my face and dropped onto my T-shirt which was already darkening at the neck, armpits, and even at my stomach and the middle of my back. I hadn't sweated like that since before the onset of my diabetic symptoms when my body stopped reacting normally to exercise. My fingers jerked as I sliced a tomato and I started feeling sort of airy and distant from what I was doing. I realized I was about to black out. I took four glucose tablets—something Dr. Matthews told me to keep on hand. In ten or fifteen minutes the trembling subsided, my heart slowed, and I cooled off. I was back down to solid earth. In a reaction like this, all the glucose in the blood has been used up—the body has run out of fuel—so the liver steps in to manufacture some from body tissues. The liver is the emergency engine that produces the racking and the steam. A couple hours later my blood sugar had rebounded way beyond what it needed to be. I do my best to avoid these incidents—they wipe me out for the rest of the day and sap my energy the next day too.

That's why, six to eight times a day, I poke one of my fingertips, drop the blood onto a test strip, and slide that strip into a glucose monitor. I record the readings along with when and how much insulin I inject. I'm learning how different foods and types of exercise affect my need for insulin. Timing is critical.

I take two different kinds of insulin: one at night that maintains a basal level for twenty-four hours to help metabolize fats and proteins, and one just before meals that's fast acting and handles the carbohydrates.

Not long after moving back to Arcata, I did what I thought I would never do—took the wrong insulin as I was getting ready to go to bed. Instead of taking twelve units of the long-acting version, I took twelve units of the fast acting. That's three to four times what I would normally take before a meal. Luckily I noticed my error within a minute or two. I was frightened, knowing this could throw me into full-blown shock. I started eating glucose tablets and phoned a friend to drive me to the emergency room. Over the next two hours, a nurse monitored my blood sugar while I continued to take glucose. The readings were quite high—above normal. The glucose was counteracting the effect of the insulin. I began to question whether I had mixed up the bottles after all. Thinking I was out of the woods (the fast-acting insulin is supposed to be gone from the body within two to three hours) I went home and was in bed by midnight. But at 2:15 I woke to the thunking of my heart. I was vibrating and dripping sweat. Apple juice and more glucose brought me back to normal in minutes.

When I got the bill for the emergency room visit, I was stunned to see that the hospital had charged me twenty-three dollars for each of the three test strips the nurse had used. I pay forty-five cents a piece at the drug store.

After this episode I looked into possibilities for health insurance and discovered that as a diabetic I am flatly uninsurable with the exception of a California state-sponsored plan that costs five hundred dollars a month. Even at that, I'd have to pay one-fourth of the cost of doctor visits and insulin. At under a thousand dollars a year, my out-of-pocket expenses for coping with diabetes are far lower than the six thousand dollars insurance would cost me. The problem is that insurance is the only way to protect my savings and retirement account, both of which could be wiped out in a flash if I were seriously injured. This is the kind of thing Dr. Matthews was talking about when he said to me, "Our medical system is broken."

....

Insulin, I've discovered, is a stimulant. At first it kept me buzzing at night and interfered with my sleep. In the pool, I felt like the bionic woman (at least in stark contrast to how I felt preinsulin). I can see how it could be considered a performance-enhancing drug—it makes you a super metabolizer as long as you match it just right with food and exercise.

Seeing my weight reappear was like watching a time-exposure film. The bones of my shoulders that jutted straight up in sharp points softened and smoothed and then vanished. My face filled out—it felt pudgy compared to its former concavity. I gained thirty-five pounds in four months.

After starving for eighteen months, I'd acquired a crazed attitude toward food. Very slowly, I've become less fixated on it, realizing that I don't have to fend off extinction with constant stoking. My concern flip-flopped to keeping my weight down. I watch what I eat and use exercise—running, swimming, biking, and T'ai Chi—to stay stable. I've become a proponent of weight training. Not only did it rebuild my muscles, but it increased my energy too.

My hair fell out. Not all of it, but it was considerably thinner. Doctor Matthews said that when you come back from a starved state, your old hair falls out and new hair grows in. I wore my hair chopped off short for a while. Now it's down to the middle of my back. Dry mouth disappeared in days; talking to my classes became so much easier. The leg cramps are gone. The water in my legs, ankles, and feet receded within a couple months. My distance vision came back into focus and my reading vision went back out. The bubbles of light that slid upward along the sides of my eyes when I closed them or when I turned out the lights in a room slowly vanished. I escaped permanent liver, kidney, and eye damage. The color returned to my face and my body looks solid and strong. I have some of that extra that I envied on women in the locker room in Portland.

The worst of the depression lifted and I stopped seeing Hannah about three months after starting on insulin. Now I sleep, only getting up once during the night to pee.

My new drug brought on a spate of what I referred to as "insulin dreams." Lots of male-female contact and kissing. In one, a momentous commitment was made to be life partners. I saw it as my own yin and yang regenerating and reuniting, marrying.

I got my master's degree in writing. (Free at last!) For almost a full year, I carried a memento of the Spanish comprehensive exam. I injured my wrist (hyperextended it? cut off the circulation too long?) by sitting with my elbow on the desk, my chin pressed heavily into my palm while reading the passages and answering the questions. It was a two-hour exam—the only timed, in-school test that I'd taken in thirty years, and I was nervous. I wonder if I'm the only person to have physically injured herself while taking a written test.

Some friends came down hard on me for using alternative healing methods and taking the advice of alternative healers for too long, allowing my health to deteriorate so drastically. It seemed unfair and disrespectful. They're people who never question the medical establishment and are mostly ignorant of other ways to grapple with illness. They act as if I stood idly by, being negligent. It's just the opposite. I took too much responsibility on myself. I weathered the same kind of censure twenty-six years ago while immersed in my first alternative healing program, and that time it was successful. Looking back, it seems obvious that I should have realized I needed insulin sooner, should have seen that all my efforts with diet and supplements were only slowing the tide, not stemming it. But I mistrust conventional medicine for good reason. There are at least as many quacks with M.D. degrees as there are without. I wanted to be in control of my own health, as I always have been—I didn't want to turn my body over to someone else to fix, the way I take my car to a mechanic. I think it was reasonable to expect that the professionals I consulted would know better, or at least know that they didn't know. In the end, any serious illness is fought day-to-day—it's easy not to see the forest for the trees when you're working hard, coping and hoping.

I sued both Marilyn and Maureen and filed complaints with their overseeing medical organizations. In my depleted state, it took all I had to get the story down on paper. The suit was successful—they quickly settled out of court. Not a lot of money involved, but it got their attention and may prevent others from suffering as I did. Marilyn escaped censure from the board, probably because I had only seen her for seven weeks. But Maureen was put on probation for two years.

....

I got myself back to Arcata and that's when I hit bottom. I was finally where I wanted to be and I was glad to be there, but I couldn't do another thing. I had to stop. The depression was palpable; it nauseated me. Daily meditation led me to tears every time—sometimes sooner, sometimes later. These are the things that surfaced when I became still: fear, loneliness, self-disgust, and fatigue. The events of September eleventh made it seem the entire world was collapsing with me, and for similar reasons—too much yang, not enough yin; too much aggression, not enough nurturing; people being wrenched into impossible shapes by surrounding conditions. No wonder we're deformed. Again, death looked like a relief.

I tried a counselor—once—but she was too expensive and immediately started talking to me about setting goals. Oh please. That's how I got to this state—I was always setting goals and meeting them. It was time to quit—I had no choice but to quit. If I had been a bourgeois character in a nineteenth-century novel, I would have spent a year or two in a seaside resort or a mountain sanatorium.

Come to think of it, I felt as if I had moved to a resort when I got to Arcata. I rode my bike to the marsh beside the bay every morning to practice T'ai Chi. There I faced a small, rippling lake overrun by swooping, wheeling, whooshing flocks of godwits and terns; individual pelicans wheeled in for splashy landings; white egrets tiptoed through the shallows stalking fish. I continued to make small efforts to earn money as a copyeditor and T'ai Chi teacher, partly out of dumb habit, partly out of necessity, and partly for show—to appease myself and friends. Both they and I were frightened by the idea of my truly stopping, with no solid plan for future income. So I was being minimally "productive." But there was space in my days. I read, I meditated, I practiced T'ai Chi, I cooked for friends, and I sat and stared off into space.

....

I came up with a new motto: "I give up." I recite it like a mantra when I feel the anxiety rising. It helps. I give up trying to be in control—of every part of my life and of my future. It's futile.

When I was in grade school, our class would take over a whole field beside the playground for a game called "release the Belgian." (Don't ask me where the name came from—I'm not even sure if I'm spelling it right. Liberating a country during World War II?) Half of us chased the other half, collecting our prisoners in a small circular area. I prided myself on being the fastest runner in the class, the only uncatchable one—until I literally ran into Tom McGrath. Tom was big and heavy and possibly the slowest kid in class. He had planted himself out in the open. As he marched me, dazed and humiliated, to the prison, he explained, "I knew I couldn't catch anyone so I figured if I just stood still, eventually somebody would run into me."

I decided to be like Tom McGrath. For the first time in my life, instead of chasing something, I was standing still, waiting to see what might run into me.

The corollary of "I give up" is "I open up." Suddenly the possibilities expand, unconfined by my narrow vision, my plan, my self-image. The process starts with releasing my grasp on the old exterior and curling inward for a period of stillness. The purpose is not to quickly hatch a new, self-conscious identity, trading one for another. The point is to shed the whole concept of identity. A public (and even private) identity is a shell soon outgrown, a cage. It makes us seem comfortably consistent and predictable to others and ourselves. And we know what my namesake says about a foolish consistency.

But I argue with myself: Striving for recognition—to have an image in relation to other people—is probably a basic human drive that, to a greater or lesser degree, we're all born with. One of Joanna Trollop's characters in *The Choir* asks, "Do you think all human endeavor springs from the need to be particular, visible?" The answer given by another character is "Probably."

This is what's true for me: Sometimes I've needed to be somebody and sometimes I've needed to be a nobody. The nobody phase is the replenishing, gestating time. The somebody phase is the manifestation of the new being. There has to be a balance between the two, an oscillating back and forth between dark and light—time inside the chrysalis, time outside.

I've been accused of being driven all my life. Okay, I'm driven—or I have been and maybe I will be again. I've thrown myself into my callings as they've arisen—clay, T'ai Chi, writing. Is that bad? I always suspected that my accusers were jealous of my passion and energy—I inadvertently made them feel remiss. What's wrong with going all out, doing what I feel compelled to do, burning up all my fuel? I've always felt that I had to contribute something new to the world in order for my life to have meaning. I know others who feel that way, and I know some who don't. Is it neurosis or is it genetics? If it's genetics, maybe we humans contain both ways of being, even within the same person—there's a time for striving and a time for stopping.

Retreating. Slowing. Stopping.

They say the natural evolution of Wu style T'ai Chi is toward nonmovement. Over the years, in my own practice, my gestures have slowed and become more and more muted. Sometimes any movement at all seems too rapid. Particle by particle, I release and spread out. Anything holding me in—a watchband, a knit hat—become annoyingly restrictive. I disappear into and mingle with my vast surroundings. We mingle with each other. I'm the welcomed guest; I'm the welcoming host.

. . . .

As time went on, I stopped taking editing jobs. The work was too sedentary and too tedious to induce me to work very hard at drumming up business. The long delays in payment (sometimes several months beyond their stated terms) made me think it wasn't a viable way to make money. People tell me I have to put up with that sort of thing. No, I don't have to. I won't work for people who don't respect me and don't show it in the most minimal ways, like paying on time. It's dangerous to my health.

For a while I was director of an art center where people go to work in clay and glass. The money worries and personal conflicts were too wearing—not enough time or energy was left to do the things I most want to do. Now I work part-time in a medical office to keep my head above water.

My article "Studying T'ai Chi in Korea" was finally published in *Black Belt Magazine,* three years after it was accepted by that magazine and two others. I was paid two hundred fifty dollars. It was also published in *Qi Journal* for no pay.

I'm gardening. My duplex apartment has a fenced-in back yard. After several years, I'm seeing some results. (Some things will survive and even thrive in clay!) From the beginning, getting my hands into dirt, fussing over the trees, plants, and flowers that rise up out of the mud, has been instant mood-enhancing therapy. I take my time; it's all done bit by bit. Sometimes I wake up at night, get out of bed, and open the back door just to look out at the peaceful emerging growth. For the first two springs—every day, sometimes more than once—I counted the gladiolus as they poked through, even moved aside clumps that shaded their tender, reddish points. So many plants were given to me by friends that it's as if those people are with me when I'm in my garden.

An important part of my week is the hour's standing meditation that I do with Women in Black. We're on the plaza downtown and there's plenty of traffic, but the cool green grass grounds me and we create our own silence. We're witnessing the atrocities that humans commit against each other and the planet.

The war in Iraq is foremost in my mind now. Being a part of Women in Black is one of the ways I try to exert some small influence in the world.

I'm teaching T'ai Chi in my back yard this summer, and in the fall will go back to teaching in a martial arts academy within walking distance from my home. As always, the classes bring genuine people into my life and give me an opportunity to talk with them not just about the mechanics of the movement but also about T'ai Chi as metaphor—the implications of our practice in everyday life.

....

Piglet reentered my life. I retrieved her from the friends who cared for her while I was away. They gave her littermate to an elderly woman in a nursing home because Tigger was so depressed when they brought a new baby into the house that she retreated under the bed and stayed there. Her new owner doted on her and named her Lacy Belle. I left my phone number with the woman in case Tigger ever needed a home.

It made perfect sense that Piglet and I would be together again. It was her pig tail that I felt in the dream when I held her in my arms as if she were my child. She remembered me and we quickly fell into our old routines. I combed her daily (the inexhaustible fuzz factory), played with her, petted her, and talked to her. She talked back with her various voices; bossed me around with her chirpy greetings, inflected questions, and irritable, impatient complaints and demands. Piglet acted like she owned the place. Her idea of entertainment was to see me jump, hear my startled mutterings when she pounced onto my chest from the windowsill at night. After standing watch at the cool window or on the corner of the bed for a while, she brushed her whiskers against my face to wake me. I dutifully opened the covers so she could burrow in against me where she purred, kneaded my arm, and warmed up. She was small and round and kittenish, even at the age of eighteen. Her wide-open golden eyes and delicate pointy ears made her look like an owl. Her medium-length, mottled brown fur was soft as a bunny's. She cried when I cried. Who could help but love her?

But I had to relearn how to love her. I knew I wanted her, but I was out of practice at lavishing love on another being. She became my roommate—the person I said hello to when I walked in the door and said good-bye to when I left.

Last summer I arrived fifteen minutes early as usual for a T'ai Chi class in the park. It gave me time to chat with one of my long-time, dedicated students who also arrives early. I could have asked Bob about his son who had just come back from fighting in Iraq, but I chose a more general question this time, "What's new?" He said he and his wife, Ann, who are in the business of rescuing animals, had taken in an exotic chicken from a zoo that was downsizing its collection of fowl. Also, Ann had dropped by the animal shelter and seen a cat that had just arrived there the day before. She was alluringly beautiful but looked very depressed and dangerously thin. Ann couldn't resist, she took her home. Bob told me the cat was seventeen and its elderly owner, who had been living in a nursing home, had died. The family didn't want to have the animal euthanized, so they dropped her off at the shelter. Her name was Lacy Belle. As soon as Bob mentioned the cat's age, I started to vibrate—this could be my cat. As he gave me more details, I became certain. The next day I drove to Bob and Ann's home in Ferndale (where I was living when I first acquired Tigger and Piglet) and reclaimed her. I may have imagined it, but Tigger seemed to recognize me. She came out from behind the bathtub to greet me and let me pick her up. It seemed right that Bob would be the means of my reuniting with Tigger. He often expresses gratitude for my teaching and lets me know the many ways in which T'ai Chi contributes to his life. Returning Tigger to me was a wonderful way to thank me, although Bob's presence in the class is thanks enough.

Tigger was fur and bones and too weak to jump up onto my lap at first. But she quickly gained weight and strength and her familiar feistiness. I couldn't tell if Tigger and Piglet recognized each other. But Piglet made it clear that she resented the interloper. She growled when Tigger approached and took to sleeping in the meditation room. Tigger had commandeered the bed—first by hiding under it, then by spending most of the day on it. She became my nighttime companion. Piglet was on me at every opportunity during the day. Gradually, Piglet became more tolerant.

I've wondered if my taking in Tigger hastened Piglet's death. Tigger had always been the dominant cat and Piglet blossomed when it was just the two of us. Her world of contentment was disrupted by Tigger and she was angry at both of us. Yet I knew Tigger belonged with me and I had to give her a home. About six months after Tigger's arrival, Piglet died of acute renal failure at the age of eighteen.

I've had to parcel out my grief for Piglet. It's as if her loss was too big for me to look at all at once. I've only been able to look at it peripherally, a piece at a time. This will be a slow process.

Tigger's reappearance in my life seems auspicious. It's like a pass I threw to myself—over time. I see her as physical evidence that I'm supposed to be here, postdiabetes. I had to be here to catch Tigger. And she had to be here to catch me, post-Piglet.

....

I created a meditation room in my home. My apartment has two bedrooms; I emptied one of all its furniture. Originally I thought I might use the space as a studio for clay or finger painting. But the room quickly told me otherwise. I guard it as a place to sit every morning.

I arrange myself on a pillow against a wall, facing the window. (When Piglet was alive, she was in my lap.) A white linen curtain covers the bottom half of the glass so that all I can see are trees against sky. I painted the ceiling, the window wall, the wall I sit against, and the top border on the other two walls pure white. White may be my favorite color right now. Saturated colors—deep blues and bright greens—flow through a misty sky on the wall to my left. It's an evocation of Crater Lake, the site of my annual pilgrimage. The lace cap hydrangea in my back yard was the inspiration for the lavender pinks and blues that wave their way across the wall to my right. Several rounded river rocks are piled in one corner of the floor.

I marvel at how I—people—manage to manifest who they are. Despite all life's distractions and imperatives, we inevitably find our way—like water flowing downhill. I'm conscious of what a luxury it is to have a room set aside for nothing but meditation. I've made my choices, forged my life, and followed my own path. It has led me (now) to this clear room. It honors my yearning for stillness and quiet introspection. It holds me and invites me to expand inward and outward.

....

Early mornings are precious to me and the true focus of my life. I get up, step outside, and give myself a face massage. It's self-applied acupressure that uses the head as a microcosm of the body to stimulate all its systems. Next I warm up my knees and stretch my leg muscles before going on a four-mile run. The road is deserted and lined in places with ferns and forest. I see deer almost every morning and an occasional fox. At the end of the run I practice T'ai Chi in my back yard or in a nearby school playground. Then I go inside and take a bath before sitting for forty minutes or more. Everything leads to sitting. Progressing from strenuous activity to gentler movement to utter stillness ushers me into a profound meditative state.

This is what happens when I sit: I sink into my tan t'ien (the center of my abdomen) and whatever's occupying that space—whatever has been consciously suppressed or unconsciously repressed—is displaced. It's forced to leave by rising up and out through my body, venting from the crown of my head. My eyes turn upward as if drawn that way by the current. I experience all of it as it passes—anxiety, impatience, anger, sadness, excitement, joy, tenderness. My mind tries to evade the uncomfortable feelings by creating diversions—triggering mind chatter, thought loops that pin blame on people and circumstances outside myself. Not that those things aren't partly responsible for the unpleasant feelings. But for the moment they're irrelevant. Now it's just a matter of taking a look at what's inside and letting it float upward and out—releasing it. It's a daily bath, a daily cleansing that keeps things moving, not allowing them to build up and fester and infect. Trapped in there, forced to be unnaturally confined, they do their damage. I don't always feel so good when I first start meditating (or practicing T'ai Chi), but as I persist, I transcend this stage, I clear out. Eventually, on a good day, I reach a state of clarity and peace.

....

Theodor Fontane (in a quotation I found in the *Korea Herald*) says there are two secrets to happiness: first, comfortable shoes and a good night's sleep, and second, being where you belong.

Being where you belong. One of my first T'ai Chi students had an interesting encounter with that concept. He went for a solo hike on a favorite trail that led through redwood trees to a bluff overlooking the ocean. He stopped there and practiced the sequence of T'ai Chi. As he pressed his hands downward to conclude, tears fell onto his T-shirt in big, heavy drops—"like rain," he said. Then he heard a voice: "It's okay. You belong here." Did it come from inside or outside his head? He couldn't tell. While he told this story, he kept interrupting himself to say what a practical man he was—as a physician who saw human disease and suffering every day, he was not what he considered a spiritual person. Yet at that moment he not only felt as if he had been embraced by the universe, but as if he had been "blessed." It was a unique experience—he was used to being liked, respected, and thanked by his patients. This went beyond that.

Why did he need to be reassured that he belonged? He has a family, a position in the community. He has been in the same home for decades. Why would he be so relieved, so grateful to be given this gift?

A vision during meditation connected me with an ancestral archetype and made me feel I too have a place here, in the long continuum: The head of a woman hurtled toward me, light brown hair rippling behind. She was sheer power—overwhelming and irresistible. I was flooded with a sense of familiarity: I know this woman. Then she was gone and these words were typed out in front of me in capital letters as if by my old Smith-Corona: IPONA - IPECHTA.

I researched the words. Ipona (or Epona) was a Celtic goddess who was worshipped wherever the Celts lived—from the British Isles to Eastern Europe. She could appear as a white horse or as a woman riding a white horse; she could appear as a black horse or as a woman riding a black horse. If she came to you in her white incarnation, she rewarded you for your good deeds. If she came in her black incarnation, she punished you for your mistakes. I saw both her names—both sides of her, yin and yang. For centuries British kings were crowned while standing beside a white horse. The ceremony was a symbolic marriage between the two. The white horse—Ipona—brought plentiful harvests and prosperity to the realm.

I am related to Ipona. Perhaps many of us are. I saw her fourteen years ago and having seen her makes me think I'm part of some vast web extending in all directions of time and space. I use her name as a mantra—Ipona as I breathe in, Ipechta as I breathe out.

Horses are a recurring motif in my dreams. Within the last few months I had this dream: I'm searching for a place to swim, looking for water that's clear enough and deep enough. A stream that lies beneath my feet and even the ocean just beyond are shallow and coated with algae. But out of a tide pool among the rocks emerges an enormous translucent horse made of water. Its powerful body glistens; well-defined muscles ripple. It turns first its head, then its body to face me. Smoothly, gracefully, a woman emerges from the horse—the horse transforms into a woman. I was struck by the fact that this majestic double being came from such a meager source. Again, I felt a sense of power and connection.

I have often lived as a foreigner, feeling as if I don't belong, even in my own country. My homes have been T'ai Chi, meditation, clay, writing, dreams, visions, precious friends, and the natural world.

My closest relationship while in Portland was with the fir tree that I faced so many mornings to do T'ai Chi. I visited it just before I left—sat about twenty feet away and looked at it. The words "Will you miss me? Will you miss me?" repeated like a round in my head. They seemed to be coming from the tree.

There's a group of three trees in a corner of the Rose Garden. I'd stand under them, place my palms on them one by one, and look up into their blue-green branches. I felt a running pulse inside each, but one hummed stronger than the others. Morning after morning, I'd wrap my arms around it, press my heart against it, and rest my temple on its feathery bark. We belonged to each other.

I feel compelled to be in the redwood forest at night. Daytime is nice, but not nearly as fulfilling. I camp by myself. I have the same feeling that I've had with a lover—I want time to stop and the night to last forever. I look up to see trees silhouetted against a black sky. Fat stars, bright moon moving in and out of branches.

On one camping trip I dreamt that Piglet was purring inside the tent and Abe, a Labrador-golden retriever cross that I had an uncanny closeness with back in Illinois, was lying outside the tent.

In the dark time when I first returned to Arcata, I camped at Crater Lake in southern Oregon. Before I even got there, as I gaped at the Rogue River gushing through volcanic chasms overhung by clinging pines I could only vaguely remember that I'd been depressed about something. ("Wasn't I depressed?") For me, Crater Lake is a sacred place. I drink in the stunning blue of the lake from the height of the caldera or from the rocks at its shore. I'm besotted by the contrast of the bright green pines against the unique color of the water. I go there every year. As soon as I start the drive from Arcata, I feel released, totally unconstrained, and euphoric. After my last visit, I had this dream: I was standing on the trail that winds to the top of Mt. Scott, a peak overlooking the lake. I was facing the lake and my arms hung at my sides. I was dressed in a full-length white wedding gown. My palms turned outward to better absorb the lake's inspiring blue. That was all—that vision. Bride of Crater Lake.

As for human companions, some of my best friends are scattered across the country and some are around me now.

Looking back on my life, it's interesting how a few people have maintained a presence within me—growing larger and more vivid over time—whether I have contact with them or not. Many others (including two husbands) have evaporated except for the thinnest intellectual memory. I resonate with some people as I do with some trees. An old man who used to visit me in my studio told me over and over again, "You can't substitute people." (I thought maybe his wife had left him for another man.) Now I understand him. It's true. There are no substitutes for individuals. Humans have "infinite particularity" as Iris Murdoch put it.

When I'm in between books, I still reread *Pride and Prejudice.* Elizabeth Bennett expresses my general feeling toward people: "The more I see of the world, the more I am dissatisfied with it; and every day confirms my belief of the inconsistency of all human characters, and the little dependence that can be placed on the appearance of either merit or sense." She adds, "There are few people whom I really love, and still fewer of whom I think well."

By now it's evident that following my own path leads me away from most people. I'm accepting the fact that I have a lot of hermit in me.

....

When I read women's stories, I want to know about their romantic relationships, their intimate partnerships. Of course most people are reluctant to describe this part of their lives in detail—they want to protect their privacy and the privacy of the people they've been involved with. I feel the same way. But the picture isn't complete, especially because relationships have been one of my principal teachers.

I'll say this much. My relationships have been with men. I've been legally married twice and I've cohabited twice. By choice, I have no children. There was a period of a few months when I was startled by an intense "baby urge." I was thirty-two years old and had just witnessed the birth of my brother's daughter in their home. That emotional experience must have jarred some hormones loose, because I returned to Illinois after two months of travelling with a single fixation. The man that I wanted to have a baby with was not ready to have children. I resumed the work in my studio, my creative energy had an outlet again, and the baby urge receded, never to return.

I've had several mutually loving experiences that endured for two or three years and added vastly to my life. I've had other relationships that were hurtful and destructive and I've stayed too long in some of them.

I stayed for a combination of reasons. I was grasping for sex and comfort and a sense of belonging. I was afraid of hurting the man's feelings. I felt guilty that I didn't want to "work on" the relationship as almost all my friends, acquaintances, and counselors advised me to do. (Even if someone knew nothing about the man, very little about me, and nothing about the dynamics of our relationship, this advice was quickly volunteered.)

I'm sorry to say that I've been swayed by the force that society exerts—on women in particular—to couple up and stay that way. The fierceness and ubiquitousness of that force keeps taking me by surprise. It shouldn't by now. Why do people want to stuff others into boxes and then hold the lid down? Is it because they're living in cramped and painful boxes themselves and don't have the courage or strength to break out? Is it because if one person escapes it calls into question their years—maybe decades—of imprisonment? Their urgings are ostensibly in the name of love, forgiveness, and compromise. But people often have a poor understanding of these qualities. A woman is held responsible for doing most of the compromising, the distorting and suppressing of herself to assure the survival of the relationship. Nothing is worth relinquishing my values and self-respect. I have to live with dignity. Until mature women require the same level of nurturing from men that they themselves provide, men will not mature and the human species (and our environment) will continue to be endangered.

People have accused me of being cold and unforgiving. If I had less heart and less warmth, I'd be married right now and telling myself that the prestige and material comfort marriage can provide is more important than being true to myself and to the other person.

Good relationships are rare because only people who value themselves can value other people. And both members of a couple have to be on approximately the same plane—they have to know the same things and not know the same things. The fact that a relationship endures does not mean it's a good one. The fact that a relationship dissolves does not mean it wasn't good for both people for a time.

I'm no longer susceptible to society's pressure to pair up. I'm finally getting the hang of not only recognizing my intuition but having the fortitude to act on it too. They are two different things. To all those people who get cold feet before getting involved with or committing to another person, I say don't do it. Go with your feet.

Perhaps the main reason I've chosen repeatedly to be single is that living alone is a viable option for me. I do well that way. I know that many don't and would never choose that state willingly.

People talk about "something missing" or feeling "incomplete" without a partner. I feel more complete without a relationship than I do within one. I think I always have, but my sex drive periodically obliterated the drive to become myself. I know that the drama of romance and sex has kept me from facing my incompleteness. Relationships mask my loneliness for myself and hinder me from evolving into my own peer, my own partner.

Romantic love is too confining for me. On my own, I'm free to go my way at my speed. I may be intimate with a man again, but I don't yearn for it and it's not a goal of mine. Anyway, I'm evidently married to Crater Lake.

....

"It's terrible to get old," my sixty-something mother said more than once. That was over twenty years ago and I thought she was getting old because she smoked and didn't exercise and was disappointed with her life. Now I catch on to the fact the we do all get old eventually. "Don't you just love getting older?" a friend my age asked. Does *she* love it, I wondered. She's on hormone replacement therapy. What do I think?

I think I look much older on the outside than I feel on the inside. I look in the mirror and think it's a fascinating process, this steady approach to my mortality, this conveyor belt I'm on no matter what, 'til death do me meet.

I reap the advantages of middle age—a growing comfortableness with myself and a diminishing concern with what others think of how I live. I also know myself better.

This pattern recurs: When life is too full and I'm too busy and pressured, I get tired. Being tired makes me depressed. Being depressed means I have to withdraw in the interest of self-preservation. It's as simple as that. Ideally I'm exerting myself and engaged in creative work, but I also require some placid lakes of time dotting the landscape. Knowing this helps.

....

The harsh culture of South Korea was a mirror of my life. And diabetes—the insatiable hunger and thirst, the slow dying—was also a reflection of me. Butting up against a wall of fatigue, disillusionment, and anger engendered a metamorphosis. Insulin gives me time to realize the change.

In other words, I took a shortcut to reincarnation.

I do believe we get more than one chance. My dreams, visions, and experiences tell me that the death of our bodies is not the end of us. I think there are several possibilities after death.

Someone like my mother, who was very dissatisfied with her life, came right back and started over. She urgently wanted another chance. Mother had not come close enough to becoming who she wanted to be, so she willed herself into another life. The night before her funeral I dreamt that we were all in her house, dressing for the ceremony. She was there too, standing in the hallway outside my bedroom. I said, "What are *you* doing here?" She said, "Well I'm not here. I'm in Tucson, Arizona and I feel great." I pictured her as a newborn.

Then there are people like my Great-Aunt Lessie. I didn't know she was dying, but when I came home from a sweaty summer day in my Illinois ceramics studio, I got into the shower and was overwhelmed by a thrilling feeling of weightlessness and infinite expansion. I said again and again to myself out loud, "I feel as if I've left my body." My mother called within hours to tell me Lessie had died. I felt her benevolent presence for some years after her death.

One night she appeared beside my bed as I was drifting into sleep. It was just after a phone conversation with my sister who has been insulin-dependent diabetic since she was a child. She was worried her life would not be long enough to allow her to accomplish all she wanted to do. (At the time I was in my early thirties and a long way from becoming diabetic myself. Great-Aunt Lessie's only child, my Aunt Margaret, was also diabetic. She died from complications of the disease in her fifties.) I went to bed feeling my sister's anxiety—and my own. Lessie spoke to me, "Don't worry about time. We think it moves in only one direction because we're trapped inside out bodies, our bodies are aging, and we measure time by that standard. But time moves in all directions—forward, backward, and sideways." Then she left. Forward and backward are easy to envision, but sideways? Does this mean alternate, simultaneous realities? Do we reach a point when we can choose which direction we go? Can we—do we—exist in all possibilities at once?

Lessie gave me a legacy—in that initial hit in the shower and in her words and lingering presence. I don't know what happened to her. Perhaps she eventually decided to come back for another round; or maybe she had other places to go. My mother immediately dove back in. Some souls need to start again right away. Some souls don't.

Because of insulin, I'm able to embark on a new journey in the old body. There are advantages. I remember my previous life and can apply what I've learned.

The changes in me are internal, not external. There's a sense of joy and anticipation when I wake up on an ordinary day. Sometimes I wonder why. I'm aging; diabetic; have very little disposable income after necessities; and much of my work is uninspired, indoors, and computer-fixated. But I savor so many "little" things—T'ai Chi, meditation, dreams, visions, intuitions, running, swimming, being under the trees or at the ocean, reading, writing, finger painting, seeing a good movie, interacting with my cat, real conversations with real friends. Mostly I'm riveted by the glimpses I get of the web-like spirituality that infuses and connects every living and nonliving particle through space and time. I want to explore this. Knowing that it's not arrogant or wrong to live by my intuition; trusting all the messages that come from my body, mind, and spirit means that I have a guide, I have a way in. Many years ago I dreamt that I was a blind man with a guide dog. I am all the characters in my dreams, so all I have to do is follow myself.